Understanding Electronic Commerce

David Kosiur

Understanding Electronic Commerce

Published by **Microsoft Press**
A Division of Microsoft Corporation
One Microsoft Way
Redmond, Washington 98052-6399

Library of Congress Cataloging-in-Publication Data
Understanding Electronic Commerce
      p. cm.
   Includes index.
   ISBN 1-57231-560-1
    1. Electronic commerce.   I. Title.
HF5548.32.K67   1997
658.8'00285--dc21   97-4201
                                  CIP

Printed and bound in the United States of America.

3 4 5 6 7 8 9   QMQM   1 0 9

Distributed in Canada by ITP Nelson, a division of Thomson Canada Limited.

A CIP catalogue record for this book is available from the British Library.

Microsoft Press books are available through booksellers and distributors worldwide. For further information about international editions, contact your local Microsoft Corporation office or contact Microsoft Press International directly at fax (425) 936-7329. Visit our Web site at mspress.microsoft.com.

Macintosh and the Mac OS logo are registered trademarks of Apple Computer, Inc. Intel is a registered trademark of Intel Corporation. ActiveX, Microsoft, the Microsoft logo, the Microsoft Internet Explorer logo, Microsoft Press, the Microsoft Press logo, Visual Basic, Windows, and Windows NT are either registered trademarks or trademarks of Microsoft Corporation in the United States and/or other countries. Other product and company names mentioned herein may be the trademarks of their respective owners.

Companies, names, and/or data used in screens and sample output are fictitious unless otherwise noted.

Acquisitions Editor: Eric Stroo
Project Editor: Stuart J. Stuple

Table of Contents

Chapter Six

Offering Custom Products on the Internet 117

Chapter Seven

An Electronic Marketplace of Buyers and Sellers 133

Acknowledgments

I owe a lot to my colleague David Strom, David Fugate of Waterside Associates, and Eric Stroo at Microsoft Press for initiating this project. Eric in particular was a good sounding board for some of the ideas that eventually made their way into this book.

Many individuals at the companies covered in this book shared their insights into electronic commerce. Dave Mawhinney at Nets Inc. was particularly inspiring and informative, as were Jim Kessler at AMP Inc., Charles Kirk at Fruit of the Loom, George Brill at AeroTech, and Paul Cimino at Snickelways. Some of the people who helped "smooth the path" for obtaining crucial information, and who deserve special thanks, are Jennifer Christensen and Mike Spataro at Nets Inc., Thea Hocker at AMP Inc., and Kim Phillips at Snickelways.

I especially appreciate Eric Fleischman's efforts at Microsoft for arranging a visit that enabled me to get a better understanding of how Microsoft itself is using the Internet and intranets for electronic commerce. I found the conversations with Eric, Jim duBois, Chris Nefcy, Al Alston, and Jonathan Shuval to be particularly informative and exciting. Thanks to you all.

The Herculean efforts of Devra Hall and Steve Sagman, my book editors, as well as those of Stuart Stuple at Microsoft Press, have helped make this a better book and one that was produced on time.

Lastly, I owe a special thanks to my wife, Sue, for putting up with the vagaries of book authoring while I worked on this book. It's amazing how supportive and understanding she can be.

Chapter One

What Is Electronic Commerce?

For some time now, large business enterprises have used electronic commerce to conduct their business-to-business transactions. **Electronic data interchange**[1] (EDI) on private networks began in the 1960s, and banks have been using dedicated networks for **electronic funds transfer**[2] (EFT) almost as long. Recently, however, with the increased awareness and popularity of the Internet, electronic commerce has come to encompass individual consumers as well as businesses of all sizes.

The Internet is already changing the way that many companies conduct their business. As that influence grows, and more companies use the Internet, the possibilities for conducting business-to-business commerce on the Internet will expand greatly, and become more of a routine part of commerce than it is today. We've not yet reached that critical

EDI and EFT can be conducted over the Internet

---

1. Electronic data interchange allows companies to exchange business documents in a standardized form.

2. Electronic funds transfer was designed to optimize the transmission of electronic payments.

mass where everyone thinks of conducting business-to-business commerce on the Internet everyday, but we will. This book focuses mainly on the business uses of electronic commerce, but, of course, consumers are the source of much business revenue, so you will find some discussion of consumer markets as a revenue source later in the book.

An Overview

Electronic commerce is more than just handling purchase transactions and funds transfers over the Internet

To many, electronic commerce is defined as the buying and selling of products and services over the Internet, but there are many more aspects. From its inception, electronic commerce had included the handling of purchase transactions and funds transfers over computer networks. It's grown now to include the buying and selling of new commodities such as electronic information. And the opportunities for companies seeking to take advantage of the capabilities of electronic commerce are greater than merely adopting our present view of commerce to performing those same transactions over electronic networks (although that's a good place to start an exploration of the topic).

Focus on electronic commerce involving the customer has increased

Despite electronic commerce's past roots in transactions between large corporations, banks, and other financial institutions, the use of the Internet as a way to bring electronic commerce to the individual consumer has led to a shift in viewpoint. Over the past few years, both the press and the business community have increased their focus on electronic commerce involving the consumer.

Businesses of all sizes can lower costs by using the Internet

Meanwhile business-to-business electronic commerce is rolling along, stronger than ever. The Internet has also given business-to-business electronic commerce a boost—in some cases, smaller companies are now discovering that they can conduct business on line, just like their larger counterparts. And businesses of all sizes are finding that they can take advantage of the Internet to lower the cost of electronic commerce—either by replacing other networks, or by using the Internet as another communications medium, converting their business data to digital form, and incorporating it with their business practices.

The move for businesses to digitize information isn't new— it's been going on for more than a decade, and continues to increase as personal computers become standard business equipment for more and more corporations. What's making a notable difference to businesses is that a significant synergy has formed between the use of digital information, computerized business practices, and the Internet. This synergy is what enables electronic commerce.

Integrate digital data, computerized processes, and the Internet

Before we define electronic commerce, consider for a moment what makes up traditional commerce. Traditional commerce involves more than just selling an item and collecting the money. Here is what's actually involved in the sales cycle of a purchase managed without electronic commerce.

To meet the needs of the marketplace, businesses design and manufacture new products, market their products, distribute them, and provide customer support, generating revenue for themselves along the way. Customers first have to identify a need for something, whether it is a physical product, a service, or information. Then they must look for information about that product or service, find places that sell it, and compare the options they have found (prices, service, reputation, and so on) before they actually purchase the product. Making the sale might also involve negotiating the price, quantity, terms of delivery, and maybe even some legal issues. And the sales cycle doesn't end with the delivery of the product or service, either. Customer support adds more steps while working to the benefit of both parties—customers get what they need to keep their products performing

The sales cycle describes the linear series of tasks that support the buying and selling of goods and services

well, and suppliers learn more about market needs. Meanwhile, banks and other financial institutions handle the transfer of funds between buyers and sellers, whether they're individual consumers or large multi-national corporations.

Once you realize how many tasks and processes are involved in traditional commerce, you discard the simplistic definition of commerce as just the buying and selling of products. You should also discard the equally simplistic definition of electronic commerce as merely the conducting of business transactions over electronic networks instead of paper, telephones, couriers, trucks, planes, and other means of moving products and information.

Electronic commerce includes the tasks that support the buying and selling of goods and services, and interactions among those tasks

Electronic commerce is a system that includes not only those transactions that center on buying and selling goods and services to directly generate revenue, but also those transactions that *support* revenue generation, such as generating demand for those goods and services, offering sales support and customer service (see Figure 1-1), or facilitating communications between business partners.

Electronic commerce can facilitate internal department interactions, improve customer relations, and eliminate the constraints of time and place

Electronic commerce builds on the advantages and structures of traditional commerce by adding the flexibilities offered by electronic networks (see Figure 1-2 on page 6). By operating with digital information in electronic networks, electronic commerce brings with it some new opportunities for conducting commercial activities. For example, by using digital information for commercial activities, electronic commerce makes it easier for different groups to cooperate. The groups could be departments sharing information within a company to plan a marketing campaign, companies working together to design and build new products or offer new services, or businesses sharing information with their customers to improve customer relations.

The cycle of electronic commerce. *Figure 1-1*

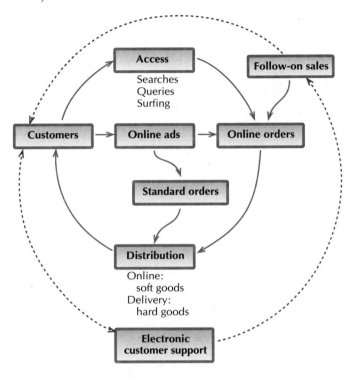

Conducting commercial activities on electronic networks also removes certain physical constraints. For example, computing systems on the Internet can be set up to provide customer support 24 hours a day, 7 days a week. Orders for your products and services can also be accepted on an anytime, anywhere basis.

Electronic commerce enables new forms of business, as well as new ways of doing business. Amazon.com, for example, is a bookseller based in Seattle, Washington. The company has no physical stores, sells all their books via the Internet, and coordinates deliveries directly with the publishers so they do not have to maintain any inventory. Companies such as Kantara and software.net take this a step further.

Electronic commerce enables companies to close stores, reduce inventory requirements, and distribute products over the Internet

Because all of their products (commercial software packages) are electronic, and can be stored on the same computers that they use for processing orders and serving the Web,
their inventory is totally digital. As another example, AMP
Inc. is offering its clients the opportunity to purchase electronic connectors and related components directly from its
Web-based catalog, bypassing the need for EDI-based purchase orders and confirmations.

Figure 1-2   *Components of electronic commerce.*

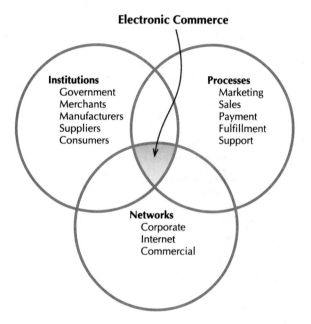

The definition of electronic commerce is not a static one.
Even as the new opportunities offered by our current technological capabilities have yet to be fully exploited, new
networking technologies or applications software can arrive
tomorrow. Thus we'll be presented not only with new ways
of doing what we've done in the past, but we'll also find
new things to do.

Traditional vs.
Electronic Business Transactions

Consider what tasks your company has to perform when an employee wants to buy something, for example, a filing cabinet. First that employee generates a request for the filing cabinet, including some specifications (four-drawer vs. five-drawer, with lock vs. no lock), and passes this request on through an approval process involving one or two managers, depending on the cost. That request finally makes it over to the purchasing department, where someone has to check through the office supply catalogs to select an appropriate model and supplier. Assume the company doesn't have a single preferred supplier for office supplies, so the purchasing agent has to check more than one catalog and call the suppliers to determine the availability of the filing cabinet. Once a supplier is selected, the agent can issue a purchase order, and either fax or mail it to the supplier. (Phone orders aren't accepted because a paper trail is an important part of the process.)

The purchaser generates a request, gains approval, selects an appropriate supplier, determines availability, and issues a purchase order

Once the order has been received, the supplier verifies the credit and sales history of the ordering company, checks the warehouse for inventory, and finds out when the shipper can pick up the cabinet from the warehouse and deliver it to the appropriate location. Satisfied that the item can be delivered within the time requested, the supplier creates a shipping order, notifies the warehouse, and creates an invoice for the filing cabinet. The invoice gets mailed, the filing cabinet gets delivered, and somewhere along the way, your company pays the bill for the cabinet.

The seller must verify credit and sales history, check inventory, schedule shipping, notify the warehouse, and issue an invoice

Now consider how this might be done using electronic commerce. The employee would visit the Web site of either the distributor or the manufacturer, and select the appropriate filing cabinet by matching the needs (color, number of

Using electronic
commerce, the pur-
chaser can select
products from a
Web site, request
approvals and forward
orders to purchasing
via electronic
processes

drawers, lock, size) with the data in an online catalog.[3] The
employee would then use electronic mail to send a digital
request (perhaps appending the Web page of the selected
product) to the manager for approval. Once approved, the
manager would simply use e-mail to forward the request to
purchasing. Purchasing could then copy the necessary
information into their order database, and send an electronic order to the supplier, via EDI or another form, also
using e-mail.

The seller can add
orders to a database,
check warehouse
inventory and
customer status,
arrange delivery, and
handle communica-
tions all via elec-
tronic commerce

When the supplier receives the order, a computer program
might automatically insert the order into a database of
pending orders, check inventory at the warehouses, check
your company's credit status, and earmark the item for
delivery. This same program might then pass a shipping
order electronically to the appropriate warehouse and create
an invoice. If a shipping agent were used, the warehouse
would notify the shipper via e-mail. Once the filing cabinet
was received, accounts payable would instruct the bank, via
e-mail, to transfer the appropriate funds to the supplier.

Compare the traditional way of doing things to the electronic commerce version (as shown in the table on the
facing page). Many of the steps are the same, but the way
that information is obtained and transferred along the cycle
is different. Many different media were needed in the traditional method, making coordination more difficult, and
increasing the time required to process the order. But with
electronic commerce, everything starts out and stays digital;
only different applications are needed to transfer and process the data as it winds its way through the order process.

---

3. In the future, you might instruct a computer program called a mobile
   agent to search the online catalogs of office suppliers to find the
   products you want and have the agent present comparably priced
   products in a spreadsheet.

New and Old Ways of Purchasing an Item

Sales Cycle Step	Traditional Commerce (Multiple Media Employed)	Electronic Commerce (Single Medium Employed)
Acquire product information	magazines, flyers online catalogs	Web pages
Request item	printed forms, letters	e-mail
Get order approved		
Check catalogs, prices	catalogs	online catalogs
Check product availability and confirm price	phone, fax	
Generate order	printed form	e-mail Web pages
Send order (buyer); Receive order (supplier)	fax, mail	e-mail EDI
Prioritize order		online database
Check inventory at warehouse	printed form, phone, fax	online database Web pages
Schedule delivery	printed form	e-mail online database
Generate invoice	printed form	online database
Receive product	shipper	
Confirm receipt	printed form	e-mail
Send invoice (supplier); Receive invoice (buyer)	mail	e-mail EDI
Schedule payment	printed form	EDI online database
Send payment (buyer); Receive payment (supplier)	mail	EDI EFT

The traditional sales
cycle involves many
different media

The initial desire for the filing cabinet might have been spurred by a flyer from a manufacturer of office furniture, or the cabinet might have been featured in a magazine. Even before the product was delivered and paid for, other means of communication were used—more printed media (catalogs, ordering forms, and so on), interoffice mail, the telephone, and perhaps fax or the United States Postal Service. The payment itself might have been made by writing a check, using a corporate purchasing card, or including it in a larger monthly payment to the supplier.

Use of a single
medium for all steps
would be most
efficient

Imagine how much more efficient this process would be if you were able to obtain all the information you needed right at your fingertips, and also make your purchases, all using one medium. That's the promise of electronic commerce, reflected in the last column of the table shown on the previous page. Of course, you can't deliver filing cabinets over the Internet, but some goods and services are more amenable to electronic transfer than others.

More Than the Sum of Its Parts

All information
can be expressed
and stored as
computer bits

For those of you in the business of providing information products and services, or content, your production options vary from traditional print media to various forms of multimedia, either for the Web, movies, or television. The crucial fact is that all of this information can be expressed and stored as computer bits, which makes the product more versatile as new media are embraced or new opportunities arise. For example, catalog data stored in a database can be presented electronically via the Web, but it can also be printed in customized catalogs targeted at specific market niches. Or the data might be included on a CD-ROM, along with multimedia presentations of your products. Your production infrastructure is going to rely on computers and other electronic devices. If you're publishing information on the Internet, you'll be using such computer applications as **Web servers**, databases, and multimedia authoring tools.

This section looks at the five processes shown in Figure 1-3: information sharing, ordering, payment, fulfillment, and service and support. All of these are part of the new electronic commerce life cycle.

Electronic commerce and business processes.   **Figure 1-3**

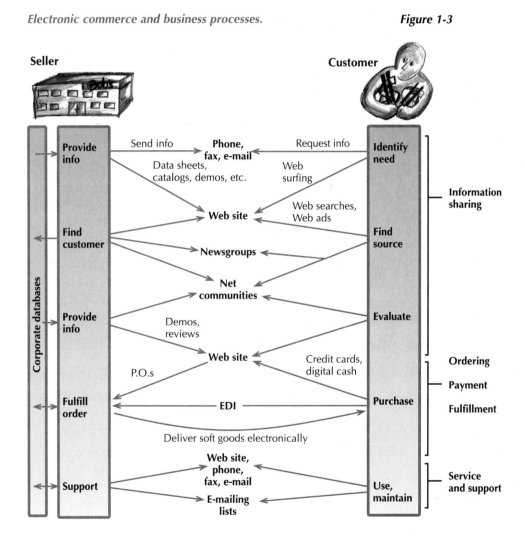

Information Sharing

Use the Internet to provide information while learning about your markets

Even before you make a sale, you need to make your clientele aware of your products and services. That means advertising and marketing, or, more generally, providing data for your customers' information gathering process. Potential customers must get information about your company and its products, while you learn more about your markets in order to reach your customers better, and design your products and services to meet their needs. With electronic commerce, the two goals (both yours and your customers') can go hand-in-hand.

Use networked communities to distribute product information

You also may find that networked communities can be useful for distributing information about your products. Chat rooms, multi-party conferencing, bulletin board systems, and newsgroups (the Usenet newsgroups on the Internet, for example) are all ways that you can foster discussion of your company and its products. Many of these systems can be integrated with a Web server.

Gather data from Web site visitors

The World Wide Web (or more often just "the Web") provides one effective medium for communicating with your customers. You can design Web sites to include product catalogs that can be searched electronically and that provide new types of product information. If you maintain an online catalog of products using the Web, you can obtain data on which products are requested in searches, and how often those requests are made. Or you can actively request information from visitors to your Web site by providing them with a page for comments. Asking Web visitors to provide some information about themselves as they search your catalog, or prepare an online order, can help you tie demographic data to product searches and information requests—information that can help your marketing and sales departments (see Figure 1-4). You can also send periodic notices about product upgrades and new features to interested parties by e-mail.

Gathering information from your customers.   *Figure 1-4*

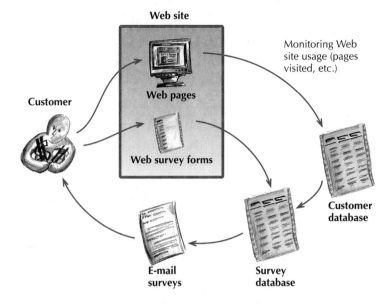

The Internet offers you a number of different ways to provide customer support. For example, if you're maintaining a Web server,[4] you can include a form to accept questions from customers using a **Web browser**,[5] and direct those queries to your support staff. You can compile questions that arise repeatedly into what are known as Frequently Asked Questions (FAQ) files, and distribute them via e-mail, Usenet news, and the Web. Even before Web sites became a mechanism for accepting questions, customers have often been able to correspond with support staffs via e-mail.

Distribute FAQs via e-mail, Usenet news, and the Web

One part of customer support that you shouldn't overlook is actively seeking customer opinions. You can design forms-

---

4. Web server software manages data at the Web site, controls access to that data, and responds to requests from browsers.

5. Web browser software allows you to connect with servers to access HTML documents and their associated media files (that is, Web pages) on the network or World Wide Web, and to follow links from document to document, or page to page.

based surveys for your Web site, or use e-mail to distribute similar surveys to select customers.

Opportunities exist for intermediaries to guide consumers through the mass of information

While a large number of Web sites are aimed at the general public, a significant number of sites are aimed at business markets. In some cases, you can find intermediaries, or brokers, offering sites that allow buyers and sellers in a particular market to interact, trade information, bid, and make sales. As you'll discover in Chapter 4 (see "Examining the Role of Intermediaries" on page 109), the likelihood of an Internet-driven information explosion in many markets is an opportunity for intermediaries to help guide clients through the mass of information.

Ordering

Use electronic forms and e-mail to process orders

It should be a routine matter for customers to electronically place orders for your company's goods or services. Electronic forms that mirror traditional paper order forms are a good way of handling this. Client/server applications have often been designed to handle this, but because most Web systems support electronic forms,[6] many companies are now turning to the Web instead. But don't overlook such an obvious opportunity as accepting orders via e-mail, either. Even if you do not use forms-based e-mail on the Internet, it is not too difficult to write a **CGI script** to process ASCII-text messages and place the order information into a database.

Payment

EDI setup costs were prohibitive for small businesses, but the Internet is leveling the playing field

Now comes the heart of the sales process—actually receiving the money for your goods or services. With a wide variety of payment mechanisms in place or proposed, this is perhaps the most fluid and fast-changing part of electronic

---

6. A Web server can send requests for information that appear as a form to be filled out in the user's Web browser; when the information is completed, the browser sends the info back to the server, which then processes the data and stores it in a database.

commerce. Consumers can use credit cards, electronic checks, **digital cash**, and even something called **microcash**, when the payments are only a few pennies or dimes. (For more detail on these payment schemes, see Chapter 3, "Handling Money on the Net.") Some businesses have long been users of EDI, but the setup costs have made it prohibitive for smaller businesses. However, with the advent of EDI over the Internet, small businesses, and even home businesses, can use EDI. Soon, your business will have both consumer-based and business-based payments processed through the Internet.

Entrepreneurs are experimenting with a variety of electronic payment systems on the Internet. Many are electronic equivalents of the systems we're accustomed to using every day, such as credit cards, checks, and debit cards. Even digital cash, an attempt to electronically represent the hard currency in your pocket, is also available. But all of these electronic methods for paying for goods and services over a network are still in a fledgling stage when compared to all the transactions completed every day using cash, checks, and credit cards in the traditional world.

Digital cash now exists, but is still in a fledgling stage

Businesses have responded to the popularity of the Web by putting their product data sheets and catalogs for ordering on Web servers, so tying payment systems to the same medium makes sense. Many vendors offer commerce-server or merchant-server Web software specifically designed to handle accepting payments over the Web; some also include facilities for generating product catalogs.

Commerce or merchant Web server software is designed to handle payment transactions

Businesses are also starting to use EDI for transactions over the Internet with their suppliers, either by using Web-based forms for entering EDI transactions with a services company on the Internet, or by using secure e-mail to forward EDI transactions to their business partners.

In addition to all the methods for making payments electronically over the Internet, there are still the tried-and-true methods used every day, such as giving credit card numbers over the telephone, or faxing an order with a credit card number. These methods are slowly being replaced by electronic commerce, so they are not covered in any detail in this book.

Fulfillment

Use the Internet to transfer your information products to your clients

Whether you call our current era the Electronic Age or the Information Age, our economy depends on the daily transfer of massive amounts of information. Many companies make money generating, transferring, or analyzing that information. If your company is one of these, then you can use the Internet to transfer your information products to your clients. Aside from the forms of information, such as newsletters, news, analysis reports, and stock prices, don't forget that electronic data also includes software. Documentation, program patches, and upgrades are also well suited to Internet-based distribution.

Use EDI to communicate with shippers, suppliers, and distributors

If you deal in physical goods, you can't actually deliver your products via the Internet, but you can use EDI to inform your shippers of goods that need to be transferred. And the Internet lets you use e-mail to communicate with suppliers and distributors about matters such as the status of deliveries. In some cases, shippers such as Federal Express, United Parcel Service, and American President Lines now let you check delivery status using the Web.

Provide information, but do not bombard your clients

No matter how innovative and popular your products are, they are no good if you cannot deliver them to your customers. Once you create a product, you need a way to distribute it. You also need ways to inform your current and potential customers about the product. Whether your product is *soft goods*, that is, information, or **hard goods**, that is, tangible products, you can use e-mail and a Web site to make product release information available. As a customer, I personally like e-mail because I don't have to remember to check a Web site; others don't like being bombarded by e-mail, so you have to seek a happy balance according to your customers' wishes. Web sites are good for making a lot more information available than you'd probably transmit via e-mail.

If you come to rely on intermediaries or other distributors to distribute your products and product information, sharing product release schedules, product development and marketing plans, and similar types of information between your company and the intermediaries can be invaluable. Maintaining shared databases accessible by outsiders, and allowing them to enter data as well as review it, helps strengthen ties with your partners.

Strengthen ties with your partners by maintaining shared databases

Service and Support

Rarely does a company's relationship with a customer end with the sale. In fact, the sale may be only the beginning of a long and fruitful relationship with a customer. Not only might the customer need some sort of assistance with the product or service, but your company might want to work with the customer to improve the products and services it can offer to other customers in the future.

Items such as technical notes about your products' features and uses, FAQs (frequently asked questions) that provide answers to your customers' most commonly-posed inquiries, software updates, and bug fixes, are only some of the information you can make available to customers on the Internet. Cleverly designed systems can provide this information to customers through a variety of channels, such as fax, e-mail, and the Web, all at the same time. And these systems don't have to be static; you can let your customers help decide

Provide information and invite questions and comments via fax, e-mail, and the Web

what information you should provide. Providing a form for questions on a Web site, or simply accepting questions by e-mail (and not just to your technical support people), can go a long way toward ensuring that you're getting the right information into the right hands.

New Opportunities

Electronic commerce can simplify communication and change relationships

The comparison of how traditional and electronic commerce can be used for ordering items such as a filing cabinet was a simple, rather straightforward example of commerce. When you consider the different applications that can be used to work on digital information, such as those briefly outlined in the previous section, you should realize that electronic commerce can not only simplify the delivery of information and goods, but it can also change the relationships between them (see Figure 1-5). That adds up to new opportunities.

New online opportunities include easier comparison shopping for your customers

Electronic advertisements for office furniture could lead right to information about local stores carrying that item, along with that store's business hours and directions, even pointers to reviews of the products. If a consumer doesn't need to see a product in person before buying, orders could be placed and paid for electronically.

Electronic commerce offers other new opportunities to both individuals and businesses. As electronic commerce matures, and more companies conduct business on line, you'll be able to do comparison shopping more easily.

Even through direct buyer-seller communications will increase, there are still new opportunities for intermediaries

In addition, vendors will be able to electronically notify potential customers about sales of items in which they are particularly interested. Despite all the talk concerning *disintermediation*, the increase of direct buyer-seller interaction at the expense of the middleman, electronic commerce will open up new opportunities for new kinds of

Some of the opportunities of electronic commerce.   *Figure 1-5*

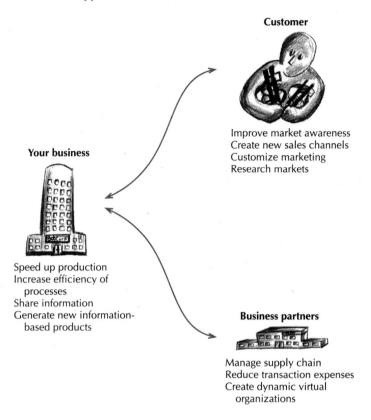

Customer

Improve market awareness
Create new sales channels
Customize marketing
Research markets

Your business

Speed up production
Increase efficiency of
  processes
Share information
Generate new information-
  based products

Business partners

Manage supply chain
Reduce transaction expenses
Create dynamic virtual
  organizations

intermediaries. For example, some businesses will become
intermediaries or brokers to track special markets, notifying
clients of bargains, changing market conditions, and hard-
to-find items, and even conducting periodic searches for
special products on their behalf.

We've only begun to see the opportunities and synergies
that electronic commerce can offer. In the past three to four
years, the Internet has become more appealing to consumers. The World Wide Web has allowed more consumers to
confidently use the Internet, and it has offered individuals
and businesses new ways to present and find information.

Using the Internet for
business-to-business
transactions is less
expensive than using
private networks

Business-to-business transactions can now take place at less expense using the Internet than they did using private networks offered for EDI and bank transactions. This has offered not only potential cost savings for large businesses, but also the opportunity for smaller businesses to use the electronic processes they found prohibitively expensive in the past.

The Benefits of Electronic Commerce

Network-based systems can reduce paperwork and allow greater focus on customers' needs

Electronic commerce can offer your company both short-term and long-term benefits. Not only can it open new markets, enabling you to reach new customers, but it can also make it easier and faster for you to do business with your existing customer base. Moving business practices, such as ordering, invoicing, and customer support, to network-based systems can also reduce the paperwork involved in business-to-business transactions. When more of your information is digital, you can better focus on meeting your customers' needs. Tracking customer satisfaction, requesting more customer feedback, and presenting custom solutions for your clientele are just some of the opportunities that can stem from electronic commerce.

The View Ahead

This chapter contains a brief overview of the concepts that are crucial to implementing electronic commerce on the Internet. This information serves as the basis for the discussion of actual electronic commerce applications later in this book.

Before you get to the series of real-world examples of how businesses are taking part in electronic commerce on the Internet (Chapters 6 through 11), you need to understand a few more important topics. Chapter 2 examines the technologies of the Internet, Chapter 3 surveys the various electronic payment systems, and Chapter 4 covers many of the technologies and issues surrounding security on the Internet. Finally, Chapter 5 examines consumer and business markets on the Internet, including a discussion of some of the important issues and opportunities that are different about electronic commerce. Then you'll move on to analyzing actual electronic commerce scenarios that show how real businesses have used the available technologies, and what business processes they've followed.

In keeping with the business focus of these later chapters, Chapter 12 discusses business strategies for taking advantage of electronic commerce, covering such issues as corporate structures, how information is shared in, and between, companies, and what business models fit best with the concepts of electronic commerce.

The book ends with Chapter 13, a look to the future to examine some of the newest technologies likely to affect commerce.

Chapter Two

The Importance of the Internet

One of the components of electronic commerce is the network used for communications; among the various available networks, the Internet has certainly gotten the most attention in the past year or two. Although the rest of this chapter focuses on electronic commerce on the Internet, keep in mind that the definition includes other networks as well. The following pages should serve as introduction to some of the more important business and technical issues of the Internet.

Internet Structure and Growth

The Internet is global in scope and strongly decentralized; that is, it has no single governing body. The physical networks comprising the Internet form a hierarchy, the top level of which is the high-speed backbone network maintained by MCI. The majority of Internet traffic is funneled onto the backbone through the **network access points** (NAPs), which are maintained by Sprint, MFS, and others, and are located in strategic metropolitan areas across the United States. Independently created national networks (created by PSInet and UUNET, among others) mostly tie into the NAPs, but some service providers have made their own arrangements for

The Internet structure is hierarchical, with high-speed backbones at the top, and regional and individual networks at the bottom exchanging Internet traffic in order to sidestep the NAPs, which are becoming bottlenecks. Lower levels in the hierarchy are composed of regional networks, and then the individual networks found on university campuses, at research organizations, and in businesses (see Figure 2-1). This grand network of networks shares a common set of communicating protocols, known as the TCP/IP suite (discussed later in this chapter).

Figure 2-1   *The Internet hierarchy.*

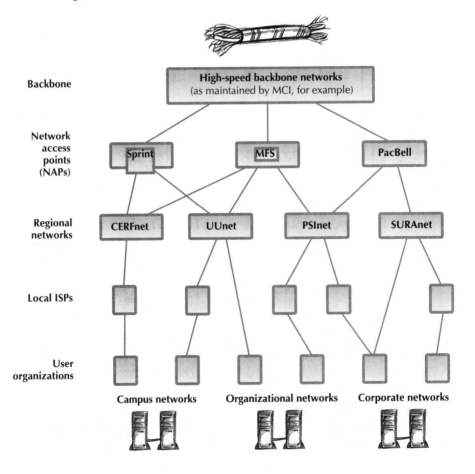

The growth of the Internet has been phenomenal by any measure. The Internet's predecessor, ARPANET, started in 1969, connecting together only four computers at different locations in the United States. Over the past few years, the number of computers attached to the Internet has been doubling annually. According to the survey of Internet host computers that's run periodically by Mark Lottor, there were almost 13 million computers connected to the Internet as of July 1996. Depending on whom you ask, there may be 50 million users of the Internet in the United States alone. With this growth has come a change in the direction of the Internet. What was once a network designed primarily for academic research is now a network populated largely by individuals outside universities, as well as a large number of commercial enterprises.

As of July 1996, nearly 13 million computers were connected to the Internet, with over 50 million users of the Internet in the United States alone

The change in the demographics of Internet users has led to tremendous business opportunities, many of which have grabbed the financial headlines. It has also produced friction between entrepreneurs with proprietary tendencies, and many of the original designers of the Internet who consider openness fundamental to the continued evolution of the Internet. The value of openness is at odds with the often-proprietary demands of businesses and markets. And the rate at which the demographics of the Internet are changing is mind-boggling. Businesses that are accustomed to working on the Internet, and even Internet technologists, are overwhelmed by the speed at which the Internet has been changing over the past few years. In fact, the standing joke among developers is that "Internet years" are seven times as fast as regular years. That doesn't seem so far from the truth.

As opportunities grow, so does the friction between entrepreneurs and the original Internet designers

As a business manager, what do the changes to the Internet mean to you? Simply put, the Internet is a very dynamic entity with a life all its own. Outside forces such as individual companies with hot new technologies, and even the marketplace itself, attempt to change the Internet and how it

The Internet is decentralized, but committees do exist to set Internet standards

functions. However, there are standards, or rules, that make the Internet work. Various standards bodies exist to ensure that the Internet runs as smoothly as possible, even though it is a decentralized collection of networks. If you keep your eye on the technologies and standards as they evolve, and pay attention to what's changing, you'll see opportunities for your company to use, and profit from, the Internet. It's the aim of this book to acquaint you with both the technologies surrounding electronic commerce on the Internet and the business strategies for using those technologies.

Although many of the systems proposed for electronic commerce on the Internet are new and, in some cases, untried, the Internet has long been a breeding ground for experimentation. It's this frenzy of experimentation in electronic commerce that makes new developments in electronic commerce on the Internet appear chaotic.

The influence of existing financial institutions lends stability to financial processes on the Internet

On the other hand, the traditional financial networks, with which we're familiar, evolved as very centralized and carefully planned systems. Some of those systems, such as those used by credit card issuers and banks, are affecting the evolution of electronic commerce on the Internet. They are bringing stability to Internet electronic commerce, and providing new ways to tie the new opportunities of the Internet to the established financial processes we use every day. Electronic commerce on the Internet will not replace our present-day financial processes, however it will be a strong complement to them. Seeing how they match each other, and also mate with your business practices, is fundamental to your effectively taking advantage of electronic commerce.

New software connects to existing banking networks or credit card clearing networks

For example, many different companies, such as Microsoft, Netscape, Cybercash, and Verifone, are all developing software that allows consumers to use **Web browsers** to pay for purchases electronically. These systems also include vendor software for processing the payments. But ultimately, they all use a connection into the existing banking networks or credit card clearing networks. Some banks are now working on systems that will use the Internet to make that connection, instead of a private network, simplifying the networking requirements for the vendors. And Visa and MasterCard have been hard at work developing a protocol called **Secured Electronic Transaction** (SET) that ties together and protects credit card information at the consumer, vendor, and network levels. (See "An Overview of Internet Security Systems" on page 181 in Chapter 4.)

Network Infrastructure

Applications that fall within the realm of electronic commerce depend on the underlying network infrastructures (see Figure 2-2). The network infrastructure covers the media required for moving information, and thus includes the Internet, as well as cable television, telecommunication networks, and private corporate networks.

Electronic commerce depends on a series of underlying infrastructures

The building blocks of electronic commerce.

Figure 2-2

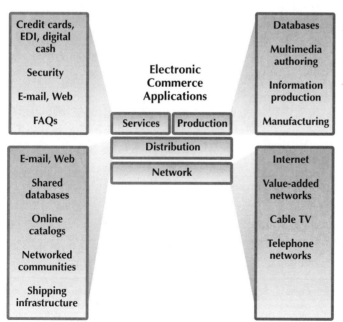

As the figure shows, other electronically based infrastructures may also be built within your business. The production infrastructure focuses on your company's products (whether they are information-related content or **hard goods**) and what it takes for you to create them. The distribution infrastructure lets you get your products and services to your customers. Lastly, the services infrastructure handles such processes as payments, customer support, and security.

The network infrastructure encompasses all the technologies of the Internet. Technologies are specified by **protocols**—the rules that determine everything about the way a network operates. Protocols govern how applications access the network, the way data from an application is divided into **packets**[1] for transmission through a cable, and which electrical signals represent data on a network cable.

In an effort to standardize a way of looking at network protocols, the International Standards Organization (ISO) created a 7-layer model (shown in the table) that defines the basic network functions. This model is called the OSI Reference Model.

Two important principles are at the heart of the OSI Reference Model. First, there's the concept of *open systems*. Each layer of the model has specific network functions—this means that two different network systems supporting the functions of a related layer can exchange data at that level. Second, the OSI Reference Model depends on the concept of *peer-to-peer communications*. Data created by one layer in the model and transmitted to another device on the network pertains only to the same layer on that device. In other words, intervening layers do not alter the data; the other layers simply add to the data found in a packet to perform their assigned functions on the network.

---

1. A packet is the fundamental grouping of data for transmission on a digital network. A packet consists of a sequence of bits that includes control information for transmitting the data, as well as the data itself.

Network Layers and TCP/IP Protocols

Layer	Functions	Information Transferred	TCP/IP Protocols
Application	What data do I send to my partner?	Application messages	FTP, HTTP, SNMP, DNS
Presentation	What does the data look like?	Encrypted data, compressed data	
Session	Who is the partner?	Session messages	
Transport	Where is the partner?	Multiple packets	TCP, UDP
Network	Which route do I follow to get there?	Packets	IP, ARP
Data Link	How do I make each step in that route?	Frames	Ethernet, PPP
Physical	How do I use the medium for that step?	Bits	Physical wiring

Protocol suites are designed in distinct layers to make it easier to substitute one protocol for another. You can say that protocol suites govern how data is exchanged above and below each protocol layer. (In fact, the graphical representation of these protocols in vertical layers is why protocol suites are sometimes called protocol stacks.) When protocols are designed, specifications set forth how a protocol exchanges data with a protocol layered above or below it. As long as a developer follows these specifications, he or she can substitute a new, better protocol for the one currently in the suite without affecting the general behavior of the network. For example, a new version of the **Internet protocol** is being implemented on the Internet that provides more addresses for network devices, along with added security, and multimedia options.

Protocol suites (or stacks) determine how data is exchanged between layers

TCP/IP Protocols

The protocols that form the TCP/IP stack are the basis of the Internet

The **TCP/IP protocols** define how data is subdivided into packets for transmission across a network, as well as how applications can transfer files and send electronic mail. While the TCP/IP protocols don't neatly fit into all seven layers of the OSI Reference Model, they do provide all the necessary functionality for productive networking.

PPP governs 'transmission across serial (or modem) communications

For example, TCP/IP makes use of many existing protocols that define network media, such as Ethernet over twisted-pair and other types of cable, as well as fiber optic cable (**FDDI**). **Point-to-point protocol** (PPP) is one of the few protocols developed specifically to govern TCP/IP transmissions over a particular medium, in this case, serial (modem) connections.

IP provides address space and handles routing, while ARP helps determine IP addresses

The network and transport layers are at the core of the TCP/IP stack, with **Internet Protocol** (IP) being the key protocol. IP provides an address space for internetworks, and handles the routing of packets across an internetwork. **ARP**, which is another protocol that's a part of the network layer, is used to help network devices determine an IP address.

The TCP and UDP protocols determine packet size

Above IP, either **transmission control protocol** (TCP) or **user datagram protocol** (UDP) can be used to determine the maximum transmission that can be used (that is, the packet size) and fine-tune transmissions accordingly. TCP is used when 100 percent reliability of the transmission is required, while UDP is used in less stringent situations.

Application Protocols

The application protocols are important to conducting business on the Internet

Everything that encompasses the network below the application layer is transparent to the computer user. (That is, until something goes wrong.) The application layer is where the user gets to do something useful with the networks, perhaps sending e-mail, browsing a Web site, or transferring a file. While all of the underlying network infrastructure is needed to make applications work, it's the applications that are of greatest importance to conducting business on the Internet, or on any other network.

Some of the important application protocols are **file transfer protocol** (FTP) for file transfers, **hypertext transfer protocol** (HTTP) for the World Wide Web, and **simple network management protocol** (SNMP) for controlling network devices. **Domain naming service** (DNS) is also useful because it's responsible for converting numeric IP addresses into names that can be more easily remembered by users. Many other protocols dealing with the finer details of applications can be included in the application layer. These include **simple mail transport protocol** (SMTP), **post office protocol** (POP), **Internet Mail Access Protocol** (IMAP) and **multimedia Internet mail extensions** (MIME) for e-mail.

There are occasions when it's necessary to retrieve files, such as applications or worksheets, from someone else's computer. On the Internet, you use the file transfer protocol (FTP) for file transfers between file servers and client computers like your own personal computer. Depending on your software, you can select files one by one and upload or download them, or you can create a list of files and transfer them as a batch.

FTP is the file transfer protocol

Certainly the most visible interface to the Internet these days is the Web, which is based on a standard set of codes called **HyperText Markup Language** (HTML) and a technology known as hypertext transfer protocol (HTTP). The browser on the user's computer looks at HTML to determine how the text and graphics should be displayed. HTTP determines how a file (such as an HTML document) is transferred from server to client.

HTTP determines how a file is transferred from server to client

Although Web-related traffic on the Internet is the single largest component of Internet activity, there are actually more e-mail users than Web users on the Internet. E-mail is

SMTP, POP, and IMAP are e-mail protocols

probably the most commonly used form of communication between people on the Internet. The simple mail transport protocol (SMTP) and post office protocol (POP) are the two essential Internet protocols for e-mail. SMTP is used for transferring mail between servers, while POP and a newer protocol, Internet Mail Access Protocol (IMAP), are used to handle the retrieval of messages.

MIME supports the use of multiple media types within e-mail

POP and IMAP were originally designed for text-only mail. MIME, which stands for multimedia Internet mail extensions, extends the capabilities of e-mail messaging. MIME-compliant messages can consist of more than one part; these parts might be graphics, video or sound clips, or other types of multimedia. In later chapters, you will find that the idea of a multi-part message, as defined by MIME, is important for securely transferring different types of commercial transactions on the Internet, such as EDI data.

Other Networks

Intranets use TCP/IP to share information within a company

Even though the TCP/IP protocols form the basis of the Internet, use of these protocols is not restricted to the Internet. TCP/IP has become *the* preferred protocol suite for companies seeking to adopt an open systems outlook. With the growing popularity of the Internet, businesses have also chosen to create what are called **intranets**, or networks using TCP/IP for sharing information only within the corporation.

Connecting two or more intranets forms an extranet

Using the Web in conjunction with TCP/IP networks allows companies to more easily maintain a single user interface to many applications, as well as simplify the distribution of new client software. Those companies that seek to share some of their data with business partners or clients, perhaps by establishing a shared database, and connecting intranets using TCP/IP, call these shared nets **extranets**. Figure 2-3 shows the connection between an intranet, the Internet, and an extranet. The major difference between each of these networks—the Internet, intranets, and extranets—is the control of access to information and how it is shared.

Intranets, the Internet, and extranets.

Figure 2-3

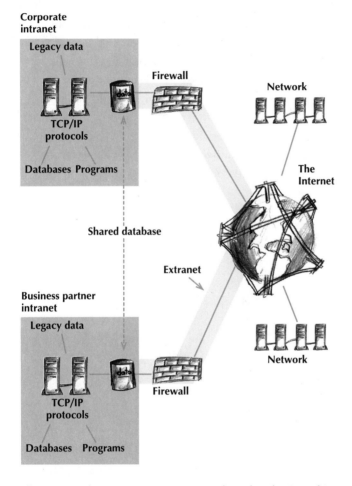

There are other non-Internet network technologies of importance to electronic commerce. These include the **value added networks** (VANs) that are maintained privately, and dedicated to EDI between business partners. Larger corporations have often maintained their own private networks for company business, and on occasion have opened them up

VANs are privately maintained, dedicated networks

to business partners for exchanging information. Bank and credit card clearinghouses also maintain dedicated private networks for electronic fund transfers among themselves and associated businesses.

VPNs running over the Internet can replace expensive leased phone lines

The network landscape is changing because of the increased influence of the Internet. The biggest change is that businesses are looking at ways to conduct financial transactions over open networks like those comprising the Internet. Companies are investigating the possibility of conducting EDI transactions over the Internet, which would greatly reduce the cost. Many of these same businesses are also experimenting with the technology to run their corporate nets as **virtual private networks** (VPNs) over the Internet, replacing expensive leased phone lines between offices.

Look for more incidents of convergence

The telecommunications and cable television networks also play a big role. Although the focus of this book is Internet-related technologies, the lines between data networks such as the Internet, cable television, and telecommunications networks are becoming increasingly fuzzy. Look for more incidents of convergence as Web applications run on televisions, multimedia and videoconferencing increases on the Internet, and the cable and telephone companies compete to bring increased bandwidth to consumers and businesses alike.

Chapter Three

Handling Money on the Net

In everyday life, you pay for goods and services in a number of different ways. If you're an individual consumer dealing with a merchant, you can pay by cash, check, credit card, or debit card. Businesses can often conduct transactions among themselves electronically, but they usually use private networks. Now with the increasing commercialization of the Internet, and the popularity of the Web, consumers and businesses are both looking for ways to conduct business over the Internet.

Use the Internet instead of private networks for electronic transactions

This chapter focuses on the systems that developers and consortia have been working on to provide electronic versions of the payment systems we use in everyday life. In addition to covering electronic versions of the standard methods for making payments—cash, checks, and credit cards—this chapter includes some background on **electronic data interchange** (EDI), because it's been used for handling payments on networks (other than the Internet) for some time, and is of particular importance to businesses. This chapter also discusses some of the unique constraints imposed by supporting real-time electronic commerce.

Transactions on the Internet

Electronic
procedures for
handling payments
are similar to those
used in regular point-
of-sale systems by
stores and toll-free
call centers

If your business is interested in allowing its customers to use electronic payment methods on the Internet, many of the procedures for handling payments are similar to those you use for a regular point-of-sale (POS) system in your store, or in a toll-free call center. The main difference is that everything takes place over the Internet using the customer's personal computer and your **Web server** (see Figure 3-1). Consumers use a **Web browser** to place an order and provide information about their form of payment, which might be a credit card, **digital cash**, or electronic check.[1] Software on your server then has to settle the transaction by verifying the order (presumably from your online catalog), and getting authorization for the funds transfer from a bank or credit card acquirer. Usually this last step is done via a **gateway**[2] that communicates with the bank using either the Internet or the bank's private network, much like a store's POS system.

Consumers are also just beginning to use new systems (such as electronic checking and digital cash, see pages 49 and 51) for making small, immediate electronic payments to information providers and others that are in keeping with the interactive, real-time nature of the Internet today.

The Internet offers
more flexibility than
traditional EDI and
EFT systems

Don't overlook business-to-business transactions, either. It's true that many large businesses and banks have been conducting business electronically for the last few decades with **electronic data interchange** (EDI) and **electronic funds transfer** (EFT), but many of these systems do not have the flexibility required to compete in current markets. Busi-

---

1. A Web server can be set up to present fields from an order form that consumers fill out in their Web browser. The information is then transmitted from the browser back to the server which processes it, usually adding it to a database.

2. Two networks using different protocols can be connected by a gateway that not only transfers data between the two, but also converts that data into a protocol-compatible form.

nesses can also order goods from suppliers via online catalogs, which is becoming a popular method of making product information available on the Internet. Companies using ledger-based purchasing might then handle the orders via EDI over either a **value added network** (VAN) or the Internet. Others might use a corporate credit card over the Internet, using methods explained later in this chapter.

The Internet payment process.   **Figure 3-1**

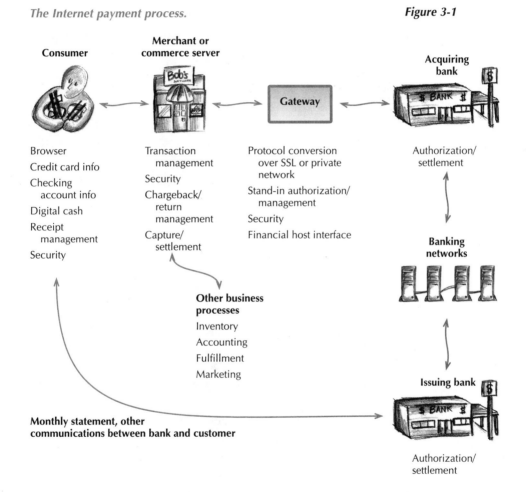

Consumer	Merchant or commerce server	Gateway	Acquiring bank
Browser	Transaction management	Protocol conversion over SSL or private network	Authorization/ settlement
Credit card info	Security	Stand-in authorization/ management	
Checking account info	Chargeback/ return management	Security	
Digital cash	Capture/ settlement	Financial host interface	
Receipt management			**Banking networks**
Security			

Other business processes

Inventory

Accounting

Fulfillment

Marketing

Issuing bank

Monthly statement, other communications between bank and customer

Authorization/ settlement

Everyone can benefit from the Internet's lower implementation and maintenance costs

As long as implementation and maintenance costs for electronic systems are low, both small businesses and large corporations can take advantage of these systems. This is one of the advantages of the Internet, with its current flat-rate pricing for access. Past business commerce systems using VANs have been prohibitively expensive, but using the Internet lowers the costs, allowing small businesses to profitably use electronic commerce for business transactions. Even if Internet service providers institute classes of fees for different types of traffic, and move away from flat-rate fees, those costs are still likely to be lower than those found on VANs.

Requirements of Payment Systems

The requirements of traditional financial transaction systems include: confidentiality, integrity, and authentication

Traditional financial transactions offer a set of special characteristics that people have come to depend on, even if they don't think about them everyday. For example, when you give your credit card number to a merchant, you expect *confidentiality*—that the number will only be disclosed to those who have a legitimate need to know it, such as the issuing bank. This situation also requires *integrity*—that neither the purchase amount, nor the goods you bought, will be altered inappropriately.

Both the buyer and the seller may require *authentication*, that is, assurance that the other is really who they claim to be. When you buy goods or services in person, you implicitly authenticate the vendor based on the location of the business and the permanence of its facilities. If you're not paying by cash, the merchant usually asks to see your driver's license or similar photo ID, or just compares your signatures in order to authenticate you. It's more difficult to authenticate a party if you're not dealing face-to-face—over the phone, for instance. In fact, many phone-based orders are conducted without any authentication at all.

Authorization allows the merchant to determine if the buyer actually has the funds to pay for the purchase. The merchant will probably want to verify that your bank account can cover the amount of your check, or get the amount of your credit card purchase approved by a credit card clearinghouse.

Requirements of traditional systems also include: authorization, assurance, and privacy

You may also want some kind of *assurance* that the merchant is competent and worthy of your trust. This might take the form of a business license; endorsements from other customers, newspapers, or magazines; or even surety bonds for more complex transactions.

There are also occasions when you want to insure the *privacy* of a sale. For example, a business conducting research might purchase a market report, but probably wouldn't want its competitors to learn what was purchased. Cash payments can offer privacy because they don't create a paper trail tying the buyer to the product that was purchased—once a cash purchase is completed, the merchant has no record of the buyer's identity to tie a buyer to a particular item. And the receipt is the only proof that the buyer purchased something at that store by paying cash. (This alone does not prove that the holder of the receipt was the original buyer—how often have you returned an item for someone else?)

If you're going to use electronic payment systems, then you ought to expect that the same requirements be adhered to. There are technological answers for providing these principles on line, but that alone doesn't mean that they can be readily practiced. For example, you can electronically authenticate yourself on the Internet by using a **digital signature**, but the infrastructure for providing your electronic driver's license, as it were, and enabling all merchants to verify it, isn't yet in place. It's almost as if a merchant couldn't read your driver's license because it was issued in a foreign language.

Methods for meeting all of these requirements on the Internet are not yet in place

Digital signatures
and certificates are
used on the Internet
to fulfill some of the
requirements

In cyberspace, it's necessary to employ encryption (see "The Process of Encryption" on page 67 in Chapter 4) to insure confidentiality, authentication, and privacy. Which requirements are met by a particular payment system depends on what is encrypted and who's allowed to decrypt it, as you'll see in the following section. For example, encrypting all the information passed by a customer's Web browser to the vendor's Web server when making a purchase maintains the confidentiality of the transaction, but neither authentication nor assurance is guaranteed if the vendor can decrypt all of the transaction information.[3] On the other hand, if the vendor is only allowed to decrypt the order information, and must pass on the encrypted payment information (checking account or credit card number) to a financial clearinghouse for authorization, then fraud is less likely to occur.

Fast-paced
electronic commerce
requires flexible
arrangements

In many cases, business-to-business commerce depends on prior negotiations and contracts. That's been extended to the world of electronic commerce by EDI, but more flexible arrangements are needed to accommodate the fast-paced world of today's business, where trading partnerships can be short-lived. The same is true for consumers—they may purchase an item on line from a vendor with whom they've had no previous dealings.

As someone once remarked, "there are no handshakes in cyberspace." To help guard against fraud, mechanisms are needed for authenticating a vendor or a buyer, as well as assuring the integrity of a vendor. In short, a buyer needs some evidence that he can trust the vendor. Such procedures include using digital signatures for electronic correspondence, and **digital certificates** to establish a company's identity. These same procedures are also likely to see increased use over other networks, such as EDI and bank

---

3. Privacy is not totally guaranteed, either, since someone monitoring the network can detect that there's traffic passed between the buyer and the vendor. That alone can be a significant piece of business intelligence.

networks, because they can support the flexible and transitory relationships that are more likely in today's faster marketplace.

Types of Electronic Payments

The methods that have been developed for making payments on the Internet are essentially electronic versions of the traditional payment systems we use everyday—cash, checks, and credit cards. The fundamental difference between the electronic payment systems and traditional ones is that everything is digital, and is designed to be handled electronically from the get-go—there's no crinkle of dollar bills, no clink of coins in your pocket, or signing a check with a pen. In a manner of speaking, everything about the payment has been virtualized into strings of bits. This virtualization will make many of the electronic payment options appear similar to each other—often the differences are due more to the companies and consortia developing the software than to the logic involved.

Electronic payment systems are entirely digital

While many of the payment systems are currently implemented for use on personal computers, you'll see other devices supporting them before long. One day you'll be able to use a **personal digital assistant** (PDA) for handling payments. Trials are already underway with **smart cards** using some of the payment systems covered here.

Many of the systems covered here have been developed with a slant toward the consumer market. If that's your market, then you'll find yourself having to support one, or more, of these options in order to conduct commerce on the Internet. But you can also use these same systems for business-to-business commerce on the Internet. Because these electronic payment methods are analogs of existing traditional payment systems, you'll probably see ways of using them within your company to supplant other purchase methods, such as corporate credit cards, for example. And

Electronic payment methods, which are analogs of existing traditional payment systems, are appropriate for business-consumer and business-to-business transactions

if you're selling to businesses, implementing these methods will allow you to provide new services for handling purchases, without resorting to more complicated, costly methods such as EDI.

Credit Cards

In a credit card transaction, the consumer presents preliminary proof of his ability to pay by presenting his credit card number to the merchant. The merchant can verify this with the bank, and create a purchase slip for the consumer to endorse. The merchant then uses this purchase slip to collect funds from the bank, and, on the next billing cycle, the consumer receives a statement from the bank with a record of the transaction.

Credit card systems should provide security and authentication

Using a credit card to make a purchase over the Internet follows the same scenario. But on the Internet added steps must be taken to provide for secure transactions and authentication of both buyer and seller. This has led to a variety of systems for using credit cards over the Internet. Two of the features distinguishing these systems are the level of security they provide for transactions, and the software required on both the customer and business sides of the transaction.

Credit card information on line can be either raw or encrypted

Credit cards can be handled on line in two different ways: sending unencrypted credit card numbers over the Internet, or encrypting credit card details before any transactions are transmitted (see Figures 3-2 and 3-3). Encrypting credit card transactions can also be subdivided according to what is encrypted. If the entire transmission between buyer and merchant is encrypted, the merchant has to decrypt at least the order details to complete a purchase. Then to further assure the customer that only authorized parties see his credit card information and protect against merchant fraud, a trusted third party can be used to separately decrypt the credit card information for authorization of the purchase (see Figure 3-4 on page 44).

Handling credit card and order data with HTML forms and CGI
script (non-secure).

Figure 3-2

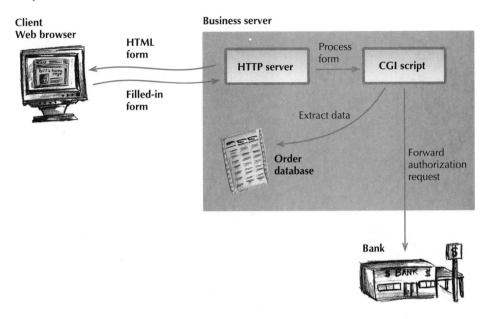

Handling credit card and order data with HTML forms and CGI
script (secured with SSL).

Figure 3-3

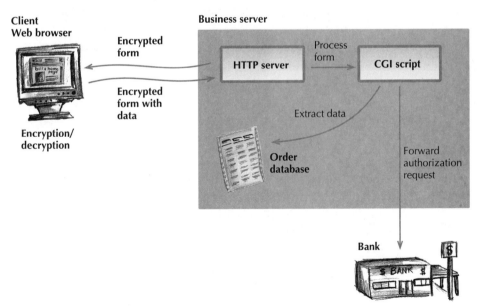

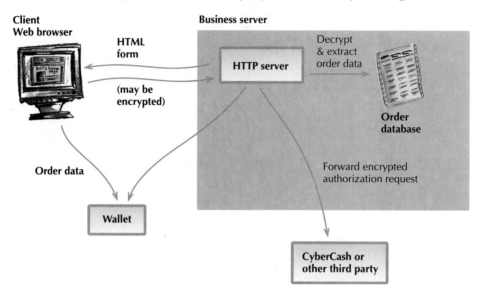

Figure 3-4   *Handling credit card and order data with a wallet as helper application and a third party for credit card processing.*

Raw data transmitted across a network is not secure

A customer browsing the Web might enter a credit card number in an order form, and click a Submit button to transmit the information to the merchant's Web server. The data would be raw, and there are no security guarantees for this type of transaction—someone could be monitoring network traffic and could intercept the transmission, or an unscrupulous merchant (or someone posing as a merchant) could use the unencrypted number for illegal charges.

For secure communications on the network, use a security protocol such as SSL

On the business end, processing the incoming credit card information only requires a Web server with a **CGI script**[4] to process the form filled out by the customer. But if you want to secure the communications between buyer and seller against snooping, a good choice is a Web browser-server

---

4. CGI, or Common Gateway Interface, is a scripting system designed to work with HTTP Web servers, and is often used to exchange data between a Web server and databases.

combination that supports the **Secure Sockets Layer** (SSL) protocol (see "An Overview of Internet Security Systems" on page 81 in Chapter 4, for a further discussion of security-related protocols).

The use of servers and browsers that support the SSL protocol only protects data against network monitors and spies. It does not guarantee that the data is protected from spying eyes on the merchant's end. To protect against merchant fraud (using a credit card for other unauthorized purchases, for example), use systems from either CyberCash, Verifone, or First Virtual. CyberCash and Verifone both use a helper application called a **wallet** for the Web browser, and pass the encrypted credit card number through the merchant to its own processor/server for authentication and approval of the sale.[5] First Virtual issues a VirtualPIN to the customer who then uses it in place of the credit card number. After receiving the sales information from the merchant, First Virtual converts the VirtualPin to the credit card account number to clear the purchase.[6] Figures 3-5 and 3-6 on the next page show a visual comparison of these two methods.

Here's a case where the electronic versions of a traditional payment system offer an added advantage—using encrypted credit card information with a trusted third party, such as Cybercash or First Virtual, instead of allowing the merchant to handle credit card processing, offers more protection against merchant fraud than is commonly seen in the everyday world.

Use systems from CyberCash, Verifone, or First Virtual, to protect consumers from merchant fraud

---

5. Verifone's vPOS system uses the SET protocol (see following pages) to transfer information to the acquiring bank. CyberCash uses their own software to process credit card information before settling accounts with the bank.

6. First Virtual uses e-mail to obtain the customer's approval of the purchase before issuing an authorization to the merchant.

Figure 3-5 *Processing a credit card transaction on line using CyberCash or Verifone.*

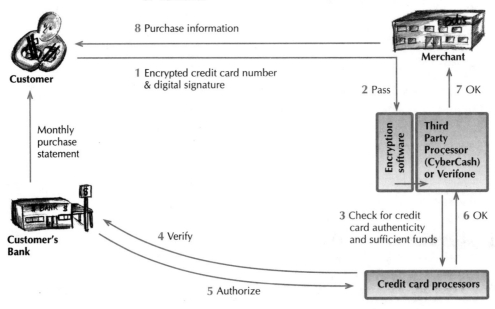

Figure 3-6 *Processing a credit card transaction on line using First Virtual.*

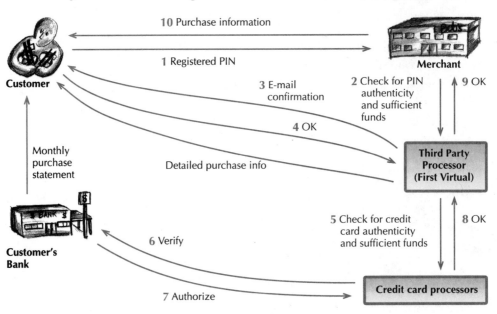

The market for handling credit card purchases on the Internet has yet to converge on a single way of doing things, or a single standard that allows the software from different vendors to work together. This lack of interoperability will likely slow down both consumer and business acceptance of using credit cards for making purchases on the Internet.

There are, however, two significant standards in the works that will make the interoperability of electronic wallet and credit card transactions simpler, both for consumers and businesses. First, there's the **Secured Electronic Transaction** protocol (SET) developed by a consortium led by Master-Card and Visa. SET is actually a combination of a protocol designed for use by other applications (such as Web browsers) and a standard (recommended procedures) for handling credit card transactions over the Internet. Designed for cardholders, merchants, banks, and other card processors, SET uses digital certificates to ensure the identities of all parties involved in a purchase. SET also encrypts credit card and purchase information before transmission on the Internet.

> The SET standard and protocol uses digital certificates and encryption to secure credit card transactions over the Internet

The second standard is the **Joint Electronic Payments Initiative**, led by the World Wide Web Consortium and CommerceNet. JEPI, as it's known, is an attempt to standardize payment negotiations. On the buyer's side (the client side), it serves as an interface that enables a Web browser, and wallets, to use a variety of payment protocols.[7] On the merchant's side (the server side), it acts between the network and transport layers to pass off the incoming transactions to the proper transport protocol (e-mail vs. **HTTP**, for instance) and proper payment protocol (such as SET). Figure 3-7 on the next page shows both sides. Because it's likely that

> To standardize payment negotiations, JEPI is an interface between the network and transport protocols

---

7. It's possible that there will be more than one SET implementation for payment systems. For example, different forms of digital signatures can be used or not all of the authentication options might be implemented by different vendors.

multiple protocols will be around for payments, transport, and wallets, JEPI makes it easier for the buyer to use a single application, and single interface, in a variety of commercial situations. It also makes it easier for the merchant to support the variety of payment systems that customers will want to use.

Figure 3-7   *JEPI's involvement in payment processing.*

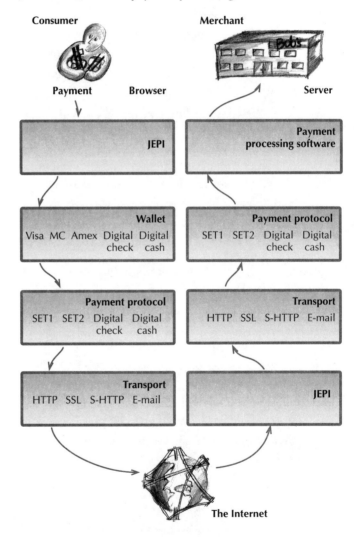

Electronic Checking

Credit card payments will undoubtedly be popular for commerce on the Internet. However, two systems have been developed—one by the Financial Services Technology Corporation (FSTC), the other by CyberCash—to let consumers use electronic checks to pay Web merchants directly.

A paper check is basically a message to a consumer's bank to transfer funds from his account to someone else's account. The message is not sent directly to the bank, but to the intended receiver of the funds, who must present the check to a bank in order to collect. After the funds are transferred, the canceled check is returned to the sender, and can then be used as proof of payment.

In virtually all aspects, an electronic check has all the same features as a paper check. It functions as a message to the sender's bank to transfer funds, and, like a paper check, the message is given initially to the receiver who, in turn, endorses the check and presents it to the bank to obtain funds.

The electronic check can prove to be superior to the paper check in one significant aspect. As sender, you can protect yourself against fraud by encoding your account number with the bank's public key, thereby not revealing your account number to the merchant. As with the SET protocol, digital certificates can be used to authenticate the payer, the payer's bank, and bank account.

CyberCash's system for electronic checking is an extension of their wallet for credit cards, and it can be used in the same way to make payments with participating vendors. Unlike the CyberCash credit card system, though, Cyber-Cash will not serve as an intermediate party for processing the checks—that function will be handled directly by banks.

The FSTC is a consortium of banks and clearing houses that has designed an electronic check. Modeled on the traditional paper check, this new check is initiated electronically, and uses a digital signature for signing and endorsing.

Electronic check systems use digital signatures and certificates

An electronic check has all the same features as a paper check

The electronic check can also protect against fraud, something a paper check can not do

To add to the flexibility of their payment system, the FSTC wants to offer users a choice of payment instruments that allow them to designate an electronic check as a certified check or an electronic charge card slip, for example (see Figure 3-8). This means that the user can use a single mechanism, the electronic check, to complete payments that vary according to payee's requirements. For example, you could decide to pay your utility bills by standard electronic checks, but you could designate that one of the electronic checks be delivered as a certified check in order to make a down payment on a new house. The instructions accompanying your electronic checks would be processed by the electronic payment handler (EPH) software installed at your bank, and distributed by the appropriate payment network.

Figure 3-8   *Extending electronic checks to existing payment services.*

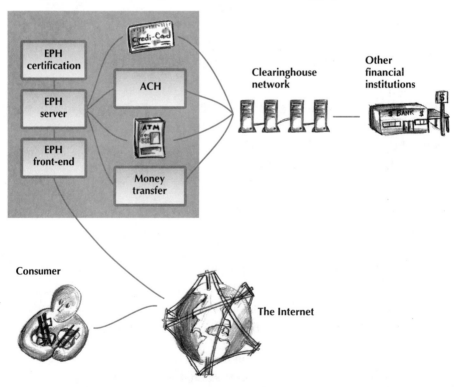

Electronic checks can be delivered either by direct transmission over a network, or by electronic mail. In either case, existing banking channels can clear payments over their networks. This leads to a convenient integration of the existing banking infrastructure and the Internet. Because FSTC's plans for electronic checking include money transfers and transactions involving the National Automated Clearing House Association[8] for transferring funds between banks, businesses could use the FSTC scheme to pay invoices from other businesses.

Ordinary consumers may prefer electronic checking to other payments systems for a number of reasons. First, more United States citizens have checking accounts than credit cards, so an electronic equivalent for checking serves a larger market. Second, at least with the FSTC system, consumers can make a variety of different payments (checks, certified checks, ATM, and so on.) using a single interface (the electronic checkbook) that gathers all transactions into a single account log. It also means that the consumer only has to deal with his bank, not a number of financial institutions, to make these different types of payments.[9]

Ordinary consumers may prefer electronic checking to other payments systems

Digital Cash

Although a digital equivalent of cash may seem like a straightforward system, digital cash, or e-cash as it's called in some circles, has raised some interesting regulatory issues regarding privacy. Digital cash also is the one system that seems to fit best with the possibility of performing commercial transactions involving small amounts of money, in real

Digital cash raises privacy questions, but it is the system best suited to small transactions

---

8. The National Automated Clearinghouse Association helps maintain the ACH Network, which is a highly reliable nationwide electronic funds transfer system governed by the ACH Operating Rules, which provide for the interbank clearing of electronic payments for participating financial institutions.

9. The CyberCash electronic checking system does not provide multiple payment options.

time, on the Internet, which many see as the next wave of applications for electronic commerce.

Digital cash, in the form of validated tokens represented by strings of digits, is both issued and redeemed by banks

In a digital cash system, currency is nothing more than a string of digits. A bank might issue these strings of digits, and debit your account with a withdrawal equal to the value of the currency (**tokens**) issued. The bank validates each token with its digital stamp before transmission to your personal computer. When you want to spend some e-cash, you only have to transmit the proper amount of tokens to the merchant, who then relays them to the bank for verification and redemption (see Figure 3-9). To ensure that each token is used only once, the bank records the serial number of each token as it's spent. If the token's serial number is already recorded in the database, the bank has detected someone trying to spend the token more than once, and would inform the merchant that it's worthless.

Digicash supports the use of blind signatures to obtain e-cash anonymously

For those wishing to preserve anonymity, the system developed by DigiCash follows a slightly different scheme. This scheme, called **blind signatures**, allows the buyer to obtain e-cash from a bank without the bank being able to correlate the buyer's name with the tokens it issues. This is much more like regular cash, where each dollar bill you get from the bank does not bear your name on it. The bank has to honor the token when it receives it from a merchant because of the validation stamp it originally attached to your tokens, but the bank cannot tell who made the payment.

Non-financial institutions may also start issuing e-cash, but they are not backed by the FDIC

It may be logical to have banks issue digital cash and, in fact, a few have already started experimenting with digital cash. But merchants and other intermediaries may also issue their own digital cash. So far, there is no system in place to provide any sort of interoperability between the different

Paying for an item with digital cash. *Figure 3-9*

Alice's PC

1 Alice uses PC to generate random number and assigns a worth of $10.

Random #

2 Alice encrypts the random number.

Encrypted random #

3 Bank decrypts message, verifying that it came from Alice, debits her account for $10.

Alice's bank

4 Bank adds its digital signature to number, returns it to Alice.

Random #

Alice's PC

5 Alice sends the number to Bob the merchant.

Bob the merchant

6 Bob sends the number to his bank.

Random #

7 Bob's bank verifies number, credits Bob's account for $10.

Bob's bank

8 Alice's number is added to "spent list."

Random #

forms of digital cash. Only the issuing institution can redeem a token, and there are no exchange rates or rules between institutions. Furthermore, non-financial institutions aren't guaranteed by government agencies, such as the United States Federal Deposit Insurance Corporation, which may well lead consumers to have second thoughts about using digital cash issued by merchants.

If consumers do embrace digital cash, this opens up an opportunity for individuals to act as **micromerchants**, offering their wares on the Internet in exchange for e-cash. They could then use the digital cash for other purchases on the Net, or redeem it at their bank.

Digital cash can be issued in very small denominations that can be used to pay for very small transactions

Since digital cash doesn't have to be divided into denominations matching those of real coins or other legal tender, it can be used in smaller denominations that are only useful for transactions undertaken in the electronic world. In both the physical and electronic worlds, transactions are often limited to some minimum amount to ensure that the transaction fees charged by banks and clearinghouses still leave the merchant with a profit on the sale.

The low cost of electronic transactions makes it feasible for merchants to charge small amounts without losing profits

The cost of electronic transactions is generally small, and using digital cash can keep them on the order of a few pennies per transaction. The small denomination digital tokens used for such payments are called **microcash**. Low-cost, real-time transactions using microcash are also referred to as **microtransactions**. With such low transaction costs, merchants can charge for small amounts of information without incurring prohibitive transaction fees and losing all profits.

Microcash can be used for items such as a stock quote, a weather report, an image or sound clip, or even a chapter from an electronic book. Players of multiplayer online games could also play games, by the minute, that are metered and paid for using microcash. Networked users could also *rent* software, such as ActiveX controls or Java applications, paying a little bit of money for each use. Designers of microcash systems also envision at least two other markets: traditional print publishers that seek to gain revenue by offering electronic versions of the information they provide in hard copy, and a new market of self-publishers who strive to use the Web to offer specialized content to discrete groups of users.

One alternative to handling and verifying microcash as each transaction occurs is to accumulate charges associated with one buyer until the amount is similar to that of other commercial transactions. Then a merchant can seek payment via a credit card transaction, for example, and not worry about whether the bank's credit card processing fees are greater than the worth of any single transaction.

Microcash thus lends itself to rapid exchange of small sums of currency for either small amounts of information or time (such as in game playing). All the currently implemented and proposed systems depend on issuance of currency before it's used, so authentication of the buyer does not become an issue. Privacy can be guaranteed by the blind signature approach.

For some of these systems, the biggest issue is security. Is security really necessary for each token that's passed from the buyer to the seller? Or are the amounts of these tokens so small as to make it not worthwhile for a cracker to break a simple-minded protection scheme? Stronger encryption schemes, such as those used in NetCash, add to the processing overhead of the system, and may slow it down to where it's sluggish and unusable.

Microtransactions might include small-item purchases, metered usage fees, rental fees, and subscription fees

Accumulating charges is one way to avoid microcash

Authentication is not an issue, and privacy can be guaranteed

Security needs must be weighed against performance requirements

EDI

VANs are private networks; so far, they are more secure and reliable than the Internet

EDI, or electronic data interchange, has been around since the 1960s, but is used mostly by large corporations and their satellite suppliers working together over a private network called a Value Added Network (VAN). These VANs offer reliability and security that has been difficult to duplicate on the Internet thus far.

The EDI service provider maintains the VAN and transfers the data between participants

An EDI service provider maintains a VAN, with mailboxes for each business partner. The provider stores, then forwards, EDI messages between partners. Each company using EDI has to agree on the contents of each form they will use for conducting business via EDI. These forms are transmitted via e-mail over the VAN; each participating company has to run EDI translation software on its computers to convert EDI data into formats used by the company's databases (see Figure 3-10).

Figure 3-10   *The basics of EDI software.*

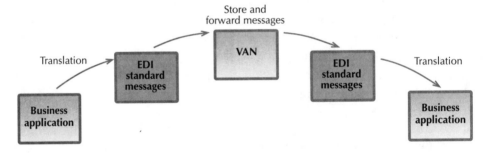

Setting up agreements for EDI using VANs is too slow and too expensive

EDI using VANs is poorly suited to the formation of virtual organizations or rapidly changing partnerships, which are becoming more of the norm in present-day business. In the past, the vast majority of EDI transactions were negotiated and set up via **trading partner agreements** (TPAs) that specified data interchange on a one-to-one basis. Setting up these agreements, and terminating partnerships, is both expensive and slow to implement, particularly by today's standards.

EDI service providers are now offering Internet access to bundled EDI services hosted at their computer centers, relieving businesses of the need to maintain much of the hardware and software. And with the move toward more flexible implementations of EDI, such as those using forms you can complete in a Web browser, small-sized and medium-sized businesses should find it easier to utilize EDI.

EDI service providers are now incorporating Internet services

EDI has been constrained by long preliminary negotiations to define transaction forms suitable to both business partners, making it unsuitable for many of the fast-paced temporary alliances in today's business world. In addition, each business sector has defined its own particular EDI forms, making cross-overs between business sectors difficult, if not impossible. **OpenEDI**, a recent series of specifications designed to make EDI transactions simpler to specify and set up, as well as use over the Internet, may make it possible for businesses of all sizes to use EDI over the Internet.

OpenEDI is a new series of specifications for handling EDI on the Internet

Businesses can use EDI to automate the transfer of information between corporate departments, as well as between companies. For instance, EDI-based data can be transferred between purchasing, finance, and receiving departments (see Figure 3-11 on the next page), to automate the purchase and payment processes. Transmitting EDI information to another company can also simplify such processes as purchasing supplies and authorizing payments between companies.

EDI is a system that encompasses more than just making payments. It therefore offers more capabilities and options than the payment systems discussed earlier in this chapter. Much of EDI can be implemented to handle purchase orders, inventory, and shipping information, without even touching on the matter of transferring funds. One use of EDI, called **financial EDI** or FEDI, specifically deals with making payments, and thus parallels the payment systems covered in this chapter, although it's strictly for business-to-business transactions.

Financial EDI specifically deals with making payments

Figure 3-11 *EDI information flow for buyer and seller.*

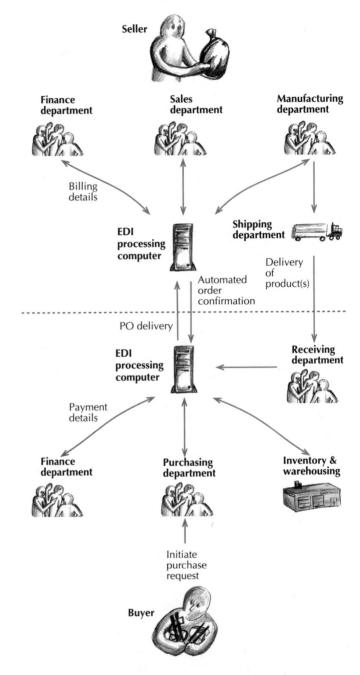

FEDI is typically set up between banks and their corporate customers to allow the banks to receive payment authorizations from payers, and make payment settlements to payees. Fund transfers between banks are handled using the typical bank networks, such as the CHIPS and SWIFT automated clearinghouses. Some banks even provide VAN-like services with their FEDI payment services, allowing their corporate customers to submit remittance information with payment instructions, instead of requiring the customer to use the bank for payments, and a separate EDI VAN for remittances.

Some banks provide extra services with their FEDI, making their service more VAN-like

Because the cost of operations on the Internet is lower than on a VAN, many companies and financial institutions have experimented with EDI over the Internet. Banks, such as Bank of America and Chase, have run limited-scale tests of financial EDI, and some industrial corporations have started to compare EDI data flow over the Internet with data flow over a VAN. Although many of the participants in these field trials seem satisfied with the methods for securing transmissions on the Internet, there are still reservations about the reliability and robustness of the Internet, and therefore also about its ability to guarantee that a transaction will get through. The table below compares the services offered by Internet access providers and VANs for handling EDI.

Using the Internet means lower costs; companies and financial institutions are experimenting

EDI on a VAN vs. the Internet

Feature	Internet Access Provider	Value-Added Network
Store & forward mailboxes	yes	yes
Secure environment	no	yes
Reliable performance	no	yes
Service provider accountability	limited	yes
Customer support	limited	yes
Interactive access	yes	extra cost
Electronic info access	yes	limited, may cost extra
Content hosting services	costs extra	costs extra

Tools for Implementation

Software is needed for interaction between existing legacy systems, databases, and Web documents

Although the customer *only* has to worry about finding the right product on your site and how to pay for it, your business has to concern itself with accepting the right payment systems and integrating them with existing inventory, accounting, and fulfillment systems. For some, this may mean building a new system from scratch. But for many companies, the process has to include legacy systems. Linking all of the business processes to electronic commerce therefore requires products such as interfaces between Web servers and databases, and back-ends (also called gateways) to financial processing systems, including banks and credit card acquirers.

Businesses looking to set up a system for electronic commerce have three paths they can follow: use a Web server with a tool kit to build their own system, buy a packaged system, or outsource the project to an electronic commerce service provider.

Tool kits require a lot of development time, but they allow you to customize your code in order to integrate it with existing legacy systems

Tool kits can range from very basic kits for implementing the important protocols (such as Terisa Systems' kits for SSL and SET, or RSA's S/PAY for SET), to add-ons that work with your server to handle credit card processing (for example, Go Software's PC Charge). Sun Microsystems has introduced its **Java Electronic Commerce Framework** (JECF), a series of Java libraries that include wallet and security options to help Java programmers handle electronic payments. The downside to using one of these tool kits is that you'll have a large development project ahead of you. You will not only have to write the software to handle the payment negotiations and transactions, but you'll also have to design your Web site and integrate its information with your corporate systems, such as customer databases and product inventories. On the other hand, the plus side to working with these tool kits is that they afford you the opportunity to customize your code as much as you need in order to integrate it with existing legacy systems.

As an alternative, there are quite a few Web commerce or merchant server packages currently available. The main program features include a Web storefront (usually with some kind of online catalog support for presenting product information to potential customers), and a means for taking orders from customers. Not all packaged systems include links to financial networks, but as time passes, more packages will include such links, either by offering their own systems, or by partnering with companies such as Verifone and CyberCash, the leading vendors of Web-based wallets and gateways to banks.

Commerce or merchant server programs support Web storefronts, catalogs, and order-processing

If the idea of setting up and maintaining your own commerce site, including links to a bank, doesn't appeal to you, you can outsource the job to an electronic commerce service provider. Quite a few **Internet service providers** (ISPs), including AT&T, MCI, Best Internet Communications, and BBN Planet, offer web hosting services that include the processing of commercial transactions. This is an ideal solution for small companies that cannot spare the resources for their own commerce server, or those that are interested in "testing the waters" before committing themselves to online commerce.

Most ISPs will host a commercial Web site for a fee

Although the Web is a good start for conducting business on the Internet, don't expect it to be the final solution. If your business is planning to incorporate Internet-based access to legacy data, and integrate it with business practices such as workflow or order fulfillment running on internal networks, then you'll have to consider more than just setting up a Web server and CGI scripts to handle database access and distribution of the data on your intranet.

The Web will not be the only means of conducting business on the Internet

The HTTP-CGI approach to linking Web servers and databases does not provide the level of high performance that's often associated with other client-server systems for handling transactions. CGI scripts lack the horsepower to pro-

HTTP and CGI alone lack the horsepower you are likely to need

cess hundreds of simultaneous requests in real time, so launching CGI scripts repeatedly to handle multiple client requests is not only slow, but an inefficient use of server resources too. In addition, the stateless connections provided by HTTP[10] do not allow an application to maintain a connection, and maintaining a connection would be the only way to ensure that a transaction (such as updating a client's purchase order) is fully completed.

Consider using transaction processing software for heavy transaction processing and interfacing with legacy databases

If you're planning a heavy-duty banking or electronic commercial site that has to handle hundreds of simultaneous user requests, and you want to insure that each transaction is completed, you should consider transaction processing software that uses the Web for the initial customer connection, but then switches to faster protocols to handle the actual transactions. Transaction processing software, particularly the type called **middleware**, is also very useful if you have to tie the data coming over the Internet with a series of legacy databases within your corporation. Expect sites designed for processing large numbers of transactions in real-time to supplement the Web with message-oriented middleware such as BEA Systems Inc.'s TUXEDO and BEA Jolt products, or Active Software's ActiveWeb.

Looking Ahead

Using the Internet for electronic commerce means solving a lot of different problems, including communications and transaction security, identifying buyers and sellers, mechanisms for submitting and processing orders, and tying it all to existing commercial systems. Electronic commerce is still in early development, and many of the players are attempting to stake out their place in the market. Standards for

---

10. When using a stateless protocol, the browser makes a single, simple request, the server responds, and the connection is immediately terminated. Once the connection is broken, the server forgets all about the request, and moves on to handle the next request.

interoperability of payment mechanisms are only now being worked out, so at this stage businesses are faced with the choice of going with early market leaders or supporting more than one payment system.

The vendors themselves are jockeying for position (and their continued existence) by forging strategic partnerships. Thus, while the Visa-MasterCard consortium that led to SET has been working with banks and server developers to implement SET widely at the back-end, companies like Cyber-Cash have been pushing their wallet, payment gateways, and related technologies to Web browser and server developers. We are only starting to see the integration based on these partnerships, and we are likely to see more consolidation of the market over the next year or two. That will be good news for consumers and businesses alike.

Chapter Four

Security and Electronic Commerce

Security is important in financial systems, whether they are based on physical or electronic transactions. In the real world we rely a great deal on physical security, while in the world of electronic commerce we must place additional reliance on electronic means for protecting data, communications, and transactions. When you're working in the world of networked computers, there are a number of different types of threats to the security of your systems. The table on the next page lists some of these threats along with security solutions. Some of the solutions provide a great deal of useful security even for those not involved in electronic commerce, such as people who need to send confidential business information via e-mail.

Electronic means must be used for protecting data, communications, and transactions

In order to show how Internet technologies can be used to secure against these threats, this chapter begins with an overview of the cryptographic background needed to understand how the systems work, and then discusses the principal standards currently developed to secure the Internet for electronic commerce.

Some Security Threats and Solutions

Threat	Security Solution	Function	Technology
Data intercepted, read or modified illicitly	Encryption	Encodes data to prevent tampering	symmetric encryption; asymmetric encryption
Users misrepresent their identity to commit fraud	Authentication	Verifies the identities of both sender and receiver	digital signatures
Unauthorized user on one network gains access to another	Firewall	Filters and prevents certain traffic from entering the network or server	firewalls; virtual private nets

The basic requirements for conducting commerce include confidentiality, integrity, authentication, authorization, assurance, and privacy (see "Requirements of Payment Systems," page 38). In this chapter you'll find that the first four requirements for electronic commerce can be solved with technology; but the last two of these requirements, assurance and privacy, depend as much on individuals and organizations acting responsibly as they do on any technological solutions. This would include adherence to laws that protect customers against fraud by merchants.

The Benefits of Cryptography

Encryption is useful for protection and authentication

Modern-day **cryptographic algorithms**, coupled with today's powerful desktop computers, now make possible the everyday use of powerful authentication and encryption methods. When you think of encryption, your first thought is probably of encoding data into an unreadable form to ensure privacy. But cryptography also satisfies other needs, such as the need to authenticate networked individuals and computers for such things as Web-based transactions. In addition, cryptography includes special methods for the digital identification of persons that can be transmitted over a network with messages or files, which is useful for authenticating messages and software.

Cryptographic techniques offer three essential types of services for electronic commerce: authentication (which includes identification), non-repudiation, and privacy. *Identification*, a sub-type of authentication, verifies that the sender of a message is really who he or she claims to be. *Authentication* goes a step further—verifying not only the identity of the sender, but also that the message sent has not been altered. *Non-repudiation* is an important requirement in commercial transactions; it's implementation prevents anyone from denying that they sent or received a certain file or data, and is similar to sending a letter Certified and Return Receipt Requested through the United States Postal Service. Finally, *privacy* is the ability to shield communications from unauthorized viewing.

Cryptography provides a means for identifying senders, authenticating message contents, preventing denial of message ownership, and protecting privacy

The Process of Encryption

Encrypting or encoding information to prevent it from being read by unauthorized parties has been the main use of cryptography since its early beginnings—Julius Caesar, for instance, used an alphabetical code when communicating with his field commanders.

For encryption to work properly, both the sender and receiver have to know what set of rules (called the **cipher**) was used to transform the original information into its coded form (often called **cipher text**). A simple cipher might be to add an arbitrary number of characters, say 13, to all characters in a message.[1] As long as the receiving party knows

A cipher is a set of rules for encoding data

---

1. This was named the Caesar cipher. Here's an example: if I applied a 13-character Caesar cipher to my name, it would appear as QNIVQ XBFVHE. (Hint: When you get to Z while counting characters, start at the beginning of the alphabet all over again.)

what the sender did to the message, the receiving party can reverse the process (for example, subtract 13 characters from each character in the message received) to extract the original text.

Basic encryption requires an algorithm and a key

Encryption is based on two components: an algorithm and a key. A cryptographic algorithm is a mathematical function that combines plain text or other intelligible information with a string of digits, called a **key**, to produce unintelligible cipher text. The key and the algorithm used are both crucial to the encryption.

An algorithm is difficult to devise, and can be used with multiple keys

Although some special encryption algorithms that don't use a key do exist (see discussion of hash functions on page 73), algorithms using keys are particularly important. Basing encryption on a key-based system offers two important advantages. First, encryption algorithms are difficult to devise—you wouldn't want to come up with a new algorithm each time you want to communicate privately with a new correspondent. By using a key, you can use the same algorithm to communicate with many people; all you have to do is use a different key for each correspondent. Second, if someone does crack your encrypted messages, all you have to do is switch to a new key to start encrypting messages all over again; you don't have to switch to a new algorithm (unless the algorithm and not the key proved to be insecure—that can happen, but it's unlikely).

The number of bits in a key determines the number of possible key configurations; more possible configurations means it's more difficult to crack

The number of possible keys each algorithm can support depends on the number of bits in the key. For example, an 8-bit key allows for only 256 possible numeric combinations, each of which is also called a key (2^8). The greater the number of possible keys, the more difficult it is to crack an encrypted message. The level of difficulty is therefore dependent on the key length. It would not take a computer very long to sequentially guess each of the 256 possible keys (less than a millisecond) and decrypt the message to see if it makes sense.[2] But if a 100-bit key were used (which equates to searching 2^{100} keys), a computer guessing one million keys every second could still take many centuries to discover the right key.

The security of an encryption algorithm correlates with the length of its key. Why? Because knowing that a key is *n* bits long only gives you an idea of how much time you'd have to spend to break the code. If security were dependent on such things as the secrecy of the algorithm, or the inaccessibility of the cipher text or plain text, unauthorized persons could derive that information from publications, pattern analysis of messages, or collect it in other ways (traffic monitoring, for example). Once the information was in hand, the unauthorized person(s) could use it to decrypt your communications.

Long encryption keys are more secure

The oldest form of key-based cryptography is called secret-key or **symmetric encryption**. In this scheme, both the sender and recipient possess the same key, which means that both parties can encrypt and decrypt data with the key (see Figure 4-1 on the next page). Symmetric encryption presents some drawbacks: for example, both parties must agree upon a shared secret key. If you have *n* correspondents then you have to keep track of *n* secret keys, one for each of your correspondents. If you use the same key for more than one correspondent, then they will be able to read each other's mail.

Using symmetric encryption, both parties have the same secret key, but you need a separate key for each correspondent

Symmetric encryption schemes also have a problem with authenticity, because the identity of a message's originator or recipient cannot be proved. Since both Ann and Tim

---

2. Trying each possible key to find the right one is called a brute-force method.

Figure 4-1 *Symmetric encryption uses a single secret key to encrypt and decrypt messages.*

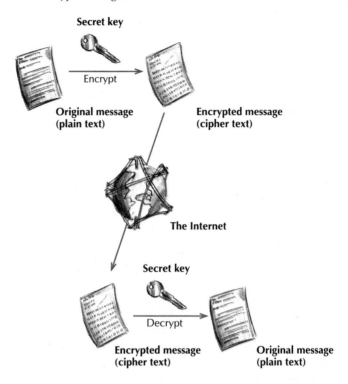

Secret key

Encrypt

Original message
(plain text)

Encrypted message
(cipher text)

The Internet

Secret key

Decrypt

Encrypted message
(cipher text)

Original message
(plain text)

Symmetric encryption cannot guarantee authenticity or non-repudiation

possess the same key, both of them can create and encrypt a message and claim that the other person sent it. This built-in ambiguity about who authored a message makes non-repudiation impossible with secret keys. The way to solve the repudiation issue is by using what is called public key cryptography, which makes use of asymmetric encryption algorithms.

The Workings of Public-Key Cryptography

Public-key cryptography is based on the concept of a key pair. Each half of the pair (one key) can encrypt information that only the other half (the other key) can decrypt. One part of the key pair, the **private key**, is known only by the designated owner; the other part, the **public key**, is published widely but is still associated with the owner. Key pairs have a unique feature—data encrypted with one key can be decrypted only with the other key in the pair (see Figure 4-2). In other words, it makes no difference if you use the private key or public key to encrypt a message; the recipient can use the other key to decrypt it. You'll see some of the power of this in the next few pages.

Public-key cryptography uses a pair of keys: one public and one private; messages encoded with either key can be decoded by the other

Using a key pair to encrypt and decrypt a message.

Figure 4-2

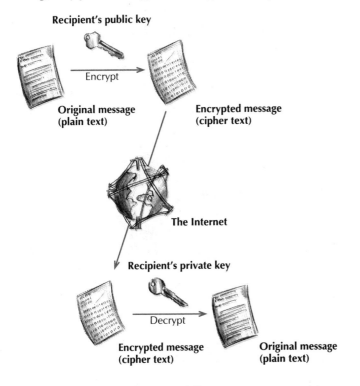

Recipient's public key

Encrypt

Original message
(plain text)

Encrypted message
(cipher text)

The Internet

Recipient's private key

Decrypt

Encrypted message
(cipher text)

Original message
(plain text)

The keys can be used in two different ways: to provide message confidentiality and to prove the authenticity of a message's originator. In the first case, the sender uses the recipient's public key to encrypt a message so that it will remain confidential until decoded by the recipient with the

The recipient's public key ensures confidentiality; the sender's private key proves the sender's identity private key. In the second instance, the sender encrypts a message using the private key, a key to which only the sender has access.

For example, in order to create a confidential message, Tim would first acquire Ann's public key. Then he uses her public key to encrypt the message, and sends it to her. Since the message was encrypted with Ann's public key, only someone with Ann's private key (and presumably only Ann has that) can decrypt the message[3] (see Figure 4-3).

Placing a public key on a network makes it easily available, and will not endanger the corresponding private key

Although encrypting a message with a a public key isn't very different from using secret-key encryption, public-key systems offer some advantages. For instance, the public key of your key pair can be readily distributed (on a server, for example) without fear that this compromises your use of your private key. You don't have to send a copy of your public key to all your respondents; they can get it from a key server maintained by your company, or maybe a service provider.

Using a private key for encryption is like signing a document

Another advantage of public-key cryptography is that it allows you to authenticate a message's originator. The basic idea is this—because you are the only person who can encrypt something with your private key, anyone using your public key to decrypt the message can be sure that the message came from you. Thus your use of your private key on an electronic document is similar to your signing a paper document. But don't forget, while the recipient can then be certain that the message came from you, there's no guarantee that nobody else has read it as well.

---

3. Because anyone with a copy of your public key can read a message that's been encrypted with your private key, intercepted messages can be decrypted. In commercial transactions, standard procedures are for the buyer to encrypt messages with his private key, while acknowledgments from the merchant would use the merchant's private key, meaning that anyone who knows the merchant's public key can read it. Other steps must be taken to ensure the privacy of sensitive information sent from the merchant.

Maintaining message confidentiality with a public key.   ***Figure 4-3***

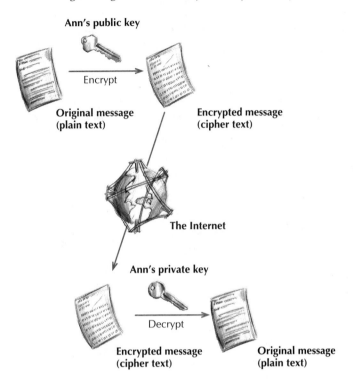

Using public-key cryptographic algorithms to encrypt messages is computationally slow, so cryptographers have come up with a way to quickly generate a short, unique representation of your message, called a **message digest**,[4] that can be encrypted and then used as your **digital signature**.

Some popular, fast cryptographic algorithms for generating message digests are known as **one-way hash functions**. A one-way hash function doesn't use a key; it's simply a formula to convert a message of any length into a single string of digits called a message digest. When using a 16-byte hash function, text processed with that hash function would

A one-way hash function converts any message into a single string of digits called a message digest

---

4. Despite its name, a message digest is not a condensation of the message's contents.

Encrypting a digest
with a private key
creates a digital
signature

produce 16 bytes of output—a message might result in the string CBBV235ndsAG3D67, for example. Each message produces a random message digest. Encrypt that digest with your private key and you've got a digital signature.

As an example, let's have the sender, Tim, calculate a message digest for his message, encrypt the digest with his private key, and send that digital signature along with the plain-text message to Ann (see Figure 4-4).

Figure 4-4 *Verifying a digital signature.*

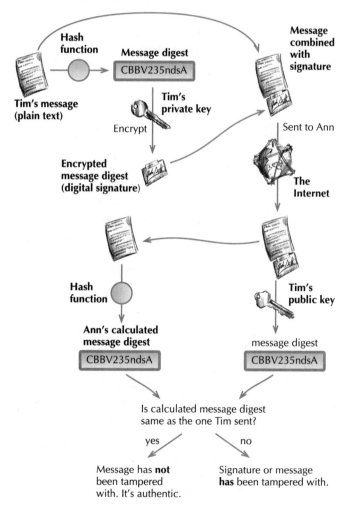

After Ann uses Tim's public key to decrypt the digital signature, she has a copy of the message digest that Tim calculated. Because she was able to decrypt the digital signature with Tim's public key, she knows that Tim created it, authenticating the originator. Ann then uses the same hash function (which was agreed upon beforehand) to calculate her own message digest of Tim's plain-text message. If her calculated value and the one Tim sent her are the same, then she can be assured that the digital signature is authentic, which means that not only did Tim send the message, but that the message itself has not been tampered with.

A matching message digest means no tampering has occurred

The one problem with this approach is that the body of the message is sent as plain text, and therefore privacy is not maintained. Although this further complicates matters, you could choose to use a symmetric algorithm with a secret key to encrypt the plain text of the message.

The Importance of Digital Certificates

In order to use public-key cryptography, you need to generate a public key and a private key. Usually that's done with the program that's going to use the key, such as your Web browser or e-mail program. Once you've generated both keys, it's your responsibility to keep your private key secure and let no one else see it. Then you have to decide how to distribute your public key to your correspondents. You could use e-mail to send your public key to all the correspondents, but that might prove unwieldy if you've forgotten someone in your address list, or new correspondents pop up. It also doesn't allow you to be authenticated with any degree of confidence; for instance, someone could claim to be you, generate a key pair and then send correspondents the public key, claiming it came from you—then they'd be free to forge messages in your name.

Digital certificates electronically verify public keys

A better, trusted way of distributing public keys is to use a **certificate authority**. A certificate authority will accept your

Certificate
authorities maintain
the responsibility for
checking a user's
identity, issuing
digital certificates,
and verifying the
validity of digital
certificates

public key, along with some proof of your identity (it varies
with the class of certificate), and serve as a repository of
digital certificates. Others can then request verification of
your public key from the certificate authority. The digital
certificate acts like an electronic version of a driver's license. As an accepted method for distributing your public
key, it provides you with a way for correspondents to verify
that you are who you say you are.

Certificate authorities such as Verisign, Cybertrust, and
Nortel issue digital certificates. As shown in Figure 4-5, a
digital certificate includes the holder's name, the name of
the certificate authority, a public key for cryptographic use,
a time limit for the use of the certificate (most frequently, six
months to a year long), the class of the certificate, and the
digital certificate identification number.

Figure 4-5   *The contents of Tim's digital certificate.*

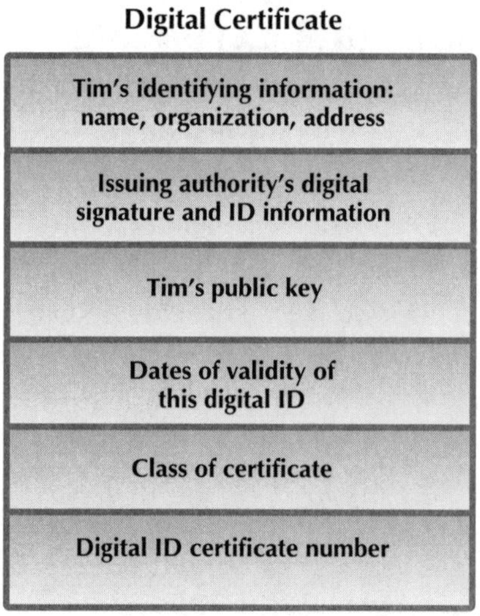

Digital Certificate

Tim's identifying information:
name, organization, address

Issuing authority's digital
signature and ID information

Tim's public key

Dates of validity of
this digital ID

Class of certificate

Digital ID certificate number

Digital certificates
come in four classes

A digital certificate can be issued in one of four classes,
indicating to what degree the holder has been verified. Class
1 is the easiest to obtain because it involves the fewest
checks on the user's background; only the name and e-mail
address are verified. For a Class 2 certificate, the issuing

authority checks a driver's license, social security number, and date of birth. Users applying for a Class 3 certificate can expect the issuing authority to perform a credit check (using a service such as Equifax) in addition to the information required for a Class 2 certificate. A Class 4 certificate includes information about the individual's position within an organization, but the verification requirements for these certificates have not yet been finalized.

Users must pay a fee to obtain a digital certificate from commercial or government certificate authorities; the fees increase for the higher classes, partly because of the effort required to check the user's background. Because of the background checks accompanying the higher classes, these class certificates serve as stronger affirmations of the user's identity.

The higher the class, the greater the degree of verification

Certificate authorities also have the responsibility of maintaining and making available a **Certificate Revocation List**, or CRL, which lets users know which certificates are no longer valid. The CRL doesn't include expired certificates, because each certificate has a built-in expiration. However, certificates may be revoked because they were lost, stolen, or because an employee left the company, for example.

Certificates have built-in expirations, and authorities maintain revocation lists

In addition to commercial certificate authorities (such as Verisign, Cybertrust, and Nortel), and government authorities (such as the United States Postal Service), corporations can also become a certificate authority by purchasing a certificate server from a vendor that has been certified by a certificate authority. Such arrangements are useful when a company needs to issue digital certificates to a number of employees for doing business, either within the company, or with other companies. As more systems use digital certificates to control computer access, corporate-maintained certificate servers will become more important. In the meantime, the United States government is trying to set up the Public Key Infrastructure for certificate authorities. Figure 4-6 on the next page shows an example of a certificate authority hierarchy.

A corporation can become a certificate authority and then issue certificates to employees or other companies

Figure 4-6   *An example of a certificate authority hierarchy.*

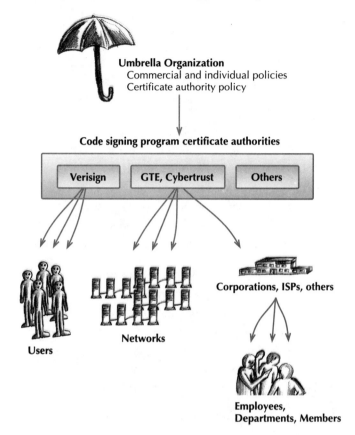

A Comparison of Encryption Methods

No one encryption system is ideal for all situations. The table illustrates some of the advantages and disadvantages of each type of encryption.

Add to this the differences of key lengths and algorithms, and it can be difficult to select the appropriate algorithm for use. The general rule of thumb is this—first determine how sensitive your data is, and for how long it will be sensitive and need to be protected. Once you've figured that out,

Advantages and Disadvantages of Cryptographic Systems

Encryption Type	Advantages	Disadvantages
Symmetric Key	Fast	Both keys are the same
	Can be easily implemented in hardware	Difficult to distribute keys
		Does not support digital signatures
Public key	Uses two different keys	Slow and computationally intensive
	Relatively easy to distribute keys	
	Provides integrity and non-repudiation through digital signatures	

select an encryption algorithm and key length that will take longer to break than the length of time for which your data will be sensitive.

One of the best discussions of key lengths, and the efforts required to break a key, is found in Chapter 7 of *Applied Cryptography* by Bruce Schneier (2nd edition, John Wiley & Sons, 1996). The following table is a condensation of Schneier's table that estimates the cost of building a 1995 computer to crack symmetric keys, and the time required to crack certain length keys.

Comparison of Time and Money Needed to Break Different Length Keys

| Cost | Length of key in bits | | | | |
	40	56	64	80	128
$100 thousand	2 secs	35 hrs	1 yr	70000 yrs	10^{19} yrs
$1 million	.2 secs	3.5 hrs	37 days	7000 yrs	10^{18} yrs
$100 million	2 millisecs	2 mins	9 hrs	70 yrs	10^{16} yrs
$1 billion	.2 millisecs	13 secs	1 hr	7 yrs	10^{15} yrs
$100 billion	2 microsecs	.1 sec	32 secs	24 days	10^{13} yrs

Remember that this is not a static situation either. Computing power is always going up, and costs falling, so it'll get easier and cheaper to break larger keys in the future. These estimates are for *brute-force attacks*, that is, guessing every possible key. There are other methods for cracking keys, depending on the ciphers used (that's what keeps cryptanalysts employed), but estimates for brute-force attacks are commonly cited as a measure of the strength of an encryption method.

Secret-key and public-key ciphers use different key lengths, so the above table cannot be used for setting all of your security requirements. The following table compares the two systems for similar resistance to brute-force attacks.

Secret-Key and Public-Key Lengths for Equivalent Levels of Security

Secret-Key Length	Public-Key Length
56 bits	384 bits
64 bits	512 bits
80 bits	768 bits
112 bits	1792 bits
128 bits	2304 bits

When it comes to selecting software or hardware for your purposes, recall that more than one encryption system might be used in the product—that's a common practice because of the different computational requirements for secret-key and public-key algorithms. For example, the table below shows how **PGP**, a common program for encrypting e-mail and files, uses **RSA**, **IDEA** and **MD5**.

Various Algorithms for Encryption Used by PGP

Function	Algorithms Used	Process
Message encryption	IDEA, RSA	(1) Use IDEA with one-time session key generated by sender to encrypt message. (2) Encrypt session key with RSA using recipient's public key.
Digital signature	MD5, RSA	(1) Generate hash code of message with MD5. (2) Encrypt message digest with RSA using sender's private key.

An Overview of Internet Security Systems

As was mentioned earlier in this chapter, there are many different types of threats that can compromise the security of electronic commerce (see the table on page 66). To counteract these threats, a number of protocols and applications have been developed using the cryptographic techniques described in the previous section.

The Internet has long been known for its dependence on open standards. This support for open standards, coupled with the open exchange of information on the Internet, may lead you to think that the Internet and security are mutually exclusive terms. That's far from the truth. While the Internet has implemented less security in the past than private **value added networks** (VANs), or corporate nets, the efforts to provide a variety of security mechanisms to Internet traffic has been moving ahead with a full head of steam.

More and more security measures are being implemented on the Internet

Common Key Algorithms

DES Data Encryption Standard is a block cipher created by IBM, and endorsed by the United States government in 1977. Uses a 56-bit key, and operates on block of 64 bits. Relatively fast; used to encrypt large amounts of data at one time.

Triple DES Based on DES. Encrypts a block of data three times, with three different keys. Being proposed as an alternative to DES, because it's been said that the potential of easily and quickly cracking DES is increasing every day.

RC2 and **RC4** Designed by Ron Rivest (the R in RSA Data Security Inc.). Variable key size ciphers for very fast bulk encryption. A little faster than DES, the two algorithms can be made more secure by selecting a longer key size. RC2 is a block cipher, and can be used in place of DES. RC4 is a stream cipher, and is as much as 10 times faster than DES.

IDEA Created in 1991, International Data Encryption Algorithm was designed to be efficient to compute in software. Offers very strong encryption using a 128-bit key.

RSA Named after Rivest, Shamir, and Adelman, its designers. A public-key algorithm that supports a variable key length, as well as variable blocksize of the text to be encrypted. The plain text block must be smaller than the key length. Common key length is 512 bits.

Diffie-Hellman The oldest public-key cryptosystem still in use. Does not support either encryption or digital signatures. System is designed to allow two individuals to agree on a shared key, even though they only exchange messages in public.

DSA Digital Signature Algorithm, developed by NIST based on what's called the El Gamal algorithm. The signature scheme uses the same sort of keys as Diffie-Hellman, and can create signatures faster than RSA. Being pushed by NIST as DSS, the Digital Signature Standard, although its acceptance is far from assured.

In fact, it now looks as though the Internet has gained an excess of riches pertaining to security, with a variety of standards covering many levels of networking, from packet-level security, all the way to application-level security (see the following table and Figure 4-7). Even if we still consider the Internet to be an insecure medium because of its decentralized nature, it's important to note that the data involved in transactions using these protocols can be secured.

Use of security standards and protocols can protect data on the Internet

Some of the Security Standards for the Internet

Standard	Function	Application
Secure HTTP (S-HTTP)	Secures Web transactions	Browsers, Web servers, Internet applications
Secure Sockets Layer (SSL)	Secures data packets at the network layer	Browsers, Web servers, Internet applications
Secure MIME (S/MIME)	Secures e-mail attachments across multiple platforms	E-mail packages with RSA encryption and digital signature
Secure Wide-Area Nets (S/WAN)	Point-to-point encryption between firewalls and routers	Virtual private networking
Secure Electronic Transaction (SET)	Secures credit card transactions	Smart cards, transaction servers, electronic commerce

Three ways security standards are used in networks.

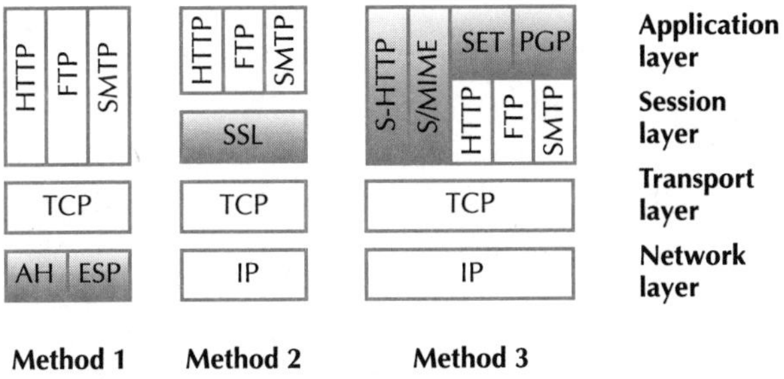

Figure 4-7

Method 1	Method 2	Method 3	
HTTP / FTP / SMTP	HTTP / FTP / SMTP	S-HTTP / S/MIME / SET / PGP	**Application layer**
	SSL	HTTP / FTP / SMTP	**Session layer**
TCP	TCP	TCP	**Transport layer**
AH / ESP	IP	IP	**Network layer**

The standards covered here can be classified according to whether they provide connection security or application security. Standards such as **Secure Sockets Layer** (SSL) and **Secure Wide-Area Networks** (Secure WAN or S/WAN) are designed to maintain secure communications on the Internet, although SSL is used primarily with Web applications. **Secure HTTP** (S-HTTP) and **Secure MIME** (S/MIME), on the other hand, are aimed at providing authentication and privacy for applications (Secure HTTP for Web applications, and Secure MIME for electronic mail and mail-enabled applications). **SET** goes a step further by providing security only for electronic commerce transactions.

Security for Web Applications: S-HTTP and SSL

The security of Web applications revolves around two protocols, Secure HTTP and Secure Sockets Layer, which provide authentication for servers and browsers, as well as confidentiality and data integrity for communications between a Web server and browser. S-HTTP is specifically designed to support the hypertext transfer protocol (HTTP), providing for the authorization and security of documents. SSL offers similar protection methods, but secures the communications channel by operating lower in the network stack (between the application layer and the TCP/IP transport and network layers, see Figure 4-7 on the previous page).

SSL can be used for transactions other than those on the Web, but it's not designed to handle security decisions based on authentication at the application or document level. This means that you'd have to use other methods to control access to different files.

Security for E-Mail: PEM, S/MIME, and PGP

A variety of security protocols have been proposed for electronic mail on the Internet, but only one or two have seen anything approaching widespread use. **Privacy-enhanced mail** (PEM) is an Internet standard for securing e-mail using either public keys or symmetric keys. PEM is seeing decreasing use because it's not designed to handle the newer multipart e-mail supported by MIME, and it requires a rigid hierarchy of certificate authorities for issuing keys. Secure MIME (S/MIME) is a newer proposed standard that uses many of the cryptographic algorithms patented and licensed by RSA Data Security Inc. S/MIME depends on digital certificates, and thus also depends on some kind of certificate authority, whether it be corporate or global, to ensure authentication.

Use of PEM is decreasing; S/MIME uses digital certificates and supports multi-part e-mail

One popular application that was developed for securing messages and files is PGP, or Pretty Good Privacy. It's probably the most widely-used security application for Internet e-mail, and uses a variety of encryption standards (see the table on page 81). PGP encryption/decryption applications are freely available for all major operating systems, and messages can be encrypted before using an e-mail program; some mail programs, such as Qualcomm's Eudora Pro and FTP Software's OnNET, can use special PGP plug-in modules to handle encrypted mail. PGP was designed around the concept of a *web of trust* which allowed users to share their keys without requiring a hierarchy of certificate authorities.

PGP is an ad hoc standard for securing Internet e-mail

Security for Networks: Firewalls

When you're connecting resources on your corporate net to a public network such as the Internet, you are putting your data and your computer systems at risk. Without a **firewall**, both the secrecy of your data, and the integrity of the data itself, is subject to attack. Like their physical counterparts in homes and other buildings, firewalls are meant to control damage, in this case, to your data and computer systems.

Firewalls help to protect your data

CryptoAPI and CDSA

There are currently two major efforts to simplify the developer's task of incorporating cryptographic methods in applications on PC platforms—**CryptoAPI** from Microsoft, and Intel's **Common Data Security Architecture** (CDSA).

Microsoft has developed its Internet Security Framework for use with Microsoft Windows 95 and Microsoft Windows NT. A significant component of the framework is CryptoAPI, which is an applications programming interface (API) at the operating system level. CryptoAPI provides Windows developers with a means of calling cryptographic functions, such as encryption algorithms, through a standardized interface. Because it's modular, CryptoAPI allows developers to substitute one cryptographic algorithm for another, according to their needs. CryptoAPI also includes options for processing and managing digital certificates.

Intel's CDSA offers much of the same functionality as CryptoAPI, but it's designed to be cross-platform from the beginning, rather than just for Windows. Some of the companies implementing CDSA in their products include Netscape, Datakey, VASCO Data Security, and Verisign.

Firewalls can provide protection against attacks on individual protocols or applications, and can be effective in protecting against **spoofing**.[5] Firewalls implement access controls based on the contents of the packets of data that are transmitted between two parties or devices on the network.

Firewalls provide a single point of control for network security

One of the major advantages of a firewall is that it provides a single point of control for security on a network. Of course, this can also work against you, because the firewall can also be a single point of failure, and is therefore likely to receive the focused attention of hackers.

Remember that firewalls are not a cure-all for Internet security problems. For example, firewalls don't check for viruses,

---

5. One party masquerading electronically as someone else.

so they cannot provide data integrity. Furthermore, firewalls do not authenticate the source of the data; and for the most part, they do not provide confidentiality of data either. However, new protocols are being developed to handle authentication and confidentiality of data **packets** on the Internet.

Although firewalls can help to protect your data and systems, corporate networks often depend on linking offices scattered around the city, county, state, or world. Work is now underway to secure IP-based networks,[6] such as those forming the Internet, at the network level, which will enable businesses to create their own **virtual private networks** (VPNs) using the Internet as an alternative to expensive leased lines.

A group of firewall and router vendors have formed an initiative called the S/WAN (Secure Wide Area Networks) initiative. They have taken it upon themselves to implement and test the protocols suggested by the Internet Engineering Task Force (IETF) for securing IP packets. These protocols include methods for authentication and encryption of packets, as well as a method for exchanging and managing the keys required for the authentication and encryption processes. S/WAN protocols will help insure interoperability between router and firewall vendors, making it easier for geographically separated corporate offices, as well as partners forming a virtual corporation, to communicate securely over the Internet.

Firewalls cannot provide privacy or authentication, nor can they protect a network against viruses

S/WAN protocols for authenticating and encrypting packets will help insure compatibility between various router and firewall vendors

Looking Ahead

Although implementation is still somewhat spotty, the software and hardware needed for secure Internet connections and applications are well along their way in development.

---

6. The software required to secure data at the IP protocol level would be installed within firewalls.

The industry has not
yet agreed on how
(or where) to
implement the
security protocols

One of the problems with implementation is that the industry hasn't yet agreed on where in the network to add application protocols to implement the cryptographic technology. The different components—workstations, **Web servers**, **Web browsers**, communications protocols, and other applications—have led to a variety of proposals, many stemming from only one portion of the market. (Compare the development of all the proposed standards for e-mail, for example.)

Market forces seem to
have more influence
on the evolution and
adoption of standards
and protocols than do
the official stan-
dards bodies

Integration of these standards, or at least dominance of certain standards, is more likely to come from market forces, rather than standards bodies such as the IETF. Vendor acceptance of ad hoc standards, such as early versions of SSL, and alliances between different developers, will show which protocols are most likely to be popular.

Chapter Five

Consumer and Business Markets

Now that you've taken a tour through many of the technologies involved in electronic commerce, it's time to turn to the heart of the book: how businesses use these technologies to actually conduct electronic commerce. This chapter's presentation of the background on consumer and business markets on the Internet, followed by its discussion of some of the important issues and opportunities surrounding electronic commerce, sets the stage for the case studies presented in the next six chapters. The case studies illustrate how real companies have found ways to integrate electronic commerce into their business models. Each chapter focuses on the concept, the process and technologies used, and the impact on business practices. Although many of the cases in this book focus on business-to-business commerce, a couple also cover business-to-consumer commerce on the Internet.

If you're getting into the consumer market on the Internet, you'll be part of a relatively new, but growing, market, with all the risks and rewards that accompany such new markets. Because you're limited to people who have personal computers and connect to the Internet, you initially might have a broad understanding of the customers you're trying to reach. But your success on the Internet will depend on how effectively your company can define and develop market niches

Success will depend on how effectively your company defines and develops market niches among Internet users among Internet users. It's significant, and important to keep in mind, that the Internet and Web technologies offer your company a greater opportunity to deal with customers on an individual, customized basis. These markets will expand as consumer acceptance of the procedures and technologies used for electronic commerce grows. You should factor the growth period due to this evolving acceptance into your plans.

The Internet supports multimedia, something EDI transactions can't handle

Business-to-business commerce has already had a sampling of electronic commerce, largely thanks to companies handling orders and payment information via **EDI** over **VANs**. But conducting EDI transactions over private networks doesn't allow for the new types of business information, such as images, sound, graphics, and video, which are becoming more a part of the business world. The Internet is better suited for exchanging and integrating such information, largely because of developments surrounding the Web.

Create new relationships, new products, and new roles

Finding new uses for internal corporate information, using it to strengthen relationships with business partners, and perhaps even creating new products from this information, are all a part of electronic commerce over the Internet. Even as companies use the Internet for building business relationships, intermediaries will be able to assist in the formation and maintenance of these relationships. Existing intermediaries will add such services to their offerings, while new intermediaries will continue to form on the Internet with these business relations in mind.

The Consumer Market and One-to-One Marketing

The consumer market on the Internet is still new and undeveloped

It goes without saying that for your business to be successful, you have to know your market. In the case of the Internet, the consumer market is rather new and undeveloped. Most users have been on the Internet for only a year or two, and many retailers are still experimenting with advertising and selling goods over the Internet.

For instance, data from Forrester Research and Cowles/ Simba Information indicates that consumer spending on line was only $240 million in 1994, and grew to $993.4 million in 1996; but Forrester Research expects online consumer commerce to reach $6.9 billion by 2000. Of this, it's projected that 32 percent of the money will be spent on computer products, 24 percent on travel, 19 percent on entertainment, 10 percent on gifts and flowers, and 5 percent on apparel (see Figure 5-1). By contrast, 1995 revenues for direct-mail catalog suppliers was $57 billion.

Online consumer spending is expected to reach $6.9 billion by the year 2000

The growth of consumer electronic commerce.

Figure 5-1

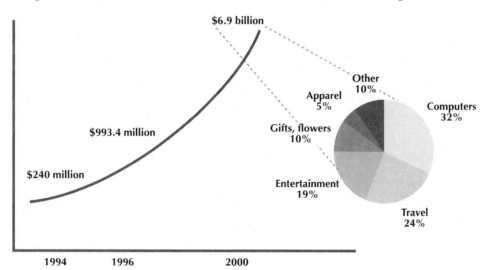

What are some of the things you should consider if you're planning to conduct business in this market? Aside from the demographics of potential customers, you'll need to concern yourself with the Internet's unique ways for staying in touch with customers, and ensuring their loyalty. The Internet probably has the greatest potential for dealing with customers on a one-to-one basis, so maintaining a customer focus is important. But don't forget that with all these new

Maintaining a one-on-one customer focus is easy using the Internet

technologies on the Internet, you'll have to experiment to see what works best with *your* customers; if they're not comfortable with new technologies and techniques, their lack of acceptance won't help your business at all.

The fundamental basis of one-to-one marketing and sales is that you need to eliminate the one-size-fits-all mentality, and tailor your goods and services to the individual's needs. Creating custom relationships with each customer has also been referred to as relationship marketing, feedback marketing, and mass customization. Whatever its name, this concept is a powerful strategy to gain and keep customers, and to fight product commoditization[1] and price competition.

Your Web server can create customized Web pages based on customer input and information from your database

Although marketers have had varying degrees of success with one-to-one marketing using other media, the technologies integrated with the Web and the Internet make it easier and more automated than before. **Web servers** can create customized Web pages on demand, incorporating a customer's preferences for product information, for example. Some of this information might come from users directly (as they sign on to your server, for instance), but other information might be derived from your past dealings with customers, information which might be accessible via a database.

Customers can design and create their own custom bundles

In the realm of electronic commerce, one-to-one relations aren't simply restricted to promotional or sales information, either. A Web system could easily allow customers to design and create custom bundles of products for themselves. And because customers are looking for solutions, rather than just products, custom bundles are likely to be of more interest to them than individual pieces. Furthermore, if you're dealing with information-only products, both the bundling and the delivery can be customized automatically.

---

1. Custom products typically can be sold for higher prices than generic ones. When products begin to look similar, their value decreases, and prices go down. Products valued as commodities do not appear to be anything special, and are often sold in *price wars*.

Consumer Demographics, Loyalty, and Acceptance

Once you get to know your consumer base, and design ways to customize your approach for potential buyers, you can begin to build customer loyalty and gain their acceptance. Don't forget that with electronic commerce the demographics may be a little different than for consumers of the same product or service who prefer to shop via the traditional interactions, and resistance may be a little higher.

Examining Demographics

Over the past few years, various surveys have tried to determine the demographics of the Internet user. Three of the better-known surveys are the ones conducted by Nielsen Media Research, O'Reilly & Associates, and Georgia Tech, the latter of which has been conducting a semi-annual survey for the last three years.

While the surveys don't agree on the number of Internet users, citing numbers from 12 million to 50 million in 1996, they do agree on certain general characteristics of those users. The Internet demographic is an attractive one for many companies as it is an upscale, well-educated market. For example, the typical user has a median age in the mid-30s, with a median income between $50,000 and $60,000, and often has a college education or better. Compare that with the median United States income of $37,000. Although initial populations of users were predominantly male, the proportion of female users has been increasing rapidly.

The typical user is thirty-something, college educated, and makes $50,000-$60,000 a year

In addition to the usual demographic descriptors of a market, such as age, income, geographic location, and education, it's useful to categorize Internet users according to their means for accessing the Internet. With access methods ranging from 14.4-bps modems, **Integrated Services Digital Network** (ISDN), and **cable modems**, to high-speed T1 connections, you have to give some consideration to the

Lower the potential for customer frustration by designing *your* site for *their* equipment

time it takes to get information to your customers, as well as to the type of computer and monitor they us to access your Web site. For example, downloading large graphics or animations in a Web page, over a slow modem, can take a very long time. Long download times, and slow processing of Web-based searches or orders, will only lead to frustration on the part of your customers; it may well convince them not to return to your site, leading to lost sales.

First look at your likely customers from the point of view of the technology they are using, because this determines how they can access the information, and possibly the products, you provide. If these are home-based customers, they may not have the latest, fastest computers, or a fast way to connect to the Internet. For the majority of the home-based computer users, a fast modem is a 14.4-kbps modem. Sales of 28.8-kbps are constantly on the increase, and a small percentage (only 1.4 percent, according to a report by International Data Corp. in Fall 1996) have ISDN lines to the home. Future technologies, such as cable modems, satellite access for personal computers, and **asymmetrical digital subscriber line** (ADSL) will provide greater bandwidth to home users, but don't expect a significant portion of the consumer market to use these new technologies any time soon.

This means that technically well-designed Web sites, with fast-loading but informative graphics, should be used to reach these customers. Stay away from the more graphic-intensive multimedia Web add-ons, such as ShockWave and large Java applets, unless you feel that these technologies must be used on your Web site (for presenting demos of games or presenting dynamic data, for instance). In those cases, try to keep their use to a minimum and, if possible, make their use optional.

Also, don't overlook how Internet users exchange information. As popular as the Web is for providing information, the number of people who use e-mail is still larger than the number of people who surf the Internet. Keeping in touch with your customer base via e-mail can be an effective way to provide them with useful information. If you want them to visit your Web site, include your **URL**[2] in your e-mail.

Be sure not to underestimate the usefulness of e-mail

Building and Maintaining Loyalty

When dealing with physical products in our everyday world, brand name and image are very important influences on consumer buying habits. If you're not already a brand-name business, and consumers on the Internet can switch services and find alternatives at the drop of a hat, how can you ensure that you keep your customer base?

It may sound trite, but the answer is all a matter of building customer loyalty. And customer loyalty comes from contin-ued interactions between the customer and your business. As long as you can provide information of value to your customers, they're likely to treat you as a trusted partner.

Continuous and informative com-munication with your customers builds loyalty

To maintain continued loyalty, you have to offer products and services that customers perceive to be of high value. This means that you should provide ready access to infor-mation about your products and services, make them easy to select and acquire on the Internet, and charge prices that reflect the perceived value of both the products and transac-tion process.

A customer's perceived value of a product is based on a combination of factors including product features, service, transaction cost, risk, and the maintenance costs over the life cycle of the product. Even if the features of the products you offer on the Internet do not differ from those offered in stores or catalogs, electronic technologies offer you the

Increase perceived value by decreasing transaction costs and increasing service

---

2. URL stands for Uniform Resource Locator, a means for identifying a resource on the Internet.

opportunity to increase the perceived value of your products by reducing transaction costs and increasing service.

Because customers on the Internet can switch vendors easily, your business must build an electronic relationship that makes them reluctant to leave your business. For example, using Web technologies with databases allows you to tailor your services to individual customers. The more you individualize your services, the more your customers will feel that you are treating them as someone special.

Customers can directly provide you with some of the information you need to customize offerings by filling out a Web form when they first visit your Web site. You can then monitor each customer's browsing and buying history on your site, and continuously use this information to further refine the customized offerings you present to them (see Figure 5-2). As customers build this history with your business, they will become increasingly reluctant to switch to a competitor with whom they have no history. The time they've invested with you may offset any other advantage your competitor can offer. It's to your direct benefit as well—marketing professionals estimate that it costs businesses five times more to gain a customer as it does to keep an existing one.

Figure 5-2 *Building and maintaining relations with customers by offering custom electronic information.*

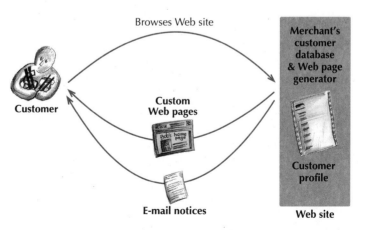

Browses Web site

Customer

Custom Web pages

E-mail notices

Merchant's customer database & Web page generator

Customer profile

Web site

If you're dealing solely with electronic goods and services, the Internet can be an ideal platform for delivering these items. But if you're a retailer dealing with physical goods, there's always the danger of channel conflict[3], leading to fewer total sales rather than more. This often happens when a company doesn't devote sufficient time and resources to maintain both channels. Disappointed customers who have been loyal to the company using one channel may not make the switch to the other sales channel, while the new channel doesn't gain enough of a following to offset the losses. One way to minimize this potential problem is to segment your products, and offer products on line that are not available through your traditional channels.

Moving from one channel to another can lead to lost customers

However, switching to a new channel isn't necessarily bad. Some businesses have grown by being able to close down store locations and replace them with fulfillment houses at a lower cost. And the cost of online full-color catalogs is much less than the cost of printing and mailing a four-color catalog that cannot be easily updated.

Gaining Acceptance

A bell-shaped curve called the Technology Adoption Life Cycle (see Figure 5-3 on the next page) has often been used to explain how businesses adopt new technologies. At first, technical enthusiasts within the company try a product early on, simply because they love technology and like to play with the latest and greatest toys. Visionaries get involved early because they're interested in revolutionizing some aspect of their business to gain a competitive advantage. Eventually, products make it into the mainstream, being accepted as an established part of the high-tech landscape. Pragmatists want to use technology products to improve their productivity in a non-disruptive fashion, while conser-

Visionaries are early adapters of new technology, but a change in marketing strategy is needed to reach the mainstream

---

3. Channel conflict occurs when one means of selling goods cannibalizes sales through another channel.

vatives look to get by with the safest, cheapest technology they can find. And then there are the skeptics, who might never purchase your product. Some high-tech marketing gurus have also postulated that a chasm exists between the visionaries and the mainstream, requiring a shift in marketing strategies.

Figure 5-3   *The Technology Adoption Life Cycle.*

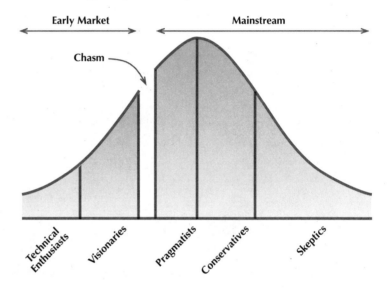

Demographics play a role in the rate of technology adoption

Consumers fall into these same categories when it comes to embracing new technologies and products—there are technical enthusiasts, visionaries, pragmatists, conservatives, and skeptics, when it comes to technologies such as fax machines, ATM cards, voice-mail, personal computers, and electronic commerce. Some of this acceptance of new technologies and procedures may be correlated with age, education, income bracket, or various other factors, and you should take this willingness into account when planning your ventures into electronic commerce. For example, many younger people have grown up with personal computers, and they are more likely to use them for electronic banking and surfing the Web than adults in their 50s or 60s.

The growth and acceptance rates of personal computer and Internet technologies continue to affect the probable success of electronic commerce, especially in the consumer market. To many people, the Internet can appear to be a large, unknown entity with new technologies and terminologies. This can be true even to those who have used computers for some time. Add to that the multitude of payment systems proposed for electronic commerce, and the stories about hackers and insecure Internet systems, and it may take a considerable effort to interest many more consumers to shop on the Internet. Again, it's a question of showing them the value of the experience, and that's as much your job while you're running a business on the Internet as anyone else's.

You will need to show consumers that the Internet experience is of value

A new technology is more readily accepted when it offers more convenience to the user than the technology it's re-placing. Consumers will use the Internet for commerce when they see that it's a more valuable way of doing things. Some of the ways that your company can make using the Internet more valuable include:

Consumers look for convenience and value

- providing more information on your products on line

- combining catalog searching and product ordering into simple point-and-click operations using a single application on the Internet, instead of requiring a faxed order, or calling a toll-free number, once they've found the product on line

- suggesting alternatives to out-of-stock items

- allowing customers to track the status of their orders

- tracking customer purchases and catalog searches as a guide to bring new items to their attention, or to mention related products (a ski rack when they're buying skis, for example)

Don't overwhelm potential mainstream customers with complex systems

Once you move into the mainstream, beyond the technical enthusiasts and visionaries, you should strive to maintain simplicity in your systems. This includes not only the technologies you employ on the Web or e-mail, but also the payment systems you use. The more complicated a system is, the less likely it is that mainstream customers will use it.

One more issue that is central to consumer acceptance of electronic commerce is the issue of trust. Business is based on trust between two parties, whether the business is conducted in person, by phone, or over the Internet. Many of the ways we currently conduct business ensure trust by means of well-established legal and financial instruments. Purchase order/invoice payment systems in businesses are one example; paying by a credit card or check, backed by an established bank, are two more examples.

Consumers are more likely to trust brand identities, even for electronic commerce

Unless you treat the Internet as more than just a communications tool, the trust and credibility between two parties will continue to be established and maintained outside of the network. In such situations, brand names and established companies are likely to have an edge for engendering trust among consumers for electronic commerce on the Internet. But using rating systems (such as that implemented by eTrust[4]), participating in online communities (see "Taking Advantage of Online Communities" on page 112), and using secure technologies such as **digital signatures** for guaranteeing identities, can all help a company use the Internet to establish and maintain its credibility and customers' trust.

Digital signatures can help maintain trust in electronic transactions

As electronic commerce becomes more prevalent, it's likely that the Internet will often become the sole link between business parties. In traditional commerce, we're all used to

---

4. eTrust audits how a Web site collects visitor information and what the company does with that information (maintaining a customer history, for example). eTrust provides each site with a special graphic that the site can use to alert users about the confidentiality of the data collected while they're visiting the site.

being able to resort to a paper trail for sales, negotiations, and other contracts. In electronic commerce, electronic analogs must be developed to replace this paper trail.[5] Because digital signatures offer a way to verify a party's identity, buyers and sellers can use them to verify each other for electronic transactions, making it a bit easier for them to trust each other.

The Business Market

The business-to-business market is even larger than the online consumer market. BIS Strategic Decisions has estimated that the amount of merchandise purchased electronically by businesses though EDI, e-mail, and proprietary order entry, is 100 times greater than that purchased electronically by consumers through home shopping, online commercial networks, and home bill paying. Just as with the consumer market, this is expected to grow significantly during the next decade. Thanks to the low cost of Internet access, and the popularity and versatility of the Web, small-sized and medium-sized businesses will be able to conduct electronic commerce that previously was limited to larger corporations, further enlarging the market.

The electronic business-to-business market is reported to be 100 times greater than the online consumer market

Business-to-business use of the Internet, especially for commercial transactions, differs from the way a consumer conducts business on the Internet. Business buyers are typically time-constrained to accomplish a job or task, having little time to surf the Internet to find what they need. On the other hand, consumers usually don't shop with such a sense of urgency, and they can wander through the Internet looking

Business buyers have little time for online browsing

---

5. Commercial transactions require some sort of acknowledgement, and electronic transactions are not an exception. EDI and some e-mail systems automatically generate e-mail receipts for each message received. If you're processing orders via either the Web or e-mail, sending e-mail to the customer informing him of the receipt of his order, when the order's processed and when the goods are shipped are good ways of keeping him posted.

at more sources and choices. When you're dealing with business customers, you ought to make it simple for them to search for items and place an order. If they're repeat customers, for example, storing their billing, payment, and shipping information on your server, and allowing them to reuse that data when they place an order, makes the order process faster. Consumers are more likely to make impulse purchases, so showing them different product lines, or adding product information on a Web site, is less likely to keep them from shopping than it would a business customer who knows exactly what they need to purchase.

Value Chains and the Marketspace

All activities are part of the value chain

Consider the activities that your company performs to produce and sell a product or service. There's design, production, marketing, fulfillment, and customer support, among other activities. Each of these activities adds value to the product or service you provide to your customers. And don't forget that these activities depend on a support structure, including human resource management, procurement, and so on. Each of these activities form what's often called a value chain (see Figure 5-4). Each of the activities that you define in your value chain provides opportunities to add value to your product, hence the name *value chain*.

Figure 5-4   *The value chain.*

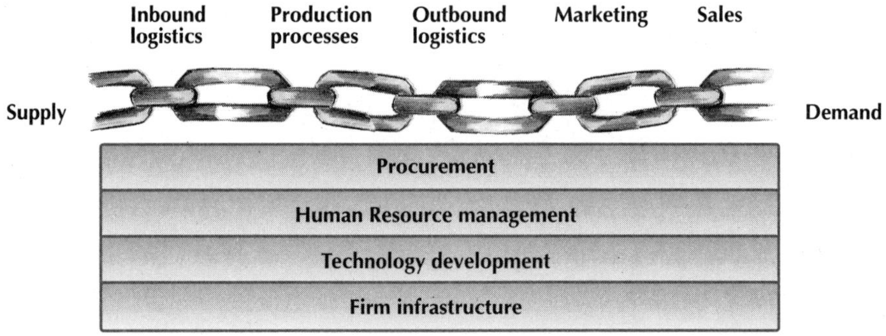

| Inbound logistics | Production processes | Outbound logistics | Marketing | Sales |

Supply   Demand

| Procurement |
| Human Resource management |
| Technology development |
| Firm infrastructure |

Think of how a company adds value to its **hard goods**—if you look at the value chain, some examples would be designing products that meet the needs or desires of the customers, creating well-manufactured products, delivering them in a timely and safe fashion, and providing proper help with installation. In the traditional model of value chains—for hard goods, for example—information is treated as part of the support structure to help other activities produce value, and it remains internal to the company. For example, sales data might be used to throttle manufacturing, or market projections might be used to plan material stockpiling.

Traditionally, information stays in house and plays a secondary, supporting role

Adding value by converting your raw information into new services and products in the information world creates a new type of value chain, the virtual value chain. When you can think of new uses for corporate information that go beyond the monitoring and controlling processes—perhaps by sharing that information with customers or partners, or by creating new products that consist of information—these become new opportunities that can be exploited over the Internet as part of a virtual value chain. The use of the word *virtual* in this case emphasizes that the activities are performed with information, rather than something physical, like the raw materials used to make an automobile.

Placing information in a primary role, by sharing it, and using it to create new products and services, creates a virtual value chain

For example, suppose your company manufactures microwave ovens. Over time, your customers have sent you their favorite recipes for use with your ovens. And customer support has been collecting special cooking hints from customers, as well as tracking the questions buyers ask most often when they call your toll-free support line. As part of the traditional value chain, all of this information might make it back to your research and development department and be used for designing the next generation of microwave ovens. Or marketing might use the recipes as a way of targeting special promotions.

Share information in
the form of FAQs or
searchable question-
and-answer databases

Now think of what your company could do with this information within the context of the virtual value chain. If you
maintained a customer support voicemail system, customers
could hear prepared answers to the most frequently asked
questions. Providing this information in an electronic bulletin board system that customers can call from their personal
computer, using a modem, is another way of offering the
information. Or if you're using the Internet, a Web site
could have a list of questions and answers, as well as a
database of problems and solutions, that users can search by
keyword or product. So far, this approach provides additional customer support by offering the information you've
gathered back to your customers. It improves customer
relations, and may be more cost-effective than answering
phones, but it hasn't directly added to your revenues.

Now consider all the recipes your customers volunteered—
your company could either decide to publish them in a
cookbook directly, or in a deal with a book publisher. And if
your next generation of microwave ovens includes a computer connection, you might sell a CD-ROM cookbook. In
the first case, you've used information to add value to your
product by offering customers more useful information than
they'd been able to get by other means. In the case of the
cookbook, you've used information to produce a new product, one that's composed only of information, and is an
outgrowth of the virtual value chain.

When it comes to creating value in a virtual value chain,
five different activities can be involved—gathering, organizing, selecting, synthesizing, and distributing information (see
Figure 5-5). Because you can generate new products, or
value, using each of these activities at any of the points
along the value chain, you can, in effect, create a value
matrix where the intersection of each information-related
activity with each step in the value chain is another opportunity to add value.

Linking the value chain and the virtual value chain.   **Figure 5-5**

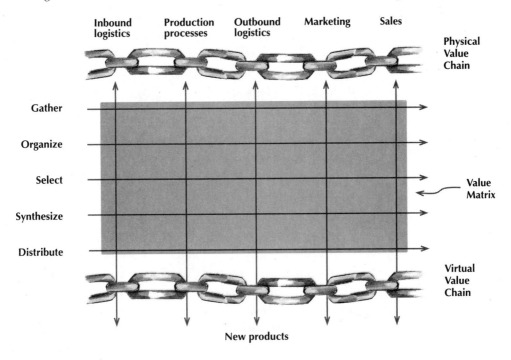

Businesses often adopt their value-adding processes to the virtual value chain in three stages: *viewing*, or keeping an eye on physical operations by means of information; *mirroring*, or substituting virtual activities for physical ones; and *forming new relations*, where managers use the flow of information in their virtual value chain to deliver value to customers in new ways.

As an example of keeping an eye on physical operations, consider what Frito-Lay has done to integrate marketing, sales, manufacturing, and distribution, with information gathered from its distributors. Frito-Lay employees collect product sales information from each store across the nation on a daily basis, allowing managers to quickly visualize the links between different parts of the value chain—sales, promotions, locations, and so on. For example, they could

You can use information to visualize relationships between links in the value chain

determine if a recent television promotion for a Frito-Lay product has led to increased sales, in which neighborhoods it's been successful, and for how long. The emphasis is on monitoring data, and responding quickly, across the board. This electronic system gives Frito-Lay a flexibility that's difficult, if not impossible, to match by any other means.

Mirroring refers to the use of online technology to replace activities that were previously performed only in the physical world

Beyond monitoring, you can ask yourself if certain processes might be performed more efficiently on the virtual value chain, rather than on the original value chain. Think about shifting activities originally performed as part of the physical value chain to parallel activities on the virtual value chain. In short, you can mirror the original value chain. A good example of mirroring is Ford's use of videoconferencing and **CAD/CAM** (computer-assisted design/computer-assisted manufacture) systems during development of the Contour sedan (their "global car"). Rather than physically bringing together team members from around the world to develop the car, Ford chose to create a virtual work team using their best people, regardless of location. The team collaborated via videoconferencing and exchanged CAD files over a worldwide network, practically eliminating the need for them to meet face-to-face. Even the testing of prototypes was done via computer simulations on systems that were available 24 hours a day.

Electronic commerce is conducted in the marketspace, where information adds value

Work in information-driven markets, such as utilizing only virtual value chains and the products they create, has led to a new term for the market where electronic commerce is conducted—the **marketspace**. The marketspace encompasses the transition from physically defined markets to markets based on, and controlled by, information. In this transition, information adds more than efficiency to a transaction, it also adds value. By participating in the marketspace, businesses can establish tighter and more dynamic links with partners.

One way to do this is to establish further relationships with your customers within the marketspace. Digital Equipment Corporation allows prospective customers to contact sales representatives, search for products and services, and take a Digital machine for a *test drive* over the Internet. Oracle Corporation offers some of its software for downloading over the Internet, usually 90-day demonstration copies that can be converted to fully licensed products by obtaining a key code from a sales representative or the company's Internet site. These are all examples of how a company can add value to its products and services, and satisfy its customers, by keeping processes *virtual*.

Form new relationships by using electronic processes to allow customers to communicate with sales representatives and test-drive electronic products

Business Evolution on the Internet

As businesses use the virtual value chain, and generate more information-based product opportunities, they will gain ways to benefit from electronic commerce (see Figure 5-6).

The evolution of business functionality on the Internet.   **Figure 5-6**

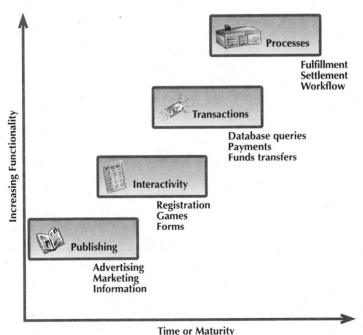

This increased functionality starts with simple processes such as publishing information about products via the Web, then progresses to customer and product registration via e-mail and Web-based forms, then on to database queries, payment handling, and finally actual fulfillment via the Internet (for information-based products). In short, the interface with your customers evolves from simple static information to a more interactive role, one that ties to your internal data, which previously might have been considered inaccessible to customers or partners.

> Businesses may begin by publishing and collecting static information, and then evolve to support interactive queries and process transactions

The most fully evolved, fully functional Internet presences integrate real-time interactions with their databases to offer what's been termed **transactional commerce**. The idea is to use customer-specific information to guide the transactions between company and customer, and to do so in real-time. Some good examples of transactional commerce include Federal Express and United Parcel Service offering their customers the ability to track a package's status on the Web. Other applications of transactional commerce include order entry, credit and payment processing, order status reporting, transaction or order confirmation and status, and delivery or fulfillment of virtualized content.

> Transactional commerce occurs in real-time, and uses customer-specific information to guide the transactions between company and customer

The fact that many businesses are following this path on the Web doesn't mean that it will be the ideal model for your company, or that the path will be smooth. Implementing electronic commerce as outlined here can be a difficult task. Friction can arise from such problems as an inefficient market structure, inefficient organizational structures in your company, and inefficient mercantile processes.

> Processing transactions may not be the ideal goal for your company

Not knowing your customers, or not reaching the right customers in the right way, can lead to an inefficient market structure. Inefficient organizational structures in your company may be structures where there is too much hierarchy, control is too tight, or there is not enough information-sharing between groups. Internet ordering and payment

> Inefficiencies in structures or processes can pose problems for online implementations

systems that are not well integrated with a business's structure and procedures can lead to inefficient mercantile processes. Be on the lookout for such problems as you plan and implement. Chapter 12 ("Strategies for Electronic Commerce," page 219), covers these issues in more detail.

New Roles and Marketing Opportunities

You've seen in this chapter that conducting commerce on the Internet can provide both consumers and businesses with new ways of doing things. In many ways, the Internet can become an ideal vehicle for initiating and strengthening relationships between businesses and their customers.

Two ways to build relationships that are important to electronic commerce, are, in some ways, unique to the Internet. The first way is the online community, where groups of users interact with each other largely, if not solely, via electronic means. Intermediaries and integrators provide a second way of building business relationships, by helping both buyers and sellers deal with the information glut and large numbers of possible interactions found on the Internet.

Online communities and intermediaries can be used to initiate and strengthen relationships

Examining the Role of Intermediaries

Intermediaries have long played a valuable economic role, even before the rise of the Internet and electronic commerce. Intermediaries make a living by meeting several critical economic functions: they overcome one-sided or prejudiced information about products and parties in a transaction, they make markets by providing a place for buyers and sellers to meet, and they often provide technical knowledge that would be too expensive for buyers or sellers to have on hand. But keep in mind that being an intermediary, or middleman, does not automatically make them nonpartisan. For example, real estate agents are intermediaries, but they represent the best interests of either the buyer or the seller.

Intermediaries can make markets, guide consumers, and provide technical expertise

The Internet has provided new potential for intermediaries. By providing a communication and transaction infrastructure, the Internet enables intermediaries to lower their transaction costs. It's also expands their potential customer base by making operations global.

Intermediaries can play a crucial role in each of the business steps between buyers and sellers. They can:

- Support buyers in identifying their needs and in finding an appropriate seller

- Provide an efficient means of exchanging information between both parties

- Execute the business transaction

- Assist in support after the sale

As more information is placed on line and scattered throughout the Web, and as more businesses seek to conduct business on the Web, the role of intermediaries and integrators will grow tremendously. Not only will people need assistance in finding information that's pertinent to them, but they'll also want to do comparative shopping on the Internet. Obtaining product information and prices from a few sites won't pose much of a problem, but finding and comparing tens of sites will cause such methods to cease to be effective, both in terms of time and cost (see Figure 5-7).

Intermediaries serve an integration function for customers and businesses alike. In doing so, they provide value for both sides of the market. For instance, an intermediary might focus on a small number of interrelated markets in a comprehensive way and would therefore deal only with certain companies, tracking their products and inventories. For the customer, this specialized knowledge would likely mean faster responses and a better understanding of the market. For the businesses involved, this intermediary can offer them a focused look at their market.

Commercial transactions with and without an intermediary.   ***Figure 5-7***

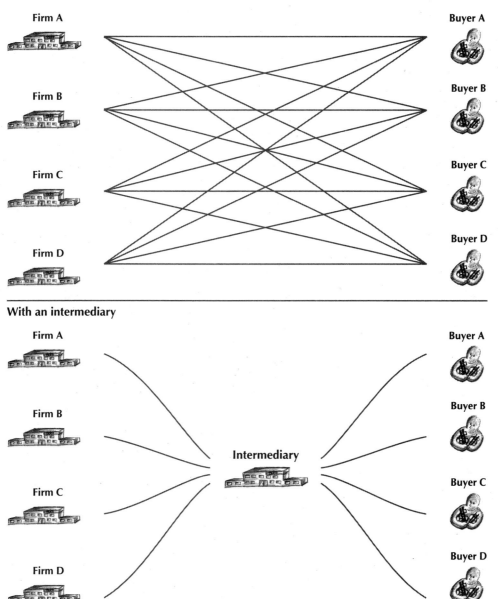

Without an intermediary

Firm A   Buyer A

Firm B   Buyer B

Firm C   Buyer C

Firm D   Buyer D

With an intermediary

Firm A   Buyer A

Firm B   Buyer B

Intermediary

Firm C   Buyer C

Firm D   Buyer D

Specialized intermediaries like this will also be able to provide another type of integration. Because they are intimately involved with all the major players in a particular market, they can use their interaction with, and knowledge of, their own customers to bundle products from different manufacturers to meet the customers' needs.

As we move more into the world of information, a number of new types of intermediaries suggest themselves. These include:

- Search and directory services (including intelligent agents) for finding goods, services, and people

- Virtual malls (another form of community) for consolidating certain types of merchants

- Virtual resellers

- Web site evaluators

- Auditors for measuring audiences and advertising efficacy on the Web

- Spot market makers and barter networks

Businesses must actively seek customer feedback, either directly from customers or through intermediaries

Of course, businesses that participate with such intermediaries have to exercise some caution, because in order to develop new products and foster growth they, too, need feedback on customer desires and product requests. If all the customer information stops at the intermediary, the suppliers and other businesses gain little more than the sale of their products, which is a sure formula for disaster.

Taking Advantage of Online Communities

Intermediaries can gather customer options in a single location

We've probably all dealt with a human agent, or intermediary, face-to-face in the past. Real estate agents are often the first to come to mind, but don't forget some of the suppliers' warehouses and similar stores that stock a seemingly endless selection of products; in their own way, they're agents as well because they've amassed all your choices in one location. Dealing with these intermediaries isn't too difficult, especially when it comes to deciding whom to trust. You can get a sense of the company and the person from face-to-face discussions, the look and location of the office or store, and, as a last resort, by asking the Better Business Bureau.

But this element of trust is difficult to reconstruct in electronic transactions. There's the old joke about no one knowing that you're a dog on the Internet. Now take that a step further for commercial transactions—how can you get a sense of a potential business partner from their electronic storefronts or e-mail exchanges? Is he or she a "dog"? If you've dealt with the merchants or suppliers before, or your electronic transactions have a counterpart in the physical world, then it's easy. But if all you know about them is what you see on their Web sites, and you've never heard of them before, then you need to be cautious.

Seeing isn't always believing, especially on the Internet

Creating trust on the Internet depends on fostering relationships via electronic means. One of the best approaches depends on word-of-mouth and guerrilla marketing methods. The basic concept is to share as much information about your products, services, and company, as you possibly can with the Internet community. And this doesn't mean just putting static information on a Web site. You have to be more dynamic and participatory in sharing information. That means participating in Usenet news groups that relate to your products or services, maintaining e-mail mailing lists for more than your current customers, and even offering chat services between employees and potential customers.

Participate in Usenet groups and maintain e-mail mailing lists to share information about your company and generate word-of-mouth

When it comes to marketing your company and its products in the electronic world these days, your company organization must be relatively flat—every employee should be encouraged (and trained) to share appropriate information with potential and current customers. (This point is discussed further in "Flexible Organizations" on page 223 in Chapter 12.)

Encourage employees to share appropriate information on line

All of these actions help form a sense of community among your current and future customers. Building relationships in Internet-based communities allows current and potential customers to learn more about your business—your recent past is going on line for all to see and comment on. The exchange of information and opinions between customers also builds a base that you'd find difficult to create by other means. And, as long as this base of opinions and information is favorable to you and your products (remember Intel and the negative press about problems with its Pentium chip?), customers' trust in your company will increase.

Customers who are part of a community exchange information and opinions; when their opinions are favorable, trust in your business will increase

Online communities can also be a good way for customers to discover alternative products and solutions that you offer—as long as you've seen to it that the information is known to the community. If people have a sense of belonging to a community, they will often seek advice from, and air their problems with, others in the community. Tapping the communal knowledge base in this way can be particularly beneficial when dealing with the large amounts of information on the Internet. If you do the groundwork, by getting information on your products to the right communities, then the people in those communities may well become your unofficial salespeople.

Online community members can act as unofficial sales people, so be sure they have plenty of accurate information

Business-to-business commerce can benefit from such communities as well. Although many businesses may already have non-electronic communities that might parallel online ones in purpose, putting these communities on line can improve communications, and new communities may also form.

Online business-to-business communities can improve communications

A business community might be a simple association, such as a partnership between two businesses, or it might be a more complex arrangement where a group of businesses form a consortium to meet a goal (see Figure 5-8). Coordinating teams within different companies, or groups of sub-

Partnerships, consortiums, virtual organizations, and business organizations, are all forms of business communities

contractors, to form a **virtual corporation** with the express purpose of accomplishing a task is another form of business community. There are also membership-based and regional business communities.

Different types of business communities.

Figure 5-8

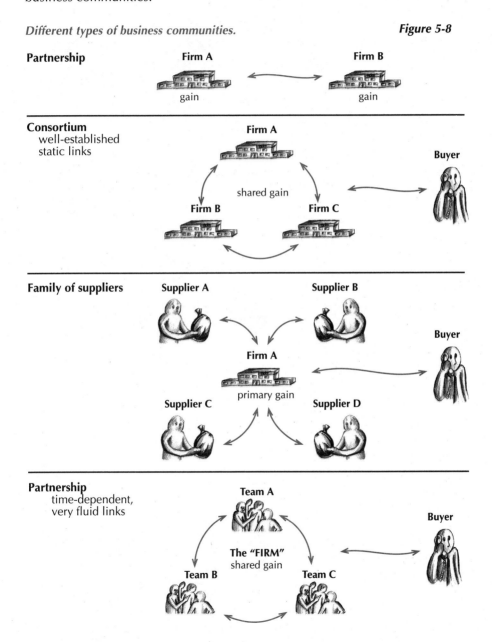

Partnership

Firm A Firm B

gain gain

Consortium
well-established
static links

Firm A

Buyer

shared gain

Firm B Firm C

Family of suppliers

Supplier A Supplier B

Buyer

Firm A

primary gain

Supplier C Supplier D

Partnership
time-dependent,
very fluid links

Team A

Buyer

The "FIRM"
shared gain

Team B Team C

Online business
communities need
secure communica-
tions, and the ability
to alter shared data

To support business communities in the electronic world, information systems must be secure, yet easy to enter. In order to be most effective, members of the community have to be able to share information, as well as alter it, regardless of where it resides.

Electronic communities will eventually have a great impact on every company that produces consumer goods and services, not just information services. These communities will redefine the structure of industries. And some communities will be defined and driven by intermediaries.

The next six chapters contain some real-life examples of how businesses have actually applied the technologies and business practices discussed so far.

Chapter Six

Offering Custom Products on the Internet

When it comes to electronic commerce, many vendors are looking to use the Internet as another sales channel. This sales channel can mimic that of the stores and malls that consumers are used to, in what have been called virtual malls that are hosted on Web servers; alternatively, the channel can parallel existing channels such as direct mail and telephone ordering.

One company that built itself solely on direct sales is Gateway 2000, Inc., the well-known supplier of personal computers. Gateway has grown from a direct-order powerhouse that took orders only over the phone, to one that now accepts individual and corporate orders using the World Wide Web. Using the Web has allowed Gateway to put more product information into the hands of the customers, resulting in customers who are well educated about their choices.

Gateway customers using the Web are better educated about their choices

It has also provided Gateway with the opportunity to improve the integration of the online ordering process with their inventory and scheduling systems, which run on the corporate computers using legacy software. Gateway was able to take its initial Web-based ordering process, a process where received orders were entered by hand into legacy sales software, and improve the handling of online orders by electronically transferring the order data to the legacy systems. In doing so, Gateway improved the turnaround time for processing orders and scheduling product assembly, as well as reduced errors in the ordering process.

Gateway improved order processing and scheduling by linking orders from the Web to their legacy systems

The Gateway story is typical of how a direct-order business can set up a commercial site on the Web. But Gateway also faced some unique problems stemming from the wide variety of customizable products that it offers its customers—you'll discover how they solved that problem shortly.

Concept: Moving from Phone Sales to the Web

Founded in September 1985, Gateway has always taken the approach of selling PC products directly to their customers. By 1987, the company had begun to sell completely configured PCs aimed at technically sophisticated and price-conscious customers who were willing to buy their products sight unseen if the price was right. This strategy catapulted Gateway's revenues from $1.5 million in 1987 to $5.04 billion in 1996.

Gateway chose to mirror its phone services on the Web

In 1996, Gateway decided to use the Web as another sales channel for their products. Prior to using the Web, Gateway customers had to place their orders by phone or fax. Gateway's new approach would offer the same ordering services, allowing customers to select either previously configured systems or configure their own system, on the Web.

Gateway replaced its custom programs

At first, Gateway developed a Web site just to provide product information to potential customers using the Microsoft

Internet Information Server (IIS). When Gateway implemented its first Web ordering system, they continued using the same server software, and added custom-written software to process orders. Later in 1996, when Microsoft released its Merchant Server software for handling Web-based purchases, Gateway decided to use Merchant Server, instead of its custom software, with IIS for all online ordering.

Merchant Server's features would allow Gateway to more easily generate Web pages dynamically from its databases, use the **Secure Sockets Layer** (SSL) protocol for protecting transactions, calculate product prices with its original custom-written software, and manage the system. However, before Gateway replaced the custom software with Merchant Server for all online ordering, their Information Systems department wanted to learn more about the capabilities of Merchant Server, so they set up a pilot project for the sale of non-computer products bearing the Gateway logo, such as mouse pads, T-shirts, and coffee mugs.

The pilot was limited to non-computer products such as mouse pads and coffee mugs

Building on the experience they gained with ordering on line using these systems in 1996, Gateway's first step was to move ahead with plans to use Merchant Server for all online orders. After that, they planned to improve the system by integrating it with their legacy systems (that is, the existing accounting, inventory, and manufacturing systems) thereby offering them better control over their inventory and manufacturing processes.

Full-scale implementation plans included an online store for all products, followed by systems integration with legacy systems

Implementation: The First Online Store

The first system for ordering Gateway's computer products on line offered the same options that were available when customers chose to order a system over the phone: they could select a pre-configured system, and either take it as

Web shoppers could finalize their orders on line or by phone; Gateway entered the orders manually packaged or add options. Once the customer had chosen the system's features, the order could be finalized over the Web, or by calling a sales representative. Both Web and phone orders were then manually entered into Gateway's ordering and inventory management system. If the order was placed via the Web, someone on Gateway's staff also sent an e-mail confirmation of the order to the customer.

Order tracking was available only by phone

Because the original system was not connected to the inventory system, they could not yet support order tracking on line. Gateway supports an automated phone system, available via a toll-free number, so that customers can track their orders and find out estimated delivery dates. Customers also can call customer service directly if they have any questions about their order.

Gateway simply expanded their original informational Web site to include online ordering

Gateway had a rather extensive Web site even before it started accepting orders on line, and they continued to offer this support information as they added Web-based ordering. The Web site (see Figure 6-1) now includes a technical support area containing troubleshooting notes and software patches, a computer glossary, descriptions of some of the latest PC technologies, and communications from Gateway's management. The Spot Shop, a separate online shopping area, offers items such as coffee mugs, mouse pads, and other goods featuring cows—Gateway's famous logo.

All of the information for the Gateway Web site is stored on a Gateway G6-200 PC with a 200MHz Pentium Pro processor, three 2-gigabyte hard drives, and 256 MB RAM, running both Microsoft NT Server and Internet Information Server. In addition, Microsoft Merchant Server was used to handle the products available in The Spot Shop. Using Merchant Server for all of its online orders was part of Gateway's plan for automating as much of the system as possible, and for integrating the order data with other **back-end processes** such as inventory and accounting.

Selected content and basic organization of Gateway 2000's Web site, not including cross links.

Figure 6-1

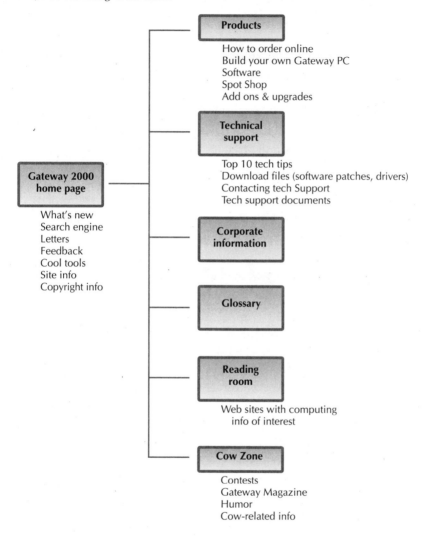

Gateway 2000 home page

What's new
Search engine
Letters
Feedback
Cool tools
Site info
Copyright info

Products

How to order online
Build your own Gateway PC
Software
Spot Shop
Add ons & upgrades

Technical support

Top 10 tech tips
Download files (software patches, drivers)
Contacting tech Support
Tech support documents

Corporate information

Glossary

Reading room

Web sites with computing
info of interest

Cow Zone

Contests
Gateway Magazine
Humor
Cow-related info

Expansion: Full-Scale Integration

The first online ordering system that Gateway implemented exhibited some of the problems common to similar ventures in which the Web-based store was not electronically linked to the rest of the company's data processing systems. The

Integrating the
ordering system with
legacy systems
would require less
manual handling,
reduce data entry
errors, and be more
efficient over all

involvement of people was required for such steps as sending the e-mail confirmation of an order, manually entering the order information into a legacy database, checking the status of orders when called on the phone, checking parts inventories, and issuing manufacturing orders. It was easy to see that processes like the e-mail confirmation, entering orders, and checking inventories could be automated and linked with the customer's input from the Web. By reducing the number of manual data entry steps, Gateway could also reduce errors and make the entire process of accepting an order and building the desired product more efficient.

**Maintaining the
security of legacy
data was an
important issue**

As Gateway moved to integrate its online ordering process with inventory management and general accounting, the systems developers faced a few challenges. Although it was relatively simple to convert its online store to Merchant Server, Gateway wanted to maintain the security of its legacy data. As the first version of the system using Merchant Server was rolled out, order data generated by Merchant Server was saved as a series of data files and then transferred to the AS/400 computer by one of the system administrators. This insured that no one on the Internet could hack the **Web server** to gain unauthorized access to Gateway's internal data systems because there was no direct electronic link between the two. Although all details had not been finalized as this book went to press, Gateway has plans to automate the process of transferring the data using **middleware** linking the Web server and the legacy databases.

**When customers
have many con-
figuration choices,
compatibility be-
comes an issue**

How to deal with the large number of possible system configurations that Gateway offers was another big challenge in automating more of the order process. Gateway needed to be able to ensure that a customer would not select incompatible hardware parts or choose software that was incompatible with the hardware. As a solution, they programmed expert-system software from Intellisys to check the validity of each choice in a customer's configuration.

Gateway used a third-party fulfillment service to handle product orders from The Spot Shop. As part of the automation effort they also wanted to improve the efficiency of the fulfillment service. Initially, the fulfillment service checked the orders and processed the credit card information manually. As part of their plan to automate more of the process, Gateway standardized the order forms found at the Spot Shop and created a series of scripts to grab the order information and send it electronically to the fulfillment service.

Automation also opens opportunities for integration with the systems of partners or third-party services

Web Site Description: Guiding the Customer Through Choices

Ordering a personal computer using Gateway's Web site (see Figure 6-2) parallels the same process followed when talking to a Gateway sales representative over the telephone, except that all of the choices are presented within the **Web browser**. Customers start out by deciding what kind of system they want (home vs. professional), what speed microprocessor, and what size monitor they'd like.

Gateway 2000 home page.

Figure 6-2

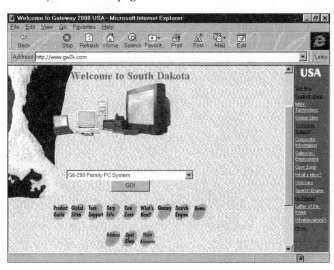

Customers can se-
lect a pre-configured
computer system or
choose individual
options

Customers who have no special needs can select one of
Gateway's pre-configured systems from an extensive list. If
customers have only one or two special requirements, such
as additional RAM or a larger hard drive, they can start with
a pre-configured system and simply add their requests as
options (see Figure 6-3). Options for each part of a system
are presented to customers in a pop-up menu that shows
each possible choice and its price.

Figure 6-3   *The initial screen for selecting options in a PC system.*

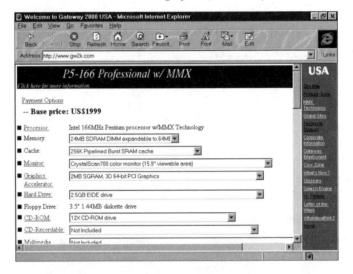

Photos, specifi-
cations, and
performance
data are avail-
able on line

Whichever process customers follow, the Gateway Web site
offers online information about the various options that are
available, including photos, product specifications, and
processor performance (see Figure 6-4). This flexibility of
product configuration adds up to over 1.6 million different
configurations.

Once customers review the system configuration on line
and decide to order it, they can place the order via the Web,
or call Gateway's sales department to place the order by
phone. Web-based purchases are conducted using the

Online product information comparing microprocessor upgrades.   ***Figure 6-4***

SSL protocol to secure the customer's credit card information from illegal snooping and capture during transmission. After the customer enters the appropriate billing and shipping information in the Web browser form, the order is delivered to a Gateway sales representative, and a confirmation of the order with an order number is sent to the customer via e-mail. If necessary, a sales representative may also call to confirm the status of the order and check the configuration with the customer. In the original Web system, confirmed orders were manually entered into legacy databases running on IBM AS/400 minicomputers, which also stored information for accounting, inventory, and manufacturing. In the current Web ordering system, electronic files with the sales data are transferred to the legacy databases.

The Spot Shop was a good candidate for testing Merchant Server because products offered in The Spot Shop are individual items that cannot be customized, and as opposed to Gateway's PCs, they do not need to be built from scratch. Before Gateway could switch its PC sales system to Merchant Server, it had to link its custom PC configuration

Orders placed on line are protected using the SSL protocol, and Gateway sends e-mail order confirmations

software to Merchant Server and develop the expert system for checking that a requested configuration was possible and didn't include hardware or software conflicts. Putting The Spot Shop on Merchant Server allowed Gateway's Information Systems department to learn more of the details of Merchant Server in real-life situations while it was developing the rest of the software it needed to convert all online orders to the new system.

The shopping cart metaphor allows customers to browse and shop as they go, finalizing the purchases when they are done

In The Spot Shop, Gateway uses the shopping cart metaphor, which is a metaphor common to many consumer-based commerce servers (such as Merchant Server). Customers can browse the selection of products, select an item to purchase (see Figure 6-5) by adding it to their shopping cart, and continue to browse, until eventually deciding to finalize the purchase. The customer then reviews the content of the shopping cart (see Figure 6-6), deletes unwanted items or changes the quantities of the items, and finalizes the purchase by providing the required credit card information.

Figure 6-5   ***Selecting an item to buy in The Spot Shop.***

Reviewing your shopping cart in The Spot Shop.   ***Figure 6-6***

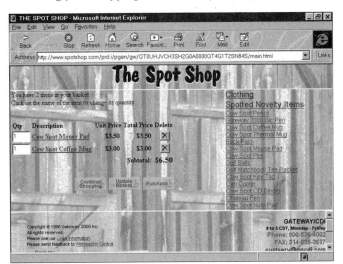

Analysis: Not Banking on a Single Sales Channel

Gateway's Web-based ordering system serves as a logical extension of their phone-based direct channel. And, even though Gateway management feels that Web sales will constitute only a small fraction of total sales for some time, they also feel that it will continue to grow. For example, Web-based sales, which first started in April 1996, accounted for $100 million in sales by the end of the year, yet this was but a drop in the bucket when compared to total sales of $5.04 billion for the year.

Web-based sales constitute a small, but not insignificant, percentage of the business

Because Web-based sales were not expected to be the main source of revenue for Gateway, the company's management wanted to be able to set up their commerce server as cheaply, quickly, and easily as possible. These were some of the main reasons they chose to first use Internet Information Server, and later added Merchant Server, for their operations. At the time when Gateway wanted to move to online ordering and integrate more of the processing with their

Using the inexpensive, customizable Merchant Server reduced the impact on Gateway's bottom line

legacy systems, they felt that only Merchant Server offered them the desired degree of database connectivity and software customizability.

Even when customers do not place an order via the Web, having the system configuration software on line and accessible via a Web browser has helped make many sales over the phone easier and faster. Gateway has noted that customers have often used the Web to investigate the system options and configure their system on line before calling a sales representative to place an order. This relieves the sales representative of having to take the customer through all of the options and explain them, and thereby reduces the time it takes to close a sale.

Because of all the stories of hackers and security breaches involving the Internet, many consumers still feel that their use of a credit card to place an order over the Internet is less secure than placing a similar order over the phone. Even though protocols like SSL do a good job of protecting against illegal snooping and capturing credit card numbers, consumers still need to be educated on the security of Internet-based purchases. For example, even though Gateway includes a note about its use of SSL for transaction security on every order page on its Web site, many customers still prefer to use the phone for ordering, even after selecting their PC configuration on the Web.

Gateway has done a lot to make it as easy as possible for customers to make intelligent decisions about system options. They have provided a wealth of online information for potential customers. For example, Gateway provides photos of monitors and PC cases, graphs on microprocessor performance, and technical documentation on most of the components that make up a PC system.

Gateway also complements this online pre-sales support with strong online technical support. The company has long had an excellent reputation for its customer support. The online technical support area reflects their support philosophy, offering not only troubleshooting tips for hardware and software (see Figure 6-7), but also lengthy documentation on PCs and possible problems. Patches and driver updates for various peripherals are also available for downloading from the Web site, helping to make the Gateway Web site a one-stop shop for not only ordering a PC, but for getting support after the sale.

Gateway's Web site also provides extensive technical information for post-sales support

Troubleshooting documents available on line.

Figure 6-7

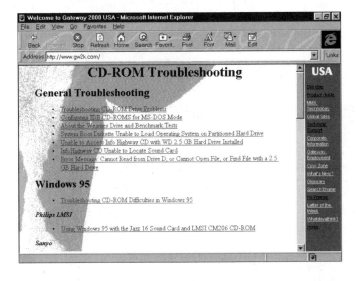

Clearly, accessing the Web site requires using a PC and a Web browser, so you might assume that Gateway's Web site is not aimed at first-time PC purchasers. However, Gateway has found that some customers will either use a friend's PC, or a PC at school, to order their first computer over the Web, so the lack of a PC is less of a constraint to sales than might be expected.

Even first-time PC purchasers use the Gateway Web site

By offering product and support information on the Web, in addition to accepting sales on line, Gateway has been able to increase the efficiency of both its sales and support de-

Integrating online orders with back-end systems minimized data entry errors, reduced processing time, and resulted in better resource allocation

partments. For example, back when the sales representative had to enter much of the data into the system by hand, a confirmation was sent out immediately, but it typically took anywhere from a few hours to a few days to check parts and schedule the assembly. When Gateway switched to Merchant Server and tied the orders to its legacy systems, the company was able to produce an e-mail confirmation of the order, check inventory of parts availability, and schedule the system's assembly within a matter of seconds (see Figure 6-8). Also, with fewer manual processes, the chance for mistakes due to data entry errors was minimized.

Figure 6-8   *Processing an order when it's digital.*

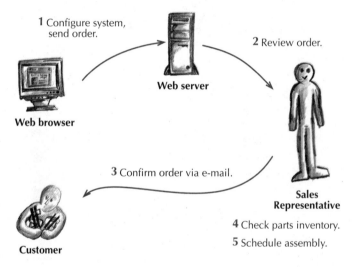

Reduced errors, faster turnaround on orders, and better allocation of resources have all combined to make Web-based ordering a low-maintenance sale, according to Gateway management.

Future Plans

Gateway has already accomplished much of what it set out
to do both in employing the Web as an additional sales
channel and in integrating the sales with their legacy systems. The company's future plans for the Web system per-
tain more to maintenance and the incremental improvement
of the system than any major changes. As the company
gains more experience with the expert system that checks
configurations, the software may be modified to improve its
efficiency and the ease of adding new configurations. Also,
as software for transferring data between Web servers and
legacy databases improves, Gateway plans to install newer
software to improve the integration of its systems.

Future plans focus
on maintenance,
enhancements, and
software upgrades

The Players, the System, the Site

Players: **Gateway 2000, Inc.**
North Sioux City, ND,
800-846-2069

System: The primary Web server ran on a Gateway G6-200 with Pentium
Pro 200-MHz processor, 256MB RAM and three 2GB hard drives,
using Microsoft Windows NT Server, Microsoft Internet Information Server, and Microsoft Merchant Server. The media server is a
Gateway 2000 P5-133 Professional PC with 128 MB RAM and 5
2GB hard drives, running Micro-soft Windows NT server, Microsoft Internet Information Server, VDOLive Video Server, and
RealAudio Server.

Site: http://www.gw2k.com

Chapter Seven

An Electronic Marketplace of Buyers and Sellers

Businesses don't exist in a vacuum. As a part of the marketplace, they participate in many types of communities and associations. These might be officially structured trading communities or business associations, or they might be something that's more loosely defined, perhaps by the casual relationships among a group of buyers and sellers, or trading partners.

As discussed in Chapter 4 ("Taking Advantage of Online Communities," page 112), building communities on the Internet can be both an important part of electronic commerce and a difficult task to accomplish. Various tools for creating services such as bulletin boards, online chat areas, and video-conferencing, are available for your use to encourage communal communications, and these services are becoming more widely used on the Internet.

Tools exist to offer online community services such as bulletin boards, chat areas, and video conferencing

One company that was formed expressly to build an electronic marketplace in the manufacturing sector and encourage electronic communications among its members is Industry.net, now a part of Nets Inc. Industry.net's story not only shows how a Web site can be developed to successfully maintain a marketplace of buyers and sellers in a particular market niche,

Creating an online marketplace resulted in a complete shift from print to electronic offerings

but also demonstrates how a company has been able to evolve from focusing on materials distributed by mail (printed information and computer diskettes) to using the Internet and the World Wide Web for all of its business.

Industry Net started with a private BBS; 18 months later they launched their Web site

The original Industry Net, founded in 1990, started out as a news service that distributed industry news and information about manufacturing practices to subscribers in print form. Industry Net also created a product called the Industrial Locator, which was a computer diskette containing an electronic yellow pages listing manufacturers and suppliers. In an effort to make the information more useful to subscribers, Industry Net organized and distributed the data by region. In April of 1993, Industry Net launched a dial-up bulletin board service (BBS), called Marketplace BBS, to offer electronic access to new technology and product announcements to manufacturers and their suppliers. It wasn't until September 1994 that Industry Net created the Online Marketplace service on the Web, which became known as Industry.net.[1]

Concept: Moving from Print to On Line

Low-cost local access is offered by most ISPs

While Industry Net was still running its proprietary bulletin board service, it had considered dealing with a service provider to offer more **points-of-presence**[2] (POPs), or locations to use for dialing into the BBS. But it decided that doing that, or constructing its own POPs, would be too expensive. That's even more evident now, with the low-cost access rates offered by so many **Internet service providers** (ISPs).

---

1. A new company, Nets Inc., was formed in June 1996 as a result of the merger of Industry Net and AT&T's New Media Services. The name Industry.net is now used solely to designate the Web-based services offered by Nets Inc.

2. A point-of-presence is a local access point to a national or international communications network.

Moving to the Web and creating Industry.net offered Industry Net three major advantages:

- **Web browsers** could be used as a universal client to all three of Industry.net's original services (industry news, directories, and the bulletin board);

- Industry Net could concentrate on developing the back-end services (and let other companies, such as Netscape and Microsoft, deliver client software); and

- the user base of Industry.net could be expanded more easily, taking advantage of the dynamic growth of the Internet.

Unlike many other sites created in the early days of the Web, Industry.net was not designed simply to provide links (**uniform resource locators** or URLs) to other companies' Web sites. Instead, Industry Net decided to actually host the Web pages for participating companies and use Web hosting as a source of revenue. Industry.net thus became a centralized location for finding manufacturers and their suppliers, creating an electronic marketplace.

By offering such a focused service, and making it easier for manufacturers and their customers to find related products and services, Industry Net was able to add value to the Web, and could justify charging participants fees for being a part of this central Web location. Because buyers may register to use Industry.net for free, the main source of revenue for this endeavor is hosting the Web pages of the sellers in the community.

The more manufacturers and suppliers that are a part of the site, the more enticing and useful it will be to customers. And the more potential customers who visit the site, the easier it will be to recruit more companies to join Industry.net.

Buying Members and Selling Clients

The Industry.net
community consists
of buying members
and selling clients

The online community, as defined for Industry.net, consists of *buying members*, who are the purchasing and specifying professionals at large corporations, and *selling clients*, such as manufacturers, distributors, and service providers. Selling clients range in size from some of the largest companies in the United States to individual skilled workers and craftsmen.

Industry.net fostered
the growth of an
online community to
share information;
future plans include
the handling of
order-related
transactions

Nets Inc.'s plans would not only make it easier for buying members to find selling clients, but Nets Inc. would be adding a further sense of community by offering online discussion areas and a periodic newsletter, along with online industry-related news. In its initial stages, Nets Inc. did not want their Internet facilities to be a channel for order-related transactions between buyers and sellers because they were not planning to offer either an ordering service or funds transfers. That situation is changing, though, as Nets Inc. moves forward with arrangements with PNC Bank (see "Future Plans" on page 147).

Implementation: Web Site Development

News, trade shows,
employment oppor-
tunities, and other
industry-related in-
formation is just as
important as the
product catalogs

Nets Inc. has taken the approach that it can build a marketplace of businesses by facilitating the transactions between buyers and sellers—not the actual financial transactions, but the processes involved in finding buyers and sellers in manufacturing sectors. Thus the Industry.net site not only contains product catalogs and related product information from a number of companies, but also offers news updates classified by industry sectors, hot product news, trade show information, employment opportunities, and links to pertinent industry associations.

The Database Approach

Nets Inc. found that taking paper-based catalogs and simply converting them to the Web using HTML (HyperText Markup

Language) would not allow them to routinely and easily maintain the information, nor would it provide customers with an easy-to-use search capability. Instead, they chose to store product data in an Oracle database and use templates for Industry.net's Web pages, transferring data from the database to a Web page when required. The templates determine how the information is presented to the customer using a Web browser; storing the data in a database allows the same data to be used in different Web pages and for other uses, such as creating CD-ROM-based and printed catalogs (see Figure 7-1)

Dynamically generated pages from an Oracle database makes searching and updating easy

Information, its storage, and presentation.   **Figure 7-1**

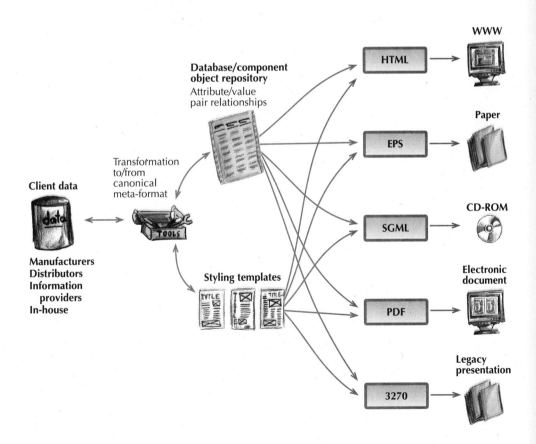

The database approach simplifies the process for updating information

Keeping the data in a database also makes it easier for a company to update its data. If product data were entered into Web pages using HTML, for instance, every page containing that product would have to be changed manually. Instead, with the database approach, the product data only has to be changed in the database; the next time a Web page is generated using that product's data, the data is obtained from the up-to-date database entry.

Three Levels of Web Services

Three levels of service are available for selling clients: the Business Center Profile, LogoLink, and a profile plus product catalog

Nets Inc. offers its selling clients three levels of Web services on Industry.net.

- The Business Center Profile service provides companies with an entry-level way to participate in Industry.net. The service also allows buyers to find sellers through searches by company name, product or service type, or, in the case of distributors, by the manufacturer represented. Sellers receive a one-page Web site hosted within Industry.net that can include company information, a list of products, and a list of distributors.

- The LogoLink service allows Business Center users to offer a link from their Industry.net page directly to their own corporate site.

- The combination service allows sellers to set up a Business Center Profile with an online product catalog.

At each level, Nets Inc. provides assistance in the design and implementation of the Web pages and catalogs.

Because the Internet is a relatively new medium for communications, many of a seller's current and potential buyers might not yet be connected to the Internet, making

Industry.net less appealing to some buyers as a channel for conducting business. To help grow the electronic marketplace and increase the synergy between buyers and sellers, Nets Inc. is helping Industry.net sellers to assist their customers in getting dial-up access through AT&T WorldNet Service via a co-branded sign-up kit.

Web Site Description: Consolidating Information for Business Sectors

The home page of Industry.net provides visitors with access to listings of companies by engineering specialty, product and market news, discussion groups, a product search facility, downloadable software, and industry associations (see Figure 7-2). The two main Web locations where customers can find products and services are the listings of engineering specialties and the product search area.

Industry.net's home page.

Figure 7-2

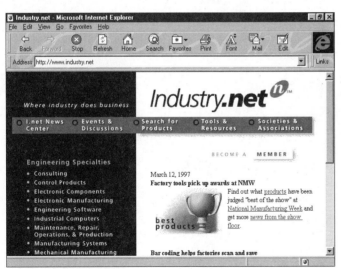

Listings of Engineering Specialties

Industry.net groups companies by specialty area

If buying members are interested in browsing a particular company's online catalog or other business information, they can enter that company's Business Center by selecting the appropriate engineering specialty, and then selecting the company name from the list that's presented. Industry.net features the following seventeen engineering specialties:

- Consulting
- Control Products
- Electronic Components
- Electrical Manufacturing
- Engineering Software
- Industrial Components
- Manufacturing Systems
- Mechanical Manufacturing
- Motion
- Maintenance, Repair & Operations
- Networks
- PCs and Workstations
- Programmable Logic Controllers
- Power Transmission
- Process
- Sensors
- Test & Measurement

Customers can use the search engine not only to find specific companies or products, but also to find vendors and distributors carrying those products, based on the customer's geographic location (see Figure 7-3).

You can search the Buyer's Guide by product, company, or manufacturer.

Figure 7-3

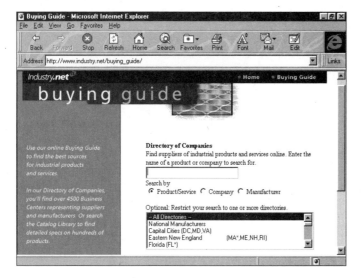

In addition to pointing the user at searchable product catalogs, the main page for each engineering specialty presents industry-specific news headlines and a showcase of the hot new products in that market (see Figure 7-4). This makes it

News headlines and new product sections help to narrow the focus

The Networks page shown here is typical of the engineering specialty Web pages.

Figure 7-4

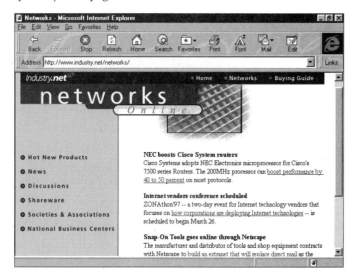

easier for customers and visitors to find pertinent information without having to work their way through information from other market sectors.

Industry.net hosts the online presence of leading associations in related fields

Industry.net also hosts a number of online association communities (24 as of March 1997). Leading associations in a given field, such as the Association for Manufacturing Excellence and the Electronic Industries Association, backs each of these online communities. These online areas usually include information about the association, a member directory, association publications, career opportunities, and guides to trade shows and association events.

Analysis: Using an Information Channel to Build Markets

Nets Inc.'s revenues have doubled, and its 280,000 registered members represent $185 billion in annual purchasing power

Nets Inc. has progressed way beyond its original online goals. As of January 1997 Industry.net had 280,000 registered members, representing more than 40,000 organizations, with a total annual purchasing power of $185 billion, and over 4500 online Business Centers.[3] Although Nets Inc. is a privately held company that hasn't released revenue figures publicly, estimates are that its revenues doubled between fiscal years 1995 and 1996, having grown from about $28 million to about $56 million.

Building on an Existing Client Base

Nets Inc.'s design plans for its online system were based on its experience with its existing client base

Nets Inc. is fortunate that it was able to build on an existing base of companies, banded together first via print-based and diskette-based information, and then through a bulletin board system. Nets Inc. was able to build on four years of experience, discovering what its clients deemed important before making any information available on the Web.

---

3. Some companies have more than one business center.

That experience shows in the organization of the Industry.net Web site, with its concentration on specific market sectors, including not only manufacturers and suppliers, but also pertinent industrial associations. Those associations, along with the discussion forums available on site, make it easier for a customer to get answers to specific problems. Even a cursory glance at the forums shows that people use these forums frequently, and that they are quite willing to exchange useful information there.

By including associations and supporting forums, Nets Inc. made it easier for customers to find answers to their questions at Industry.net

A One-Stop Shop

Nets Inc. thus not only makes it easier for customers to find the products they need, but also provides secondary information about the products through the opinions that users post in the forums. Maintaining so many different sources of related information, such as association news, trade show dates, employment opportunities, surplus equipment lists, hot product news, and chat areas, adds to a sense of community for the users, and reinforces the image of Industry.net as a one-stop shop that meets their needs.

The multiple sources of information about products, issues, companies, and associations, make their online site a one-stop resource

Buying Behaviors

Whether in traditional markets or in an electronic one like Industry.net, there are two general types of buying behaviors. There's expected buying, where the buyer is a repeat purchaser or is replenishing stock from the same supplier. And there's unexpected buying, which includes spot buys and buys that occur when buyers are looking for a new supplier. Nets Inc. estimates that there's a 50-50 split in buying activity between expected buying and unexpected buying, so their approach is to support both types of activity equally well. For instance, the search engine can lead buyers to new suppliers, while repetitive purchases with a given supplier can be arranged via e-mail or by revisiting the supplier's catalog at Industry.net.

Industry.net supports expected and unexpected buying activities equally

Catalogs

By hosting the selling members' catalogs, Industry.net creates a site standard that makes searches more efficient

Catalogs have been a mainstay on Industry.net and certainly are crucial to its success. In the absence of standards for product descriptions and interoperability between catalogs, Nets Inc. can provide a common product description for search engines by hosting the catalogs of all its selling members. As companies move to using electronic agents to search for products and prices in the future, Nets Inc. can offer them a single site that's easier to access than a number of individually hosted sites.

Two Market Models

The Industry.net format supports both open market and hierarchical market models

These catalogs can take on different forms depending on the market model that the selling member chooses to follow. By using a database to store product information, Nets Inc. allows buyers to extract different forms of product descriptions, and to customize catalogs, if needed. Many companies may choose the *open market model,* which presents general catalogs and stock catalogs as well as new product and promotional information. But other (or the same) suppliers can follow a *hierarchical market* (or *private commerce*) *model* by offering an integrated supply catalog that's customized from a variety of sources, or a buyer-preference catalog that's customized to a buyer's needs, including special pricing. Nets Inc.'s format for Industry.net supports both models. Nets Inc. has been pursuing some new ventures on the hierarchical market side with large buyers as an adjunct to what, thus far, has been an open market model.

Three Important Services

As an intermediary, a Web site host should provide assistance, analysis, and support

A business can function successfully as an intermediary only when it offers the following three services: (1) providing application or engineering assistance, (2) providing analyses or services based on capturing information about transactions at the site, and (3) offering targeting of strategic mar-

Open vs. Hierarchical Markets

The ways that businesses interact to exchange goods and services are usually classified into two market structures—open markets and hierarchical markets. Open markets revolve around the acquisition of new customers. In such markets, an electronic service like Industry.net can offer sellers lower costs for sales by making it easier and cheaper for buyers to find the products and services they need. Hierarchical markets focus more on getting known trading partners together. For these markets, Nets Inc. aims to increase the efficiency of the processes between trading partners. One way to do this is to use the electronic services that make up Industry.net (and other new services) to link together the business processes of the partners, with Nets Inc. serving as an intermediary. Intermediaries should provide assistance with applications, data analyses, and strategic market targeting.

kets based on the data collected from processes taking place on the site (such as customer searches, buying patterns, etc.). Nets Inc. doesn't offer all of these features in Industry.net now, but it's planning to. For example, Nets Inc. has been developing data warehousing techniques to process the transaction data they acquire from Industry.net, in order to provide detailed information on customer purchasing habits.

The Long-Running Transaction

The managers at Nets Inc. talk about the *long-running transaction* (see Figure 7-5). This is the term they use to describe the individual steps in assisting buyer-seller relations, from the first step of a sale (helping the buyer to locate a seller and his product), all the way to the last steps (including product support and assessment of the relationship between buyer and seller). As you can see in the figure, value can be added, in different amounts, at each step along the way. Industry.net's current structure focuses primarily on

The long-running transaction begins with buyer assistance and ends with relationship assessment

the source function with its online catalogs, but they're currently making strategic alliances and launching pilot projects to encompass more tasks of the long-running transaction.

Figure 7-5   ***The long-running transaction.***

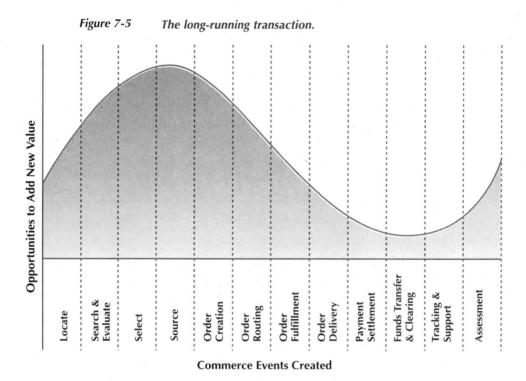

Withdrawing the printed version of the newsmagazine encouraged customers to visit the Web site more frequently

Nets Inc. stopped publishing its original newsmagazine, *Industry.net Report,* at the end of 1996. This newsmagazine had been circulated to over 165,000 subscribers and was available in electronic form at the Industry.net Web site. Although the news magazine was widely read, it was felt that the print version did not regularly lead readers directly to the Web site, and that offering the same news content electronically would encourage customers to visit Industry.net on the Web, thereby increasing repeat traffic at the site. Also, producing the print version was more costly than placing the same material on line, and the material could be updated more frequently (and easily) if it was on line.

Net Inc.'s Development Philosophy

The development philosophy for Industry Net, and now Nets Inc., has been to write applications in-house, using third-party solutions only when necessary to implement features in a timely, competitive fashion. However, when commercial solutions become available that are as good as, or better than, the in-house solutions, Industry.net replaces its applications with the commercial products. Technology has never been the driving force for doing anything at Nets Inc.; rather, the focus has been on meeting customer's needs. Often, the technology infrastructure catches up with the needs of the marketplace, and Nets Inc. can use the new solutions as part of its business.

Create proprietary applications when necessary; switch to quality commercial solutions when available

Future Plans

Although Industry.net did not start out as a transaction broker for the companies using its site, Nets Inc. has plans to expand Industry.net services to include commercial transactions. In September 1996, Nets Inc. announced that it was partnering with PNC Bank Corp. to provide online payment options to its customers (see Figure 7-6 on the next page).

Future plans include support for financial transactions

Multiple Payment Options

The payment system it is developing will provide companies with multiple payment options, including credit cards, purchasing cards, **automated clearinghouse** (ACH) transactions, and **electronic data interchange** (EDI). To simplify the use of the payment options that will be a part of the Online Marketplace, the project also includes using industry standards (EDI for exchanging purchase orders and invoices, for example) to integrate the payment methods with companies' existing accounts payable and accounts receivable systems.

Multiple payment options will be available

Nets Inc. will also create an *electronic purchasing account*, a credit facility designed to provide companies with information about purchasing practices. As part of the project,

Figure 7-6   *Electronic commerce using PNC Bank.*

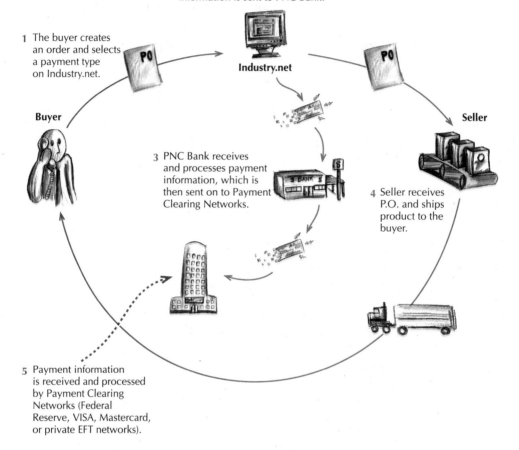

2 Industry.net receives the order and payment information. The P.O. information is sent to the seller and the payment information is sent to PNC Bank.

1 The buyer creates an order and selects a payment type on Industry.net.

Industry.net

Buyer

3 PNC Bank receives and processes payment information, which is then sent on to Payment Clearing Networks.

Seller

4 Seller receives P.O. and ships product to the buyer.

5 Payment information is received and processed by Payment Clearing Networks (Federal Reserve, VISA, Mastercard, or private EFT networks).

PNC Bank will provide traditional treasury management services, such as account activity reports, and integration of check disbursement and collection services.

Digital certificates will be used for authentication and non-repudiation

As part of the move to supporting online payment methods, Nets Inc. is also increasing the security of its systems and customer information. For instance, **digital certificates** will be used to authenticate both buyers and sellers, and to support non-repudiation in transactions.

Nets Inc. collects a lot of data about users' preferences and their usage patterns while they are on Industry.net, so Nets Inc. is considering data warehousing techniques to offer more comprehensive looks at customers that use the Web site's facilities. These preference profiles will help Industry.net develop more software to assist buyers and sellers in the near future. Part of this work is being done in conjunction with NIST's Manufacturing Extension Program, which is aimed at supporting consultants who are helping small businesses with manufacturing problems. The goal is to provide small manufacturers and the Manufacturing Extension Centers with tools and techniques to locate, search, filter, synthesize, and present information that is customized for every user. In this case, Industry.net serves as an excellent source of information about both products and practices. Nets Inc. will be able to use this information with greater ease than before.

> Nets Inc. plans to present information that is customized for every user

The Players, the System, the Site

Players: **Nets Inc.**
Five Cambridge Center,
Cambridge, MA 02141
phone: 617-252-5000
fax: 617-374-4020
http://www.netsinc.com

PNC Bank Corp.
Pittsburgh, PA
William H. Callihan, 412-762-8257

System: The system runs on Sun minicomputers using software from Netscape, Oracle, and Open Market, among others. (No other information provided.)

Site: http://www.industry.net

Collaborating on a Distribution Chain

Digital information may well prove to be the mainstay of electronic commerce over the long term. But, as you learned in Chapter 5 ("Value Chains and the Marketspace," page 102), businesses can also use information to control processes involving the manufacture and distribution of physical goods.

Electronic commerce helps processes involving physical goods

One company that's taken this to heart is Fruit of the Loom. They've chosen to use the Internet and the Web to tie together their network of distributors so that they can provide information on their mills and distributor inventories to their customers.

Concept: Distributors are Important Middlemen

Unlike Fruit of the Loom's underwear business, in which the company deals directly with large retailers like Wal-Mart, the Activewear side of the business sees a lot of competition at the distribution channel level. Fruit of the Loom maintained a traditional network for distributing its Activewear

Fruit of the Loom
wanted to help
distributors enhance
services so small
business buyers
would not seek
similar products
from competitors

products, connecting with fifty distributors nationwide via printed catalogs, telephone, and fax. Small businesses such as silk-screen shops, T-shirt printers, and embroidery shops would order Activewear goods from Fruit of the Loom distributors, who would fill the orders, if possible, from their warehouses. But customers and distributors had no easy way of finding out if items they wanted were part of the current inventory at the distributors' warehouses or if these items could be shipped in a timely fashion. If goods weren't available to meet customer deadlines, those customers would most likely look for similar products from Fruit of the Loom's competitors.

Fruit of the Loom has actively employed networks for business uses. For example, its Vendor Management Inventory (VMI) system was set up in December 1995 to facilitate exchanging order and forecasting data between the company and its distributors. The company also processes over 300,000 EDI transactions each day. But Fruit of the Loom had not considered using the Web for electronic commerce until an outside consulting firm proposed a pilot project.

A Pilot Web Project

Use the Web to
build stronger
relationships with
your distributors by
simplifying ordering
and inventory
checks

Snickelways Interactive, a digital commerce firm based in New York City, came up with the concept of using the Web as a way to build stronger relationships with distributors by simplifying ordering and making it easier to check inventory status. By working with The ConText Group, a consulting firm in the apparel market, Snickelways was able to sell their idea to Fruit of the Loom.

Although a novice to the Internet, Dave Dixon, the vice-president of marketing for Activewear at Fruit of the Loom, quickly realized that his company could gain an advantage over its competitors by using the Internet to offer closer links with distributors and the small businesses to whom they sell.

Fruit of the Loom's distribution network.   ***Figure 8-1***

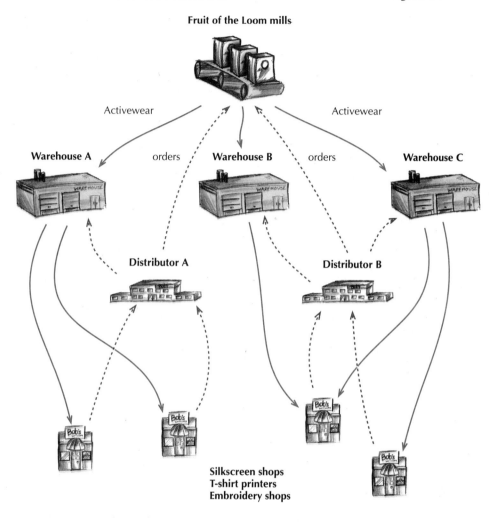

By helping distributors set up their own Web sites to collect
sales orders and offer products from Fruit of the Loom in
place of other out-of-stock items, the project would increase
customer awareness of Fruit of the Loom as well as help
distributors automate their sales process (see Figure 8-1).
He commissioned a pilot project to prove this concept.

Snickelways sought to create a system that would tie together the Fruit of the Loom distribution network electronically so that distributors and the small businesses ordering from the distributors could get the information they needed to place orders. Not only would small businesses be able to check the distributor's inventory and the status of their orders more readily, but also the system would be able to suggest alternatives to an out-of-stock item and search for alternate warehouses stocking a desired item. These last two features particularly demonstrate the power of having an electronic information network that connects customers to distributors. Without these options, the system would be little more than an online catalog; that's enough to add value to the process, but offering alternative items and warehouses adds even more value.

The system would check the distributor's inventory and the status of orders, search for alternate warehouses stocking a desired item, and suggest alternative products when an item was out of stock

Implementation: A Single Distributor

Snickelways turned their ideas into a prototype system for a single distributor, Broder Bros. Inc., a $150 million firm located in Plymouth, Michigan. The goal was to prove to Fruit of the Loom that such a system was not only possible, but offered distributors new ways of doing business and cutting costs.

Broder Bros. Inc. was interested in developing a Web site so that they could provide customers with 24-hour-a-day access to the catalog ordering system. By automating more of the ordering system, they also hoped to be able to reduce the staff in the customer service department that was responsible for taking orders over the toll-free and local phone lines. Eventually, it was hoped, they'd be able to eliminate the toll-free operator and associated facilities entirely.

Distributors could reduce costs by replacing order-taking staff and facilities with an automated catalog ordering system

Although interested in using the Internet for its business advantage, Broder Bros. Inc. was reluctant to allow customer access to its corporate databases over the Internet.

Customers don't access the corporate database directly

Because they did not have a firewall to secure their corporate data against outside access, the prototype required the system manager at Broder Bros. to periodically transfer a file containing inventory data from the corporate system to the Web-based catalog.

Creating the Prototype Web Site

With only six dedicated full-time staff, Snickelways created the prototype in 12 weeks using tools that were simple, yet powerful. The full team consisted of a team leader, an executive producer, three programmers (for interface design, **HTML** coding, and database programming), a subject matter expert, art director, graphic designer, and a production artist. (Not all these people were dedicated full time to the project.) To create the prototype Web site, they turned to O'Reilly's WebSite server program running on Microsoft Windows NT, and they used the Microsoft Visual Basic 4.0 programming environment to create the front-end. Later they added O'Reilly's WebBoard for the bulletin boards and software from Palace Software for the chat areas.

A small team created a prototype in 12 weeks

To get around the problems of transferring product data from the Broder Bros. corporate database to the database connected to the Web server, Snickelways used VMARK's HyperSTAR **middleware**[1] to extract ASCII files from a Uni-Verse database containing Broder Bros.' product data (see Figure 8-2 on the next page). These ASCII files, which were updated several times a day, were imported to an Oracle database running on Windows NT. An application written in Visual Basic 4.0 used ODBC (Open Database Connectivity) to connect to the Oracle database, construct queries using

Information is frequently extracted from the distributor's database so that the dynamically generated results of an online product search are up to date

---

1. A growing part of client/server development, middleware sits between a client application and a legacy database (or more than one). Its role is to translate both user requests into something the database can understand (SQL, for example), and the resulting data set into something the client application can use.

SQL (Structured Query Language) on the fly, and present the results of a customer's search on a Web page. Each page thus presented to the customer results of the product search that were dynamically generated.

Figure 8-2   *Components of prototype computing system and Web site.*

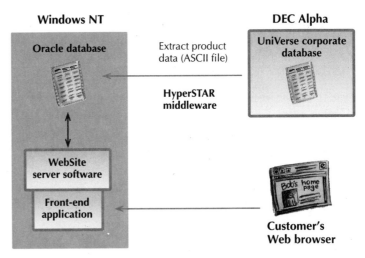

Web-based orders accounted for 5 percent of the business within the first 3 months, and savings were estimated at $10 per transaction

Broder Bros.' initial expectations for a financial pay-off were met and exceeded in a short span of time. The original projections called for Broder Bros. to reach a break-even point on the project six months after start-up; they also hoped to derive 5 percent of their business from Web-based ordering within 12 months. However, after the Web site was made available to Broder Bros.' customers, Web-based orders accounted for 5 percent of their business after only three months! At the same time, the company saved, and continues to save, roughly $10 per transaction.

Expansion:
Adding More Distributors

As the pilot project progressed and proved its viability, Fruit of the Loom Chief Information Officer Charles Kirk became more involved and aimed to expand the concept to include as many Activewear distributors as possible. The problem was that the Broder Bros. pilot site model was too expensive to apply to 30 or more sites because of all the custom work that Snickelways had put into it. The cost of the pilot site was over $500,000, which was not outrageous for a single Web commerce site, but too high for mass-produced sites such as Kirk had in mind. The solution was to use more off-the-shelf software and locate the Web servers at a single location.

Use off-the-shelf software and a central location for mass-produced sites

Expanding the Project

Kirk was able to sell Fruit of the Loom's board of directors on the idea of expanding the project to all fifty of the Active-wear distributors. Eventually, thirty of the fifty distributors signed on with Fruit of the Loom's project, called Active-wear Online (see Figure 8-3 on the next page). In return, Fruit of the Loom underwrote the cost of installation and maintenance of the Web server; the distributors have to update their catalogs and pay for the communication link to the servers, which are centrally located at Connect Inc. in California.

Fruit of the Loom's sponsorship pays for installation and maintenance of the Web server

Division of Labor

The tasks of this full-blown project were subdivided. Snickelways Interactive took over responsibility for developing the Web page design, a program for generating page templates, and the overall organization for the Web sites.

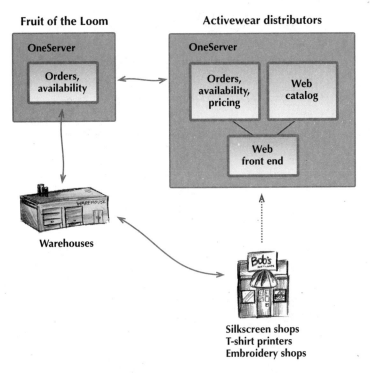

Figure 8-3   *The electronic network for distributors.*

Tasks were divided between the digital commerce firm, Fruit of the Loom, a systems integration firm, and an electronic commerce service provider

Fruit of the Loom Systems, part of Kirk's group, working with Compuware, a systems integration firm, became responsible for the installation and maintenance of the remaining distributor sites. At the same time, the project was converted from the prototype WebSite software to Connect Inc.'s OneServer Web server software to support greater scalability and the ability to handle a greater number of transactions. It took 20 programmers from Fruit of the Loom, Compuware, and Connect three months to design and implement the database for use by the OneServer software.

Using a Design Template
The program created by Snickelways walks each distributor through the creation process, in which they pick attributes such as background patterns and logos from predesigned

templates. This way, Fruit of the Loom can provide a uniform design for establishing a Web site, while still affording each distributor the opportunity for customization. This approach allowed for rapid deployment of the systems into the field; Kirk estimates that Fruit of the Loom has saved about 75 percent of the cost of a stand-alone site by adopting the pre-engineered approach made possible with the template program

The use of a design program saved money, provided consistency, and still allowed for distributor customization

Each participating distributor now has a **Web server** and a corresponding Oracle database stored on Connect Inc. hardware located at the OneServer site. Distributors can access their data by dialing the OneServer site with a 28.8-kbps modem; access is password protected. Each distributor is free to update their inventory and catalog data as often as they like, and the process for uploading a new inventory file to the OneServer site has also been automated to simplify the process.

Maintaining the System

Working with templates and the Web servers at Connect Inc. hasn't solved all the integration problems. One remaining problem is that each distributor has its own system for handling inventory and orders. For some distributors, a direct electronic link between the online catalog and the distributor's order processing system isn't possible, so orders have to be collected from OneServer and manually entered into the distributor's ordering system. Because the distributors' ordering systems varied so much, Fruit of the Loom had little choice at this stage; in order to keep inventory information up-to-date, they decided to use ordinary text files to transfer data from distributors' systems to OneServer. Once a file is at the OneServer site, the data is immediately incorporated into an Oracle 7 database so that the online catalogs are up-to-date, and customers can check their orders.

Integration with each distributor's internal inventory and ordering systems is still problematic, so ordinary text files are currently used to transfer data

Because the distributors' internal inventory and order processing systems are so varied, Connect Inc. collects incoming orders from the small business customers and forwards them to the appropriate distributor by either e-mail or fax. The distributors can then enter the orders manually, or by a batch file transfer, into their own internal systems.

Except for the Broder Bros. and Sanmar Web sites, which were the first two systems developed by Snickelways Interactive[2] before the project was converted to OneServer, the distributors' Web sites are maintained by Connect Inc. on Sun Enterprise 4000 servers running Connect's OneServer software.

Web Site Description: Ordering On Line

Each Web site follows the same organization, with a welcome message, links to Fruit of the Loom mill notes, and special promotions on the home page

By using the templates developed by Snickelways, each distributor's Web site encompasses many of the same functions (such as order forms, product substitution suggestions, and links to the Fruit of the Loom site), but the distributors also have the option to customize the look of their Web pages to suit their own company's image. To make it easier for the distributors to customize and maintain their HTML files, Snickelways developed an application called Digital Cockpit. Each distributor's Web site therefore follows the same organization as all the others (see Figure 8-4). The home page contains the welcome to customers and provides links to Fruit of the Loom's mill notes as well as to special promotions. The remaining pages, for placing orders and checking account information, branch off from the home page.

The Online Catalog

The online catalog is graphically presented to customers as a series of clothing categories, such as T-shirts, caps, shorts,

---

2. The system is now called ComForce and is used by Snickelways for other projects as well.

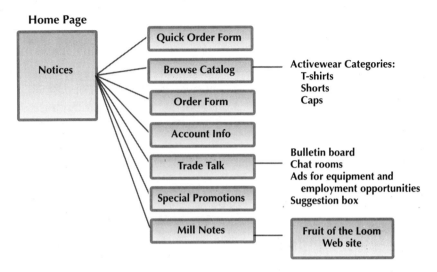

jackets, and so on (see Figure 8-5). These categories then
lead to new pages containing graphic lists of the items in
that category, along with ordering information. These pages
are dynamically generated from the product database,
ensuring that customers get up-to-date data.

A screen shot of catalog and order page.   ***Figure 8-5***

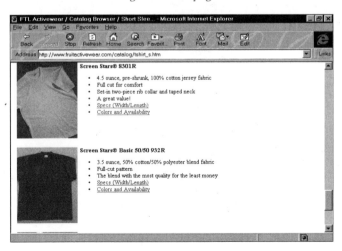

The catalog is arranged by clothing category, and the system creates order pages dynamically based on current information in the product database

Customers can store
potential or partial
orders in the data-
base for 30 days
without actually
submitting the order

As a customer orders items, the order is stored on the Web site and can be reviewed and changed by that customer at any time. This also ensures that a customer's order is retained even if the connection between the customer and the Web server is broken for any reason. Customers can keep orders on the Web site for up to 30 days, whereupon the orders will be deleted automatically by the distributor (see Figure 8-6). If there are any pending orders stored on the server, customers are notified of the orders whenever they log on to the system.

Figure 8-6   *A screen shot of a customer's pending orders summary.*

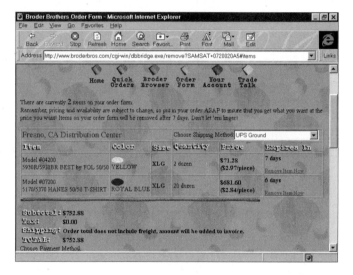

Meeting Other Customer Needs

The system checks for
multiple warehouses

The system offers added capabilities to ensure that a customer's needs are met. If a distributor has more than one warehouse and the closest warehouse doesn't have the desired item in stock, the system will automatically search the distributor's inventory in other warehouses and recommend delivery from the warehouse with the item in stock.

If the item that a customer wants to order isn't in stock at all, the system will suggest a substitute product based on the customer's stored profile; the customer can accept or decline the suggestion. Although the system allows customers to find and order merchandise made by the company's competitors, the system does favor Fruit of the Loom's own merchandise whenever possible.

Alternative product suggestions always favor Fruit of the Loom

Experienced customers may already know what products they want to order for a particular job and therefore don't need to browse through the catalog. To help such customers, every major page of the Web site includes a Quick Orders button that allows the customer to jump directly to an order page and enter the order information.

Experienced customers do not have to browse the catalog before ordering

Customer Billing

Customers must register with the distributor to get an account name and password before they can place orders. Because this limits users placing orders to those who are already customers of the distributor, there's no need to develop a system for exchanging funds on line. Once orders are placed on line, accounts payable uses its normal channels for the billing and payment cycles—in other words, they mail the bills.

Distributors provide their customers with account names and passwords.

Bulletin Boards and Chats

What's especially interesting is the inclusion of bulletin boards and chat rooms as part of the Web site. Bulletin boards have proven to be useful for exchanging information among customers, such as printing and embroidery tips. The Buylines section is also useful for placing ads for equipment and advertising for part-time or temporary help. In addition to building a sense of community between the customers and the distributor, bulletin boards and chat rooms create a sort of virtual organization where different shops can advertise for, and find, added workers according to their workload, and helpful information is exchanged as needed.

Bulletin boards and chat rooms create an online community where customers can share information

Analysis: Mastering the Distribution Channel

With Fruit of the Loom footing the bill for the cost of developing and deploying the Web servers for the distributors, you have to ask what value does Fruit of the Loom gets out of this project? After all, the distributors are better able to serve their customers and cut costs using Activewear Online, so they get direct benefits.

Fruit of the Loom benefits in ways that cannot be calculated in currency

Fruit of the Loom underwrote more than $4 million in project costs, but it has not attempted any return-on-investment (ROI) calculation for the project. They feel that an ROI calculation would be nearly meaningless because this sponsorship generates benefits (such as customer loyalty and mindshare) and paybacks that cannot be readily expressed in dollars and cents. The board of directors of Fruit of the Loom understood that from the beginning when they approved the undertaking.

Intangible Benefits

Distributors participate in a process that focuses attention on Fruit of the Loom

By implementing this system, Fruit of the Loom has improved its relationship with a majority of its sports apparel distributors (30 out of 50), and has gotten those distributors to participate in Fruit of the Loom's electronic way of doing things. In essence, they've created a group of distributors who've chosen to use the Web to provide more information electronically, and they've done it in a way that focuses attention on Fruit of the Loom and its product. This, in turn, gives them an advantage over their competitors, who now must answer Fruit of the Loom's electronic system with one of their own if they're to keep pace.

Fruit of the Loom has noticed an increase in market share as well as an increase in Web-based orders

Fruit of the Loom also gets increased mindshare from the distributor's customers because those customers see Fruit of the Loom's association with the Web sites, and because they also see Fruit of the Loom's products suggested more often than competitors' products when seeking alternatives to out-of-stock items. The increased mindshare seems to result in tangible benefits. Fruit of the Loom has reported that early results indicate a significant increase in market share for their products as well as an increase in the number of transactions booked through the Web site.

Using Channel Mastering

This approach toward providing a system that benefits members of a distribution chain without restricting them to a single supplier is reminiscent of what American Airlines did with the Sabre system for travel agencies, and Baxter Healthcare did for hospitals with its ValueLink system. This is often called *channel mastering*; while other companies have accomplished channel mastering using private electronic networks,[3] Fruit of the Loom's may well be the first attempt at channel mastering using the Web.

Fruit of the Loom has used the Web for channel mastering

Using Design Templates

The approach that Fruit of the Loom took to implementing the project also has certain dividends associated with it. As with all projects of this size, a pilot project to prove the feasibility and work out kinks is very important. But once Fruit of the Loom decided to go ahead with the larger project, their having created a set of templates for distributors significantly decreased the time and cost of implementation. Charles Kirk estimates that the system set-up could have been a multi-month project, but creating an *off the rack* system using templates took each distributor about one week. Also, having created a modular system allowed distributors to decide which parts of the system they wanted to implement without requiring more customized code from

Design templates decreased the time and cost of implementation, and a modular approach allowed for partial implementations without requiring customized programming

---

3. For example, American Airlines did this with its EasySabre online service for consumers.

the developers. This way a distributor can choose not to use the chat software, for instance, but concentrate on the online catalog and order entry.

Using the template, single-server approach is an outgrowth of Charles Kirk's philosophy for projects like this—"prepare for success." In other words, as you progress from pilot project to full-scale implementation, you need to build efficiencies into the system so that it remains easy to run even as it becomes successful. Otherwise, the cost of tasks such as customization will overwhelm the project.

Online catalogs are less expensive and more timely than their printed counterparts

The online catalog used by the distributors is itself a benefit to Fruit of the Loom. Now both Fruit of the Loom and its distributors can distribute product information electronically instead of via printed copy. Aside from the cost savings evident in such a scheme, an online catalog also allows the company to distribute updated product information in a more timely fashion, and distributors can incorporate the information into their online catalogs much more easily than they could when they handled printed catalogs.

Fruit of the Loom has the opportunity to gain favor and influence the channel at the same time

Because most distributors probably don't have the time to build their own Web sites, Fruit of the Loom hopes to gain favor with its largest distributors by offering them a Web site immediately. This is an excellent opportunity for Fruit of the Loom to influence the distribution channel in its early stages, because these distributors are unlikely to set up another Web site if they already have the site provided by Fruit of the Loom.

One unknown in the equation is how the channel will grow. The distributors may well embrace the system initially, but so far only 30 percent of the screen printers and embroiderers have access to the Internet.

Future Plans

In many ways, the electronic information and ordering network initiated by Fruit of the Loom for its distributors is only the beginning of using the Internet for electronically exchanging data between these organizations. Fruit of the Loom is already implementing plans to further integrate the system with the distributors' other computer systems and to expand the capabilities of the network.

Plans include better integration with distributors' existing systems

One area to be improved is the link between the distributors and Fruit of the Loom manufacturing processes. Right now there is no such link tied to the Web sites, but Fruit of the Loom plans to add one that will allow inventory data to provide faster feedback to the mills, and that will also allow distributors to get a better idea of what the mills are producing. An existing system, VMI or Vendor Management Inventory, came on line in December 1995, but it's a dial-up system that uses neither the Internet nor the Web; that could change and the system could become Web-based, allowing better integration with Activewear Online.

A link between distributors and Fruit of the Loom's mills will further enhance the system

Just-in-Time Ordering

Another possible enhancement would be handling inventory as a just-in-time (JIT) function. For example, if a shop orders 1000 Fruit of the Loom T-shirts and a distributor has only 800 in stock, the distributor could automatically send an order upstream to Fruit of the Loom. This would make it appear as if the Fruit of the Loom merchandise was never out of stock. With just-in-time capabilities, Fruit of the Loom distributors would eventually be able to sell inventory that they didn't even have in stock. These plans are being discussed with the distributors, but because the distributors are worried that they might be disintermediated, or taken out of the distribution channel altogether by the system, it's become a marketing relations issue, and not one of technology.

Just-in-time ordering capabilities are a possibility, but could result in cutting out the distributors altogether

All parties need to work together when formulating plans

Even though the distributors use many different types of order processing systems in house, Fruit of the Loom is working on ways to automatically deposit orders into the distributors' systems. The company is taking this step slowly and deliberately, because they don't want to seem as though they're pushing a particular way of doing things onto the distributors. Both sides of this partnership are working together to determine the best way of transferring the order information.

The Players, the System, the Site

Players: **Fruit of the Loom**
One Fruit of the Loom Drive
P.O. Box 90015
Bowling Green, KY 42102-9015
Phone: 502-781-6400, Fax: 502-781-6588
http://www.fruit.com
   Charles Kirk, CIO (Chief Information Officer)
   Dave Dixon, VP of Marketing, Activewear Division

System: The prototype system ran on a Windows NT platform with O'Reilly's WebSite Server software. Additional software used in creating the prototype included: O'Reilly's WebBoard, a chat program from Palace Software, Visual Basic 4.0, Oracle for the database, VMARK's HyperSTAR middleware, and HTML. The Final Implementation runs on Sun Enterprise 4000 servers, using Connect Inc.'s OneServer software, an Oracle database, and Digital Cockpit from Snickleways.

Site: http://www.fruitactivewear.com

(remaining players on next page)

Players: **Snickleways Interactive**—a digital marketing firm
180 Varick St
New York, NY 10014
Phone: 212-366-6000
Fax: 212-366-6456
http://www.snickelways.com
  Paul Cimino, CEO

The ConText Group—consultants for the apparel market
New York, NY
212-268-1790
  Dudley McIlhenny

Broder Bros. Co.—a distributor
45555 Port Street
Plymouth, MI 48170
800-521-0850
http://www.broderbros.com

Sanmar—a distributor
P.O. Box 529
Preston, WA 98050-6399

Compuware—systems integrators
Compuware Corporate Offices
31440 Northwestern Highway
Farmington Hills, MI 48334-2564
Phone: 810-737-7300, 800-521-9353,
Fax: 810-737-7108

Connect Inc.—Electronic commerce service providers
515 Ellis Street
Mountain View, CA 94043-2242
Phone: 415-254-4000, fax: 415-254-4800
http://www.connectinc.com

Chapter Nine

Maximizing the Usefulness of an Online Catalog

One of the most interesting commercial opportunities offered to businesses by the World Wide Web is the capability to put product catalogs on line. Online catalogs allow companies to bypass the need for costly printed catalogs, are easier to keep up-to-date, and can also be linked directly to the purchase process. For the consumer market, sales through online catalogs are usually tied to credit cards for payment, but business-to-business ordering through online catalogs can be linked to the usual purchase order-invoice cycle as well as to many of the digital payment schemes presented in Chapter 3, "Handling Money on the Net."

In the last chapter, "Collaborating on a Distribution Chain," you saw how Fruit of the Loom enabled their distributors to create online product catalogs that were linked to distributor warehouse inventories. Fruit of the Loom underwrote the development of the system to influence the distribution channel and eventually tie distributors' orders to availability of Fruit of the Loom's inventory. This chapter describes AMP Connect, an online catalog of over 100,000 electronic components that AMP, an electronics component manufacturer, created to provide current product information to its distributors and customers.

Online catalogs are easily updated, and can be integrated with the purchase process

A Single Online Catalog

AMP chose to create a single online catalog for customers worldwide

Like Fruit of the Loom, AMP wanted to provide an electronic catalog for its customers. But AMP's product lines change almost constantly, so getting timely information to customers and distributors is more of an issue for AMP than it is for Fruit of the Loom, whose product line is relatively stable and unchanging. Rather than support individual catalogs at the distributor level, AMP decided to create a single online catalog for customers to browse; in addition, AMP planned for ancillary data stored on the AMP Connect Web site to be used to direct customers to their local distributors once they'd selected products.

Planning for International Use

Geography played an important role in the design decisions

Because AMP's global distribution network includes more than 100 countries, AMP Connect needed to provide comprehensive support for international use of its catalog. AMP wanted users to be able to access its online catalog in eight different languages. To automate user selection of a preferred language and to link local distributors with a user's business location, AMP planned to maintain a customer profile for each user.

AMP designed a different search strategy

AMP Connect's online catalog was also designed to use a different search method from other catalogs. Co-developed by AMP, this *step search* method would provide users with better feedback than other methods as they attempt to narrow down their product choices based on the features they require.

AMP hoped to realize significant cost savings

By focusing on an online catalog, AMP Connect hoped to achieve significant cost savings over print catalogs, as well as to provide timely, up-to-date product information to its customers. They succeeded.

Concept: Online Catalogs are Dynamic

With annual revenues of more than $5.2 billion, AMP spent more than $7 million each year to mail and update 400 specialized catalogs to its distributors and customers around the world. These catalogs cover about 134,000 electrical and machine components. In addition, AMP maintains a fax-back system that allows customers to retrieve product information via touch-tone phone and fax. The phone bills for the fax-back system alone cost $800,000 per year.

Each year AMP spent $7 million on printed catalogs and another $800,000 in fax-back phone costs

Searching for a Better Method

Jim Kessler, the director of Electronic Commerce, had been looking for a better method for distributing product information to AMP's customers. At first, he'd looked at using CD-ROM-based catalogs to replace the printed catalogs. But, as the popularity of the Internet and especially of the Web increased, he decided to skip CD-ROMs entirely and use the Web for presenting online product catalogs. An Internet-based solution cost less than using CD-ROMs, and using the Web also would allow AMP to update product information more frequently than would using either printed or CD-ROM catalogs. Furthermore, implementing an online catalog would be a one-time cost, and updating the online catalog would still be less costly than periodically pressing new CD-ROM catalogs.

The online catalog would allow for more frequent updates, and the Web solution was less expensive than even the CD-ROM alternative

Implementation: The Pilot Catalog

The first major obstacle to developing the online catalog was the location of the pertinent data. AMP's legacy databases held product numbers but did not include product descriptions, which would be an essential part of the catalog. Information from printed product sheets, mechanical drawings, and other sources would have to be scanned or entered into a new system to create an electronic catalog.

Data had to be gathered from a variety of sources

Starting Small

Design of the actual database did not begin until after the data was classified

Rather than build a massive catalog for all of its products right at the beginning, AMP began with a pilot project in 1994. Kessler worked with CommerceNet and Saqqara Systems to design and create an online catalog of only 5000 items. Because much of the data required for the catalog was not available electronically, the first steps were to identify and classify the content before entering any data into a database. Once the information in the existing paper catalogs was classified, the database was designed, and the required product information was entered into an Oracle 7 database. This included scanning images of the products from existing catalogs.

A Unique Search Engine

A unique search engine provides ongoing feedback by indicating the number of products that match the search criteria specified thus far

In addition to providing data conversion services to create the catalog, Saqqara Systems Inc. co-developed the Step Search software that's used as the search engine for the online catalog. What makes this search engine unique is the guidance it provides to the user who's searching for an item or for a family of items. In a normal database query, the user can select a number of features all at once to narrow down the search. Ideally, the search criteria quickly yield the right product, but one also runs the risk of failing to get any match at all. Alternatively, the user may get a long list of matching items if the query is not specific enough. With Step Search, as the user selects each search criterion, the search engine indicates how many products meet all the criteria entered so far, so the user knows when he or she has narrowed down the search sufficiently to a particular product or set of products.

For example, the user is presented with a list of available product features, just like the list on a regular database query form (see Figure 9-1). But with Step Search, the user selects one feature at a time to narrow the search, ideally starting with the most desired product feature. Only a count indicating the number of products that match the features selected so far is shown to the user. In the example depicted in Figure 9-1, the user has started with 273 possible parts. The user continues entering more criteria until he or she arrives at a few products (see Figure 9-2 on the next page), or requests a comparison table to summarize the current matching set of products. Figure 9-3 shows such a comparison table for four products. The Step Search method greatly simplifies the catalog search process by allowing customers to search using their own buying criteria in order of priority.

A user can narrow the search down to find a single product, or request to see a comparison table summarizing a matching set of products

The first Step Search screen for selecting product features.

Figure 9-1

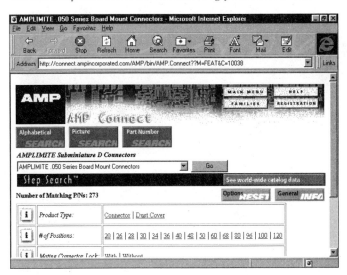

Figure 9-2   *Step Search screen after user has selected various criteria for product search.*

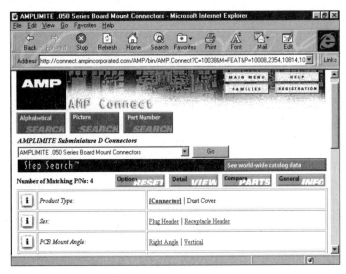

Figure 9-3   *Part comparison table from Step Search.*

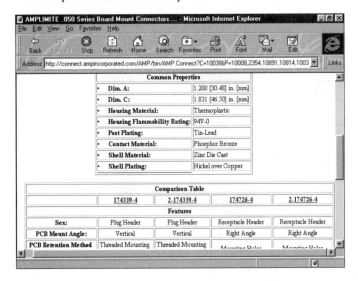

Feedback from the pilot project led to major enhancements

A number of AMP's Fortune 500 customers took part in the pilot project, and their feedback was used to refine the online catalog. The final catalog contains not only images and text descriptions of the products, but also customer drawings, application specifications, product specifications, instruction sheets, and, in some cases, three-dimensional **CAD** drawings (in IGES format[1]) that can be downloaded by customers for use in their own designs—drawings that were not a part of the original plans.

Expansion: Catalog Updates and Customer Profiles

Once the pilot project was evaluated and the online catalog fine-tuned, a full-blown version containing 32,000 items was made available on the AMP Connect Web site. The site made its debut in January 1996, and within the first nine months, more than 55,000 individuals from over 100 countries registered to use the AMP Connect online catalog. The catalog receives about 65,000 hits each day, and approximately 200 additional users register daily. By the end of 1996, over 100,000 products were in the catalog.

In less than a year, 55,000 individuals from over 100 countries were using the online catalog containing 100,000 product items

Updating the Catalog

The current catalog runs on a quad-processor Sparc 1000 system with 64 gigabytes of storage. The storage system is used to retain two copies of the database that forms the basis for the catalog—one copy of the database is the one currently used for access by visitors to the Web site, while the second copy is used to update product information. Whenever AMP wants to switch over to an updated catalog, all they have to do is redirect the link to the other database, making changeovers possible in a matter of seconds. Catalog updates were originally performed on a weekly basis, but AMP Connect has now switched over to daily updates so that they can add new products and modify the existing data more frequently. They are currently adding or modifying 200 products each day.

By maintaining two databases, AMP can update one while the other is in use and switching the two databases takes only seconds

---

1. International Graphics Exchange Standard, a file format for data describing drawings (mechanical parts, for example).

All **HTML** pages shown to a catalog user are generated
dynamically from the Oracle 7 database. According to Jim
Kessler, manually coding the HTML pages and setting static
links between them would have been too difficult and costly
for both the initial set up and the day-to-day maintenance of
product upgrades in the system.

Using Registration to Elicit Customer Profiles

In order to use AMP Connect, a user must register on line.
There is no charge for registration or using the catalog. This
is simply AMP's way of getting a customer profile from each
user. As part of the registration process, the user gets to
specify the language he wishes to use for viewing the catalog and part descriptions, and the country of delivery. The
catalog supports viewing in eight different languages, which
can either be automatically selected from the user's profile
or manually selected from one of the initial catalog pages;
the languages are Chinese, English, French, German, Italian,
Japanese, Korean, and Spanish. Specifying the user's country
of delivery is also important because all of AMP's products
are not immediately available in all of the countries in
which it does business. Knowing the user's country of delivery allows AMP to dynamically deploy lists of products that
are readily available in the user's selected location.

AMP also tracks search results to determine what products
and product information are most frequently requested.

Web Site Description: Enabling the User to Find Products Easily

When designing the online catalog, a main concern at AMP
was ensuring that customers could quickly and easily find
the products they need. The Step Search engine allows
customers to specify which product features are most important in the search (see Figure 9-1 on page 175), and that's

one reason why AMP chose to work with Saqqara Systems. That's also a reason why AMP Connect offers more than one way to search the product database (see Figure 9-4).

Main search page for AMP Connect.

Figure 9-4

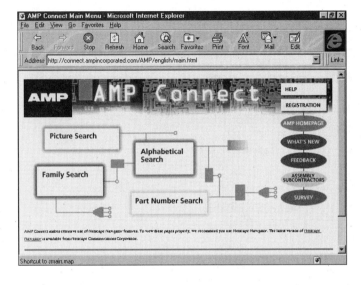

Three Different Search Types

In a general search, users of AMP Connect can choose an alphabetical search, which presents listings of each product by name. Alternatively, if users already know the AMP part number and are looking for more information on the product, they can simply enter the part number to access the catalog's product data directly. The remaining two search options, Picture Search and Family Search, are intermediate steps that lead to the Step Search forms, such as those described earlier in this chapter.

A general search can be conducted alphabetically or by part number

In a picture search, the user is presented with images of the various classes of products that AMP offers (see Figure 9-5 on the next page). Clicking on one of the images on the page either leads to another page of pictures for product sub-classes, or to a Step Search form containing the features

A picture search provides images of the various product classes and sub-classes that are unique to that type of product. For example, selecting the picture labeled PCB Switches & Shunts takes you to a second picture catalog, containing six items: DIP Switches - Standard, DIP Switches - Preprogrammed, Rotary Switches, Two-Pole Slide Switches, DIP Shunts, and Post Shunts.

Figure 9-5   *The picture search page.*

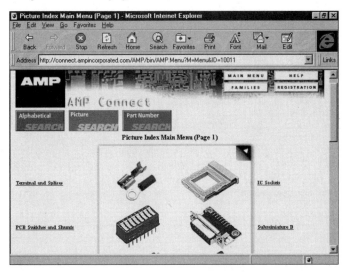

Product families offer even finer subdivisions of a product line than Picture Searches

Product families are another way of presenting product classes and sub-classes, offering finer subdivisions of a product line than picture searches. In effect, using a families search puts the customer deeper into the database right at the start, because the decision about product type was already made at the Families page (see Figure 9-6). If the customer has chosen the wrong product type, backtracking to an earlier search page is not necessary—the Step Search page makes navigation easy by including a pop-up menu of other product classes. Using the PCB Switches and Shunts example, someone reviewing part data for DIP Shunts could use the pop-up menu to quickly move to DIP Switches - Standard or to any of the other six switch and shunt types.

The family search page.   ***Figure 9-6***

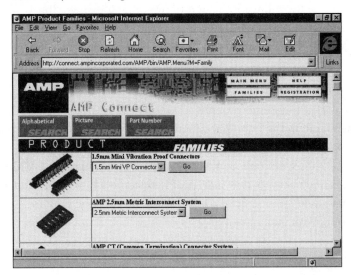

When finally selecting a product, the user can request ordering information, which includes customer service information and a list of sales offices in the appropriate country of delivery (country information is stored in the customer's stored profile). Thus, a Spanish customer finds the distributors in Spain, not in the United States.

Ordering information is provided for the appropriate country

Analysis: Tying Databases to Online Catalogs

AMP has successfully met the needs of many of its customers by switching to a product catalog that's accessible via the Web. By maintaining the catalog on line, AMP Connect serves as a central repository of useful information that remains at the customer's fingertips, 24 hours a day, 7 days a week. Much of this information wasn't available to the customer in printed catalogs and had to be specially requested, through either the fax-back system or a distributor. And because all this data is part of an online catalog, delivering information to the customer takes seconds, or minutes at the most, rather than days, which helps the user to be

Customers report throwing away print catalogs because more information is available and accessible every day, at all hours, on line

more efficient. Customers prefer the online catalog, too—many of them have indicated to AMP that they have thrown away their print catalogs and now use the online catalog exclusively to get part information.

An Example

Accessing CAD files on line is saving customers a lot of time

Making three-dimensional CAD models of AMP connectors available in the online catalog is a good example of the value of keeping the information on line. Previously, these CAD files were only available on CD-ROM. Since the CAD files have been put on line, AMP's customers have indicated that having online access to the files can save them up to two days of their design time for each product that's available.

Using the Parts Database to Generate Mini-Catalogs

The database supplies the Web data and also enables cost-effective printing of specialized catalogs in limited numbers

AMP also benefits directly from keeping all parts information in a database. Not only is that database used to dynamically generate the HTML pages that users see as part of the online catalog, but it also serves as the basis for publishing smaller, printed catalogs. These mini-catalogs are produced in small batches that are aimed at specialized markets for distribution—at shows, for example. Before it was possible to derive catalogs from data stored in the electronic database, creating such customized printed catalogs would have been prohibitively expensive.

More Frequent Updates

Product and catalog life-cycles are now in sync, because maintaining up-to-date information is faster and requires fewer resources

In the past, AMP had only enough resources to update about one-half of their 400 catalogs each year, so many catalogs had a life-cycle of two years, even though products changed more frequently than that. Creating a print catalog was routinely a nine-month project, with product data frozen roughly 30 days before printing. Now, by using database publishing, AMP is able to create specialized catalogs more easily and more frequently. They can even create a small run of a customized catalog containing only parts for the appliance industry for distribution at a show, for example, which is something they couldn't have done before. Jim Kessler estimates that by moving to the online system, AMP has been able to reduce the resources it used for catalog creation by 50 percent.

A Catalog for Global Operations

Although the Internet is an entity that spans the globe, many business Web sites have adopted English as the language of choice for presenting information, even when the company itself is an international one. AMP, mindful of its global operations, instead sought to customize its catalog for its foreign customers as well, offering support for eight different languages. Doing so can only increase its competitiveness and appeal in those foreign markets.

AMP's multi-lingual support gives them a competitive edge

Using a dynamically generated catalog based on a database also dovetailed nicely with AMP's global efforts. AMP's first bids for translating the catalog data into five Latin languages pegged the cost at about $1.5 million. By using the database as the source of multi-lingual information for the catalog, rather than hard-coding the translated information for each HTML page, the translation project cost only $100,000. Plus, this translated data can also be used in database publishing to create language-specific catalogs without requiring extensive use of translation resources.

The database also lowered the costs of other projects

Cost Savings

The cost savings that AMP Connect has realized by switching to an online catalog are considerable. As noted at the beginning of this chapter, AMP used to spend over $7 million each year to create and distribute its printed catalogs. The current estimate of the cost of getting the online catalog up and running is $1.2 million, roughly one-fifth of the previous printing costs. Of the $1.2 million, software and hardware costs were $300,000 - $400,000, with the remainder spent for language translations and catalog development.

AMP realized significant cost savings

The success of AMP Connect has led to the formation of a new company, AMP eMerce, which will take the technologies used to create AMP Connect and offer similar setup services to other companies.

Future Plans

AMP will build on its CAD model support

AMP is continually expanding its catalog, both in size and features. AMP Connect added the three-dimensional CAD models for 6000 products in mid-1996, and is preparing to offer a Model On Demand system in which customers will be able to request three-dimensional model files for AMP parts that currently do not have CAD files.

The database will continue to grow

As of July 1996, AMP Connect contained information for over 70,000 parts. The online catalog contained about 100,000 products by the end of 1996, and catalogers are adding roughly 2500 parts to the database each week, even as the company is revamping its product lines by adding or changing 200 parts each day.

AMP is using a pilot project to evaluate transaction software and develop payment options

AMP Connect is conducting a pilot project for online ordering using the electronic catalog, which should result in a fully operational system coming on line in the middle of 1997. The pilot system is being used to evaluate transaction software from both Open Market and IBM to determine which one better meets AMP Connect's requirements. This system is being developed to support alternate payment methodologies, using credit cards, banks, financial clearinghouses, and standard AMP billing processes for financial transactions. During the pilot project AMP is also investigating the potential of the Internet to service both existing customers and smaller new business opportunities for AMP.

AMP's flexible smaller business clients will probably benefit most

Although the pilot is being run with both large and small firms, Jim Kessler expects that the system will be of greatest benefit to many small businesses, because they can more

readily integrate an online ordering and purchasing process
into their existing operations. Large corporations frequently
require many steps for purchasing approval and need more
time to integrate online ordering processes into their systems.

The Players, the System, the Site

Players: **AMP eMerce Internet Solutions**
P.O. Box 3608, MS 84-26
Harrisburg, PA 17105-3608
Phone: 717-592-6706
Fax: 717-780-7477
http://www.ampemerce.com
Jim Kessler, Director of AMP eMerce Internet Solutions

SAQQARA Systems, Inc.
1230 Oakmead Parkway, Suite 314
Sunnyvale, California, 94086
Phone: 408-738-4858

Open Market, Inc.
245 First Street
Cambridge, MA 02142
Phone: 617-949-7196

IBM CommercePoint
http://www.internet.ibm.com/commercepoint/html3/main.html

System: The system runs on a Sun Sparc 1000 quad processor system
with 64 Gbytes disk storage. Software included StepSearch from
Saqqara Systems, and the Oracle 7 database.

Site: http://connect.ampincorporated.com

Chapter Ten

Electronic Customer Support

In today's push to get closer to the customer, it's hard to beat the connection between your customer support department and the buyers of your products and services. You may not be able to assign a monetary value to the feedback that your support staff acquires, but it can be invaluable to the task of improving both the quality of your product and the strength of your corporate reputation. Even so, customer support is too often viewed as a sink for resources and money rather than as a source of revenue. Service contracts are one way of adding revenue, but electronic links, such as the Internet, offer another way for companies to charge for their customer support.

In addition to providing valuable feedback, customer support can be a source of revenue

Microsoft has three different customer communities to consider when offering support for its products—individual consumers, developers, and corporate customers—and they have long offered a variety of technical support options, particularly for third-party developers and corporate customers. Support for these customers is divided into three classes, Primary, Priority, and Premier Support, as summarized in the

You may want to categorize your customers

Classes of Microsoft Technical Support table. Of the three, only Premier Support is reserved for large business customers, because it is mainly a contractual technical support and consulting option.

Classes of Microsoft Technical Support

Primary	*Priority*	*Premier*
Free online support	Range of	Contractual
FAQs	support and	technical support
Searchable knowledge bases	subscriptions	consulting arrange-
Online articles and troubleshooting	or pay per	ments with large
Drivers and update files	incident	business customers
Microsoft-hosted newsgroups	support	
Phone support[1]		
Fast Tips		
One-on-one technical support		

Primary Support via the Internet, direct modem connection, or telephone, is available to all three categories of customers. The Internet-based support features include the following: Frequently Asked Questions (FAQ) files; a searchable knowledge base of technical notes and other support information; online articles written by Microsoft's staff; a troubleshooting guide for certain products; drivers, patches, and sample files that can be downloaded; and Microsoft-hosted newsgroups for threaded discussions of products and problems (see Figure 10-1).

Growth requires reassessing the support options offered

As the company has grown, and as the breadth of its product line has increased, Microsoft has frequently had to revamp its support programs to meet the needs of its customers. This chapter takes a look at two of Microsoft's newest ventures for supporting developers and other customers: Web Response, which allows customers to submit problems to technical support; and Pay-Per-Incident (PPI),

---

1. Fast Tips is a toll-free service, but one-on-one technical support incurs telephone charges and service fees.

The Microsoft Technical Support home page on the Web.   *Figure 10-1*

the company's pay-as-you-go option, which illustrates how a system can be organized to provide chargeable customer support over the Web.

Concept: The Web Response System and PPI

The Web Response System, created in 1995, was designed to allow users of Microsoft products to submit questions to technical support via the Web. With the increased popularity of the Web, and because of Microsoft's strong commitment to using Web technology whenever possible, the forms basis of Web Response makes it easy for any user of a Microsoft product to submit a problem for solution. Because people can submit their problems through the Web, they can do so at any time of the day, on any day of the week.

And because the customer only has to use a local **ISP** or corporate Internet link to access the Internet, rather than make a long-distance phone call to Microsoft's support

Problems can be submitted anytime, from anywhere

Solutions are not immediate, but status can be monitored

lines, using the Web also lowers the cost of submitting a problem for the customer. Even though solving the problem may take some time, posting it to the Web makes it easier for the customer to check on its progress and access the solution anytime, from anywhere.

Web Response was originally designed only for subscription support customers

From its inception through most of 1996, the Web Response System was restricted to customers with annual support subscriptions. Towards the end of 1996, the Web Response System was modified to allow any individual to submit a support question via the Web using Pay-Per-Incident (PPI), thus broadening the reach of the Web Response System.

PPI provides priority response for any customer who will pay per incident

Prior to Web Response, a customer had to purchase an annual subscription to customer support in order to get a priority response to a problem. PPI was to become Microsoft's first electronic commerce offering in technical support. Its goal was to provide priority response to customers who were willing to pay on an incident-by-incident basis. In order to do this, Microsoft had to extend the Web Response design to support secure credit card purchases.

Implementation: Security and Software Modules

Much of the data used by customer support at Microsoft is stored on computers that are a part of Microsoft's internal network, or **intranet**. However, because Web Response is an interactive system that requires customer participation on the Internet, some connection between the Internet and Microsoft's intranet must be maintained. This means that it's of paramount concern to maintain a secure connection that protects Microsoft's intranet from hackers and prevents illegal access to proprietary information.

Crossing the DMZ

Along with other systems that provide information to customers and net surfers on the Internet, the main parts of the Web Response system reside in the *Internet DMZ*, as Microsoft calls it, which is on the external side of Microsoft's **firewall** (see Figure 10-2 on the next page). Data traffic that must be transferred across the firewall is converted from TCP/IP transport to IPX-based transport,[2] making it even more difficult for a hacker to defeat the firewall system.

Microsoft maintains an area outside of its firewall, and protocol conversion is required for crossing

Encrypting the Message Stream

The entire message stream between the customer and Web Response PPI is encrypted by means of the **secure sockets layer** protocol (SSL), which all the popular **Web browsers** support. The financial portion of the credit card transaction is strongly encrypted by the customer's browser using the 128-bit encryption support in Internet Explorer 3.0,[3] so the credit card number remains encrypted during the transaction.

PPI transmissions are encrypted using SSL, and credit card numbers remain encrypted

Microsoft chose to design the Web Response PPI system as a series of inter-connected software modules, each of which performed specific tasks (see Figure 10-3 on page 193). Because modules can be individually tested and new ones easily substituted, this approach not only makes it easier to maintain a large system, but also provides greater flexibility for adding new features in the future. The main modules in the Web Response PPI system are the Transaction Manager and the Commerce Engine.

---

2. IPX is a network protocol used by networks to perform functions similar to those using the IP protocol on the Internet.

3. If a different browser is used that does not include 128-bit encryption but does use encryption with a shorter key length, then the system uses the shorter key, even though it's less secure.

Figure 10-2   *Microsoft's network architecture.*

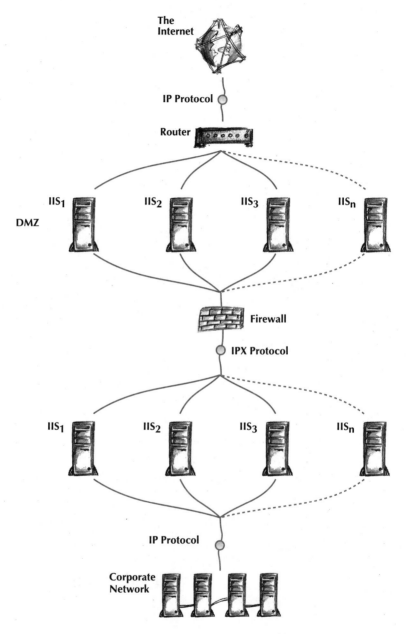

The Transaction Manager

Custom Transaction Manager software (see Figure 10-3) serves as the link between the software modules that handle processing of a Web Response PPI request and the software that takes care of accounting and credit card services. The Transaction Manager maintains the integrity of all transactions, and also manages continuity across **HTTP** sessions. Thus it is responsible for processing the basic transaction types (sale, void, refund, and adjustment), and routing the appropriate data between the financial, database, and user interface components necessary to process a transaction.

The Transaction Manager software handles transaction processing and data routing

Components of the Web Response PPI System.

Figure 10-3

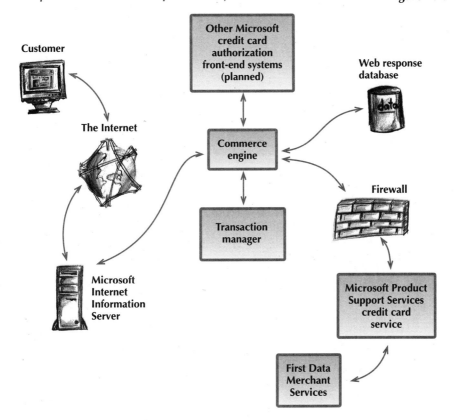

The Commerce Engine

The Commerce Engine software decrypts the credit card number and requests bank authorization

During processing of a PPI request, the customer's account or credit card information is passed from the Transaction Manager to the Commerce Engine (see Figure 10-3), another custom software module written by Microsoft's Information Services department that accepts requests for online credit card processing. As part of the flexibility built into the system (to support future uses), the Commerce Engine can accept requests from systems other than the PPI system.

Credit card data remains protected from outsiders

When negotiating sessions between itself and a client system, the Commerce Engine uses **digital signatures** to authenticate any system that requests its services. In the PPI system, the Commerce Engine decrypts the credit card number, sends an authorization request to the acquiring institution (in this case, First Data Merchant Services), and receives the response. Because account processing is restricted to the Commerce Engine and associated software designed to communicate with the Commerce Engine, the final steps of processing a credit card transaction take place on Micro-soft's intranet, protected from outside users.

Custom Alterations to the Web Response System

PPI required new software modules and enhancements to the existing system

Some parts of the Web Response system had to be altered in order to integrate PPI. For example, the Web Response database had to be changed from a system that could check users against annual support contracts to a system that handles PPI users who would pay for their support as they used it. SSL-based security for the financial transactions was also added, including storage of credit card numbers in their encrypted form.

Also, because the Web Response system was originally based on an object-oriented design, new business objects were added to support such items as database access. Some business objects,[4] such as those responsible for processing transactions and maintaining security (see Figure 10-4), interact with each other as data passes from client to server. Still others, such as those responsible for checking that proper data is entered in a data field (field validation) or setting up a user's profile, do not interact with other business objects.

Business objects fit between the user interface and the Microsoft Windows 95 operating system.

Figure 10-4

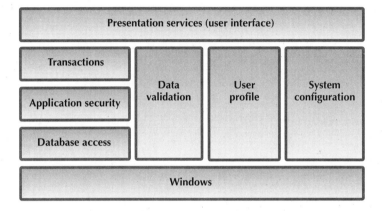

Web Site Description: Submitting and Tracking Online Problems

The Web Response form is used to submit a question to a support engineer. The form can be accessed by clicking the Select Web Response for Support option on Microsoft's Technical Support page (it's the last in the list in the top left corner of the screen shown in Figure 10-1 on page 189.

Customers use Web forms to submit questions

---

4. In programming, a business object is a software module that is written to perform a specific step in a business process. The idea is to provide a better link between the software and business tasks, making planning and modifications more organized. For example, the Transaction Manager mentioned earlier in this chapter is a business object—it handles all possible actions involved in a PPI sale, namely sales, voids, refunds, and adjustments.

The Web Response Form

Customers use the Web Response form to provide pertinent facts, a brief problem description, and the problem file (optional)

The Web Response form, shown in Figure 10-5, allows a customer to enter information about the type of software product, computer, and operating system in use. In addition, the customer can also enter a description of the problem, which helps Microsoft technicians understand whether the user is having a conceptual problem or a physical problem with the software or hardware. If the problem involves a certain file, the user can also include the file for testing by Microsoft's support staff.

Figure 10-5   *Sample Web Response form.*

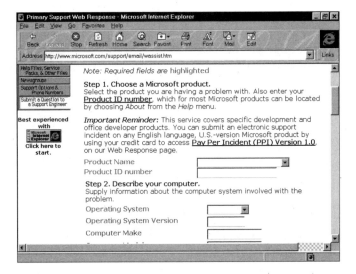

Microsoft maintains a problem database; common problems (with their solutions) also become part of the Knowledge Base

The problem data is automatically stored in a problem report database at Microsoft, and it is then made available to the support staff. Problems can be tracked using the Web (see Figure 10-6), and answers to problems are stored in a database that is also accessible via the Web. If a problem is of particular note, or if it's common to a number of situations, it may be incorporated in the FAQ file and inserted into the Knowledge Base (see Figure 10-7) that's accessible from the Technical Support page.

Search screen for checking progress on a support incident. **Figure 10-6**

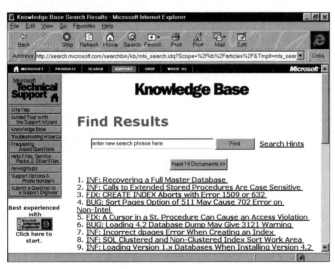

*List of example articles stored in the Knowledge Base,
displayed in response to a user's query.* **Figure 10-7**

Integrating PPI

New software modules were needed to handle credit card transactions

To integrate PPI into Microsoft's support system, the Web-based pricing had to be mapped to the existing phone support pricing policies. That also meant designing new software modules to handle credit support. Additionally, the system had to be flexible enough to accommodate future enhancements and additions to Web-based support offerings.

Analysis: Dividing Processes to Protect Corporate Information

Publishing static information is the traditional first step

When Microsoft recognized the importance of the Internet in 1995, CEO Bill Gates led Microsoft's wholehearted embrace of Internet technologies, seeking to link to the Internet as many of its products and processes as possible. Putting so much customer support information on the Web was a first step. In fact, publishing static information is the traditional first step most companies follow when using the Web. The next step was Web Response, enabling a more customized and interactive method for customers and technical support to deal with problems.

Support Pricing Strategy

Microsoft generates revenue with its many support options

Most of Microsoft's support programs have been designed to produce revenues to pay for themselves even if they don't generate significant profits. But by placing so much support information on the Web, Microsoft has also increased the availability of support for customers who were looking for more customized options. PPI is a first step in that direction, allowing customers to get their problems answered in a timely fashion, while still generating revenues for Microsoft.

Tracking locations enables proper tax apportionment

Designing a network-based system for support pricing had one additional financial benefit. In the past, Microsoft estimated the taxes associated with support calls and absorbed all these support-associated tax costs. With the implementation of Web Response and PPI, Microsoft was able to track the location for each customer and readily apportion the appropriate taxes among the states. These taxes could also then be directly tied to revenues from customer support.

A Good Framework for the Future

Because PPI was the driving force for adding financial transactions processing to Web Response, the support system can now handle transactions with greater automation and less human intervention than before. Microsoft's object-oriented approach to business objects and Web Response, as seen in the Commerce Engine and Transaction Manager, will provide a good framework for further enhancements as Microsoft adds more customizable support options to the Web.

Use of software modules makes the system easy to enhance

Addressing Security Concerns

Microsoft's location of processing resources for PPI is a good example of how transaction processing and corporate information systems should be distributed and secured when using the Internet. Only data that should be made available to outside users is supposed to reside on machines on the Internet side of a firewall (see Figure 10-2 on page 192).

Microsoft's use of a DMZ is a good model to follow

The use of multiple servers allows for *load balancing*,[5] an important issue at a site as popular as Microsoft's. Data derived from secure intranet data can be transferred over the firewall as needed. In this case, all communications between Internet-resident clients and other Microsoft-hosted applications occur via TCP/IP, while communications between the distributed applications (IIS to SQL Server, for example) occur via Novell Netware (IPX/SPX) protocols.

Server software and the use of various protocols becomes more complex, and more crucial, for popular Web sites

---

5. Load balancing prevents a large number of transactions from overwhelming a server's ability to process them. Software, acting as a traffic cop, distributes incoming transactions among a group of multiple servers, passing transactions on to the next available server in the group.

Communications with other secure sources, such as an acquiring institution for handling credit card purchases, is also handled on the secure side of the firewall.

The Future

Laws affect the availability of encryption options

Security for the financial transactions in PPI is accomplished via SSL, which is supported by all the popular Web browsers. However, United States restrictions on exports will keep some Microsoft customers from using 128 bits for encryption. A future version of Web Response PPI may include a helper application that uses a 1024-bit public key system for encryption, but the ultimate long-term choice is to use **SET**.

Built-In Flexibility

The object-oriented, modular approach will adapt easily to advancements in Microsoft OLE and ActiveX

By using business objects that are largely technology-independent, a great deal of flexibility has been built into the Web Response system. For example, the Web Response API project was developed as Microsoft was developing new technologies for use with the Internet, such as ActiveX. As the project evolves, it's likely that the business objects currently in use could then be delivered to the Web via ActiveX.[6]

Microsoft's Information Services staff is busily creating other projects to integrate Microsoft's internal processes with the Web. Some of these projects are meant strictly for internal use, but others are following the same path as Web Response, using the Web to tie customer-developer communications that takes place via the Internet, with databases and software maintained on the Microsoft intranet.

---

6. ActiveX is software technology originally developed by Microsoft for building small software modules, or components, that can be reused in different applications. ActiveX makes it possible to create, integrate and reuse software components over the Internet or intranets.

The Players, the System, the Site

Players: Microsoft Corporation
One Microsoft Way
Redmond, WA 98052

System: The system runs on Windows NT Server with Internet Information Server. (No other information provided.)

Site: http://www.microsoft.com/support/webresponse.htm

Chapter Eleven

The Beginnings of a Virtual Factory

As more information becomes digital, and information technology becomes an even greater part of the business world, pundits and management consultants alike envision the birth of the **virtual corporation.** A virtual corporation is an entity composed of geographically dispersed workers who share their work and communicate only by electronic means, with little, if any, face-to-face contact. Some small companies have taken this idea to heart, electronically tying together associates in various parts of the country. Other, larger corporations have created virtual teams to get a project done without moving the personnel to a central location—Ford's international team to produce the Contour (discussed on page 106 in Chapter 4) is one example.

But virtual organizations are not restricted to only those processing digital information. Digital information can be used as a sort of glue to bind together different companies involved in manufacturing, for instance. Such an organization, often called a *virtual factory*, allows manufacturers to stay in one location, but to access and share manufacturing data in other locations. Subassemblies can be created in

In a virtual factory, separate physical locations are coordinated digitally

different locations, but the progress (and problems) with their manufacture can be coordinated by means of digital data exchanged over networks such as the Internet.

The creation and maintenance of shared networks is an opportunity for brokers or intermediaries

In today's fast-paced world, however, the time and resources required to set up and maintain these shared networks may be too great for many companies. This is especially true for short-term partnerships or contracts, when some companies are involved for a limited period of time, and old projects are completed and new ones come into being at an ever-quickening pace. Maintaining a network of shared data for this changing landscape of contractors and partners is an ideal opportunity for a broker or intermediary, whose sole job would be to take care of these networks and control access to data.

AeroTech Service Group, Inc., an engineering consulting firm in Hazelwood, Missouri, evolved into such a brokering role for McDonnell Douglas Aerospace (MDA) and its contractors, helping to implement the first stages of a virtual factory. By serving as a facilitator and regulator for information flow, AeroTech is building a new form of electronic commerce in which it acts as an important intermediary. AeroTech's approach thus is an example of business opportunities for new middlemen to serve as information intermediaries, or *cybermediaries*, to use the latest terminology.

Concept: Virtual Coordination

More coordination roles are needed as the trend of outsourcing increases

In 1993, George Brill, the founder of AeroTech Service Group, Inc., formulated a new role for his engineering consulting firm—he planned to distribute paper drawings of MDA parts to companies that were interested in producing those parts as suppliers to the United States Government. In the aerospace industry, companies other than the primary contractor often manufacture original as well as replacement parts; this has become increasingly common as the industry increases its outsourcing. AeroTech planned to take advantage of this outsourcing trend by coordinating efforts between MDA and its suppliers.

A Prototype Information System

As he pitched this plan to McDonnell Douglas Aerospace, Brill came into contact with an internal MDA group responsible for a prototype information system called the Contractor Integrated Technical Information Service, or CITIS. MDA was developing this system as an answer to the federal government's increasing demands to reduce paperwork, and to use electronic means of collaborating on projects. When AeroTech and the MDA team met, they realized that transferring electronic copies of the drawings of spare parts could be more efficient than working with paper copies, and that the CITIS project looked like an ideal way of accomplishing this.

Digital data reduces paperwork and is more efficient for collaborations

A Pilot Project

Brill feels that AeroTech was able to move forward with CITIS because they were in the right place at the right time. MDA and AeroTech had originally planned to submit a proposal for developing CITIS to ARPA;[1] writing that proposal would have taken about six weeks. Instead, they just went ahead and set up a pilot project with one supplier in the six weeks that it would have taken to write the proposal. Then AeroTech went on to work with another supplier, one who was not familiar with computers, to prove that it could be done with just about any supplier.

Instead of writing a proposal, they created a pilot project

That led to contracts from McDonnell Douglas Aerospace to link first one, and then five more suppliers to CITIS. As AeroTech established their track record, it was a simple matter to have them set up new connections. Eventually,

AeroTech began with a design idea, and ended up as the system manager and gatekeeper for MDA

---

1. ARPA is the Advanced Research Projects Agency, a part of the Department of Defense.

some of the MDA engineers involved in the CITIS project joined AeroTech, and AeroTech made arrangements with MDA to take over the management and administration of the CITIS service in May 1994. As the maintainer of CITIS, AeroTech takes on the role of a *gatekeeper*, that is, they control suppliers' access to McDonnell Douglas data and applications. One observer likened this role to that of a butler—AeroTech sees to it that the right person gets the right item(s).

Implementation: CITIS Operations

Both the data and the applications reside on MDA computers

CITIS is composed of two parts—digital data, such as **CAD** drawings, and applications to use those data. Both the data and the applications reside on CITIS computer systems located at MDA, and not on a user's computer. The main purpose of CITIS is to provide qualified users with access to both the data and applications they need to complete a task for McDonnell Douglas Aerospace (see Figure 11-1).

A T1 line connects AeroTech with MDA, and most suppliers connect to AeroTech using modems

AeroTech maintains network communications with McDonnell Douglas via a T1 circuit.[2] Primary access for most suppliers is through a dial-up connection using a modem. Some suppliers have established higher-speed links[3] with AeroTech according to the bandwidth demands of the applications they wish to use. For example, some X Windows applications, the Unigraphics CAD program, and programs that support videoconferencing and collaborative work, perform better with greater bandwidth.

Centralized data and applications provide freedom from constraints

One advantage of providing a centralized point of access to all required data and applications is that it frees the user from both geographical and time constraints. Both data and applications are accessible at any time of day, any day of

---

2. A T1 circuit is a dedicated data line leased from a phone company; a T1 connection transfers data at a speed of 1.54 megabits/sec.

3. Some suppliers have ISDN or T1 lines.

MDA

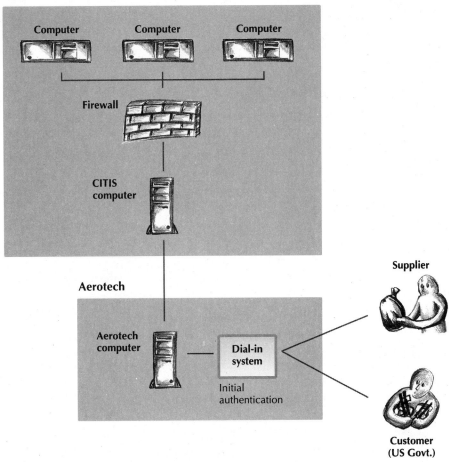

the week, by connecting to the CITIS computers maintained by AeroTech. Users also have the freedom of using whatever workstation they have available to access and process the data; if they're moving around, they can always access the original data because it's stored on CITIS computers.

Using Open Standards

Although a variety of networking protocols could have been used to set up CITIS, the project designers chose **protocols** that had been developed for use on the Internet. Internet protocols were particularly attractive because they are open standards, not owned by any one entity or company, and have been extensively tested on the world's largest network of networks, the Internet.

Internet protocols are well-tested, inexpensive, available for all platforms, and support open standards

Internet protocols have long enjoyed a history of open and shared development, with many of the protocol implementations being freely available for use on a number of computing platforms. It's not unusual to see the required **TCP/IP protocol** stacks, as they're called, included as part of a computer's operating system these days, either. This means that the cost of implementing TCP/IP is relatively low, which helped to keep CITIS costs low too. This low cost also extended to the participating suppliers, because they didn't have too much new software to get up and running.

Software to use the TCP/IP protocols is also readily available for many computing platforms, both as shareware and commercial packages; so the system wasn't necessarily tied to a single type of computer or operating system, which made it easier for contractors to participate in CITIS.

Providing Services

The CITIS system supports various communications options including e-mail, FTP, and telnet

CITIS provides a number of common ways to obtain data and run applications over the Internet. Communications between staff at McDonnell Douglas Aerospace and contractors frequently takes place via Internet e-mail. MDA contractors who need to obtain CITIS data files usually use **file transfer protocol** (FTP) to transfer those files to their local computers. Contractors or Department of Defense employees checking a program schedule are most likely to use **telnet**[4] to log on to one of McDonnell Douglas' computers to get the information they need.

---

4. Telnet is the Internet standard for terminal emulation and remote host access.

Similarly, CITIS supports the X Windows standard for platform-independent graphics displays. X Windows allows CITIS to keep all the necessary applications on its computers, only requiring that CITIS users have an X Windows display program (called the X Windows display server) on their computers. Users then have the flexibility of using many different X Windows-based graphical programs from the CITIS program library without having to store them on their own machines. This also extends the flexibility of mobile users, because they only need the X Windows display server on their computers to run the same graphical application regardless of their location (see Figure 11-2); these X Windows servers are now common components of many TCP/IP software packages so they're relatively easy to obtain. Using X Windows also makes the graphical software

CITIS also supports X Windows to provide platform-independent support for graphical applications

X Windows provides cross-platform graphics capabilities. **Figure 11-2**

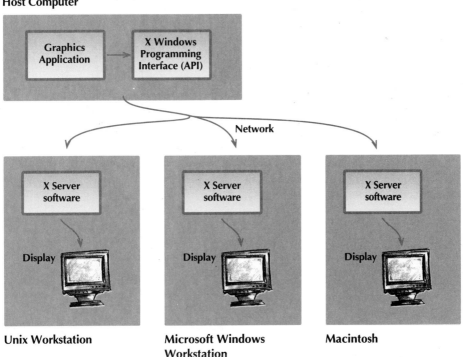

Host Computer

Graphics Application → X Windows Programming Interface (API)

Network

X Server software → Display — **Unix Workstation**

X Server software → Display — **Microsoft Windows Workstation**

X Server software → Display — **Macintosh**

platform-independent because display servers are available for most of the common computing platforms, including Unix, Microsoft Windows, and the Macintosh OS.

Controlling Access

A firewall, alone, is not enough to secure this sensitive information

Although a main goal of CITIS is to facilitate the exchange of information, there's also the question of maintaining the security of the data, and restricting access only to permitted resources. As a Department of Defense contractor, McDonnell Douglas Aerospace stores and uses confidential data that has to be secured against unauthorized or illegal access. Although the CITIS machines are separated from the rest of the MDA network by a **firewall**, CITIS also has to use other security measures to ensure that both their own and MDA's security is maintained.

The Unix operating system offers some security protection

The first level of security employed by CITIS is the security built into the Unix operating system. McDonnell Douglas system administrators perform the usual Unix tasks of assigning access rights to directories and files. Once assigned, the access rights are linked between machines using **Distributed Computing Environment**[5] (DCE) protocols. Suppliers, like other users of MDA computers, are assigned user IDs and passwords for logging on to the computers.

AeroTech uses a proxy server to monitor real-time transactions as they occur

Using a custom Oracle database, AeroTech maintains links between the list of permitted users (the outside suppliers, not MDA employees) and the CITIS directories and files that they're allowed to use. Using this database to control network activity, AeroTech serves as a **proxy**[6] for application and data access. In other words, AeroTech monitors each supplier's activity from the moment they connect to Aero-

---

5. DCE is a series of protocols that define how software objects or modules are stored and can interact across a network.

6. Proxy servers adopt a store-and-forward approach to protecting crucial data and applications.

Tech, and it compares their access commands, such as listing directories and downloading files, to the database before allowing those commands to be executed (see Figure 11-3). For example, if a user isn't authorized to download a file using FTP, AeroTech would prevent that command from being executed.

Schematic of CITIS access & security measures.   *Figure 11-3*

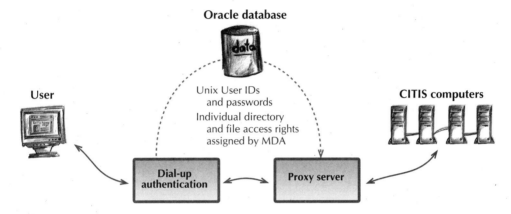

As part of a recent upgrade to support Web access to CITIS, another layer of security has been added. Because AeroTech is now using a Netscape Enterprise Server to provide access to CITIS files, secure links are set up between the server and browser using the **secure sockets layer** (SSL) protocol. SSL encrypts the data being sent in a communications session between server and browser, thus keeping unauthorized users from intercepting and viewing the data. AeroTech also provides proxied access to MDA's internal Web server from their Web server.

SSL is used with Netscape's Enterprise Server for encryption

Web Site Description: Controlling Access to Shared Data and Applications

With so many different kinds of data on the MDA computers (design drawings, part specifications, and project requirements, for example), facilitating exchange of that data with suppliers and other outside users through CITIS can prove its utility in a number of situations (see Figure 11-4). Here are some examples.

Figure 11-4   *Opening page for accessing CITIS's services.*

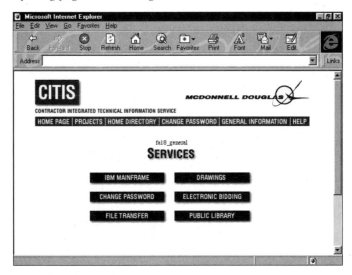

Transferring Data to a Manufacturer

When supporting individual security measures is cost prohibitive, use an intermediary

One example of how AeroTech facilitates communications is an exchange between McDonnell Douglas Aerospace and UCAR Composites, a manufacturer of tooling for high-performance composite components. McDonnell Douglas is located in St. Louis, Missouri, while UCAR Composites is based in Irvine, California. Although MDA wants to send design updates to UCAR electronically, the company does not want to allow UCAR direct access to the MDA computers because of security concerns. Setting up and maintaining security measures for a large number of trusted suppliers like UCAR would be prohibitively expensive, which is one of the reasons for CITIS and for AeroTech's involvement.

To use AeroTech's services in this case, McDonnell Douglas translates the CAD files into the numerical-control machine codes needed to operate the metal-cutting machines at UCAR, and then it transfers the CAD files and machine control codes to AeroTech's secure location. Next, Aero-Tech's system forwards the files to UCAR over a dial-up link using regular phone lines. UCAR then has the ability to review the CAD files on their own system, and to begin manufacturing the parts using the control codes provided by McDonnell Douglas. To send the same information to UCAR on magnetic tape, via express mail, would take a few days and cost about $400 per update; on the other hand, using AeroTech's services, the translation and transfer can be done in a few hours, at a cost of about $4.

By translating and electronically transferring only the required data, MDA protects sensitive information, saves time, and spends less on shipping

Speeding Up the Bidding Process

Another process that McDonnell Douglas must often undertake—providing bid-request packages to qualified parts suppliers—also lends itself to streamlining. These bid-request packages usually contain both engineering drawings and manufacturing process specifications to let the supplier determine the time and resources needed to manufacture the requested parts.

McDonnell Douglas now uses AeroTech as an intermediary in the bidding process. A McDonnell buyer notifies qualified suppliers via e-mail that a job is available for bidding. The background information for the bid-request package, such as CAD drawings and manufacturing specifications, is stored on AeroTech's computers and made accessible to the suppliers without compromising MDA's security measures or requiring that any new ones be established for the suppliers.

MDA maintains security by using AeroTech's computers to distribute bid request packages

Monitoring Projects

One other use of CITIS is to make it easier for remote overseers to monitor projects. For example, a project manager working for the Department of Defense in Washington, D.C., can use CITIS to access a project scheduling program

Remote access to
both a project
management
program and
current project
data makes offsite
monitoring easier

and project data on a McDonnell Douglas computer (see
Figure 11-5). Data from the suppliers and subcontractors can
be added to the scheduling data via CITIS as well, making
the picture more complete, and allowing the manager to
obtain warnings of possible schedule slippages by checking
the subcontractors' data.

Figure 11-5   *Web Page listing current projects for review at CITIS.*

Structuring Fees

Annual contracts
cover daily main-
tenance, but special
projects are handled
individually

AeroTech's fee structure for CITIS is fairly simple. They have
an annual contract with McDonnell Douglas for maintaining
CITIS, which covers the day-to-day expenses of running
CITIS. When special projects arise, such as revamping the
database software for better performance, or implementing a
Web interface to CITIS, those projects are separate tasks
presented as new contracts to McDonnell Douglas. In some
cases, suppliers want a higher-speed connection to CITIS (to
use a CAD program, for instance), which requires additional
funding. By the middle of 1995, McDonnell Douglas estimated that the CITIS project was already paying for itself,

based on the cost savings for disseminating information to its suppliers. (Recall the example of spending $4 to transfer data with CITIS instead of $400 to ship tapes to a supplier.)

Analysis: Entrusting Access to an Intermediary

Starting out as a small company, AeroTech was able to display a great deal of flexibility and to reinvent itself to take over the CITIS system. It helped that George Brill had already been thinking about distributing the parts specifications and drawings as a business venture; he had only to adapt his original idea to a different form—the digital representation of information.

Flexibility and vision made it possible to adapt one idea to a different medium

Brill attaches a great deal of importance to starting the project reasonably quickly, in this case with a pilot project. He feels that many corporations spend a great deal of time studying possibilities without implementing anything. Consider AeroTech's decision to create a pilot project during the six weeks it would have taken to file a grant proposal with ARPA. Much like the famous Nike slogan ("Just do it"), AeroTech seized an opportunity to prove the concept and their swift action led to the full-time implementation of CITIS. Brill also emphasizes the importance of personal relationships—he thinks the project would never have gotten off the ground if many of the people involved in CITIS and AeroTech hadn't already known each other.

A quick start and prior relationships paid off

Other Advantages of Using CITIS

In addition to the cost savings associated with using CITIS, McDonnell Douglas has been able to realize other value from the project. MDA can now rely on faster part production for its engineers; when special parts are required (as in the UCAR example), turn-around can be as fast as 18 hours.

MDA saved time as well as money

Using CITIS to speed up the bidding process has also proven to be a time-saver. In the past, it used to take up to six weeks. Now it typically takes only 24 hours using CITIS to disseminate the bidding requirements and technical specifications to the suppliers, and to receive the bids.

The system provides reliable security and is being used routinely

CITIS's success in facilitating secure links between MDA staff and outside suppliers has led to increased reliance on CITIS as the standard way of communicating with suppliers. It's not uncommon to hear MDA staff talk of *CITIS'ing* something that has to get out. As different processes have started to use CITIS as a communications channel, CITIS has also become a vehicle for standardizing processes between MDA and suppliers, which has made it easier to get the job(s) done.

Increased Usage

Within two years, the number of CITIS users grew by nearly 700 percent

The success of CITIS is readily apparent from its increased use by MDA and its suppliers. When CITIS started as an internal project in mid-1993, less than 50 people had access to it, and they were all MDA staff. When AeroTech took over CITIS in Fall 1994, they started out with 400 internal and external users. By the end of 1996, more than 2700 users were routinely using CITIS.

Brokers and intermediaries who do not charge users for access to the information, may prefer to consider themselves facilitators of virtual corporations and factories

References have been made in previous chapters to the roles of intermediaries and information brokers. AeroTech definitely fits the definition of an intermediary, but Brill doesn't consider his company to be an information broker. That's mainly because AeroTech doesn't charge its users for the information it provides; it simply facilitates communications between its primary contractor (MDA) and the suppliers. AeroTech adds value by making it easier for MDA and its suppliers to communicate and exchange technical information, which in turn makes it easier (and faster) for both sides to get their jobs done. CITIS facilitates the links between engineers, purchasing agents, machinists, and suppliers, many of whom are dispersed around the United States, thus lending credence to the idea that this is, indeed, a virtual factory.

The Future

Its experience with CITIS gave AeroTech a number of different opportunities to grow. For example, companies like Southwestern Bell were interested in using AeroTech's experience with the Internet, network security, and user tracking to offer similar services to other industries. Aero-Tech could also market, and charge for, some of the non-confidential CITIS data; demand for spare parts in the aerospace industry is high, and spare parts manufacturers other than MDA might be willing to pay for MDA's technical data.

Opportunities include new clients and data sales

AeroTech has decided to continue building virtual factories. Other major manufacturers in the St. Louis area have talked to AeroTech about building virtual factories for them, so there are numerous opportunities for the company. As a next step, AeroTech is now working with the National Institute for Standards and Technology (NIST) on the concept of a Virtual Factory Hub.

More virtual factories are on the way

CITIS, itself, is being continually refined. In the past, authentication of a supplier was accomplished using the telecommunications software at AeroTech, as a connection was made. Now Aerotech is considering using Netscape's Certificate Server and **digital certificates** to authenticate connections, which would also allow suppliers to connect via a local **Internet service provider** as well as via the current dial-up connection.

Enhancements to CITIS might include authentication of digital certificates

AeroTech is also working on more flexible licensing arrangements for the commercial software used by CITIS partici-

Alternative commercial software licensing arrangements are being investigated

pants. McDonnell Douglas had earlier negotiated site licenses for this software that included use of the software by its suppliers. Now, in an effort to move the high-performance software down to the suppliers, MDA and AeroTech are working on a system that uses Intergraph's License Manager to install Intergraph CAD software on suppliers' computers, with AeroTech controlling its use by being "keeper" of the license bits required to run the program. This would decrease bandwidth requirements and also provide for licensed use of the software on a daily basis, allowing the suppliers greater flexibility in their use of the software and making it easier to support both longtime and casual partners.

The Players, the System, the Site

Players: **Aerotech Service Group, Inc.**
12208 Missouri Bottom Rd.
Hazelwood, MO 63042
Phone: 314-895-4555
Fax: 314-895-4556
E-mail: info@aerotechsg.com
http://www.aerotechsg.com
  George Brill, President

McDonnell Douglas
St. Louis, Missouri
  Dave Utterback, 314-232-6042

System: Uses Oracle 7 database. (No other information provided.)

Site: Not available to public.

Strategies for Electronic Commerce

Any strategy you consider for integrating electronic commerce in your business should focus on information—not only its collection and dissemination, but also its use in marketing and as a salable product in and of itself. The concept of the virtual value chain discussed in Chapter 5, "Consumer and Business Markets," is important to electronic commerce precisely because it defines ways to incorporate digital information into regular business processes.

Businesses involved in traditional markets, such as manufacturing, can readily make use of information to improve their internal processes and, more importantly (at least within the framework of this book), improve their processes for dealing with customers. As you've learned, electronic commerce is more than closing a sale and transferring funds. Maintaining contact with your customers and seeking out new potential customers is important to your business. Supporting your customers once the sale is completed is equally important. Each of these processes depends on information, and much of this information can either be acquired or processed using the Internet.

Seek out and support customers using information and the Internet

How you integrate this information with your organization's processes depends on a number of factors, starting with how well you can exploit the Internet and its technologies and including the match between those technologies and your business' structure, and your perception of the marketspace.

Evolving with the Internet

While Internet developments are coming quickly, many are an extension of existing LAN technologies

Business on the Internet will continue to develop as technologies on the Internet evolve, and that evolution seems to be progressing at an ever-increasing pace. But it helps to recall that these are not earth-shattering technologies that are being developed at the rate of one a week. In many cases, the technologies (such as videoconferencing and hypertext) are refinements of existing ideas that had originally been proposed or developed for smaller networks or LANs (Local Area Networks).

But unlike LANs, the Internet uses open standards, and companies are using it to promote their products to a worldwide market

What the Internet has done is bring three important new views to the market for these technologies. First, it has encouraged the use of open standards, available for implementation by anyone who's interested. Second, the Internet is the largest network accessible around the globe and possibly the one network accessible by the widest variety of computers. And third, the Internet is becoming the common basis for introducing products and technologies to a greater market.

Keep abreast by tracking standards and by maintaining a flexible organization

Tracking innovations related to the Internet may seem to be a time-consuming and resource-intensive task, but no more so than tracking any other information systems technology, such as those related to client/server or object-oriented programming. A good course to follow for tracking Internet technologies is to watch what the standards bodies are doing, and to maintain a flexible organization so you can respond to the changes you observe.

The Standards Landscape

The Internet has long had a series of committees, mainly composed of volunteers, who carefully guide proposed technologies through a standards process. These committees, which form a significant part of the Internet Engineering Task Force (IETF), have guided a number of important **protocols** through the standards process to encourage their implementation on the Internet. Protocols such as the **TCP/IP protocols** for Internet transport, **SMTP** (simple mail transport protocol) and **POP** (post office protocol) for electronic mail, and **SNMP** (simple network management protocol) for network management, are all a direct result of the IETF's efforts.

The IETF guides proposed technologies through the standards process

Other standards bodies, such as the International Telecommunications Union (ITU), the American National Standards Institute (ANSI), and the Institute of Electrical and Electronic Engineers (IEEE), also have influence; but the IETF is the one body originally formed to guide development of the Internet.

You should realize that the IETF has not been granted this role by any government or international body, and it is a more informal standards body than formal bodies such as the ITU or ANSI. In recognition of this status, the IETF publishes its standards as recommendations; it has no authority to require vendors to implement the technologies. Even though the IETF standards may seem voluntary, they have the power of the marketplace behind them—if vendors want to tap the large market known as the Internet, they need to ensure that their products will work in tandem with other products used on the Internet, which, in turn, usually means adherence to IETF standards. And the easiest way to ensure that is by adherence to the IETF *voluntary* standards.

Standards are only recommendations, and their adoption is optional

But the networking market has seen increasing fragmentation with regards to standards over the past few years. As the Internet has grown and become more of a market for consumers and businesses alike, companies have sought to

Companies and ad
hoc groups are now
seeking to influence
standards for their
own benefit

further influence the standards process to give them some kind of competitive advantage. Even the informal standards bodies, such as the IETF, are being subjected to these pressures. And as these markets grow, businesses are grouping together to form ad hoc groups, or consortia, to push forward their own standards. Some of these groups include the Object Management Group (OMG), VRML Forum,[1] and the Java Developer Connection, to name only a few.

Often, because of the influential standing of the IETF, these ad hoc groups (or individual companies) will submit their proposed standards for consideration by the IETF. If adopted, the IEFT recommendation provides an added seal of approval. As a benefit to most businesses, if these standards make it through the IETF process, you can be certain that the protocols are defined to be as open as possible.

The slower the
standards process,
the wider the win-
dow for ad hoc
groups

One reason for the rise of the ad hoc standards groups has been the increased pace of development contrasted with a longer review cycle—many vendors feel that standards groups like the ITU, IEEE, and IETF take too long to prepare and approve standards. The IETF is the fastest of the organizations releasing standards, and it does that by basing standards on working implementations. The fact that the IETF has had to devote itself to turning out protocols that work, rather than ones that are defined in every last detail for every possible situation, should give you an indication of the pace of development, as well as the fight by businesses to control standards for their own advantage. The pace of standard development is relative. IETF does it faster than other standards bodies (such as ISO and ITU, for example), but it's still not fast enough for companies such as Netscape, Cisco, and others. In the current state of affairs, the longer a standards body takes to approve and promulgate a standard,

---

1. VRML stands for Virtual Reality Markup Language, a markup language similar to HTML that is used for describing three-dimensional objects and how they interact. The VRML Forum works on setting industry standards for VRML programming.

Chapter Twelve

the wider is the window for companies to develop their own proprietary standards and for buyers to establish de facto standards by virtue of their purchases.

Flexible Organizations

These days one of the obvious truths about the Internet is that it's always changing. The dynamics of working with, and developing for, the Internet are very different from what many businesses are used to. But that does not mean that your business has to continually change as fast as the Internet. It doesn't even mean that your business should continually change. The standard business practice of analyzing a proposed change and making sure that it is truly a benefit (either long-term or short-term) applies to changes related to technology as much as it does to changes based upon evolving market conditions. The key is that by being flexible and prepared for change, your business will be better prepared for the future opportunities afforded by the Internet and electronic commerce. And the key for being ready to adapt to change appropriately is information sharing within the organization.

Be flexible so you can take advantage of opportunities as they arise

The older, more traditional hierarchical structures found in many businesses put a high value on information and, more importantly, on its control. That's antithetical to information sharing. Organizations that redesign themselves to be flatter have structures that are better suited to exchanging information. One reason for this is that the synergies of electronic commerce depend on a greater understanding of the customer, which in turn requires free flow of information, both inside and outside of the organization. This produces a new type of alignment between buyer and seller that's more customer-driven than product-driven, with more interactions among departments and individuals rather than between an individual and an account representative (see Figure 12-1 on the next page).

Businesses with a flat structure are better suited to information sharing, making it easier to benefit from electronic commerce

Figure 12-1   *Multiple points of contact in the new customer-oriented interface.*

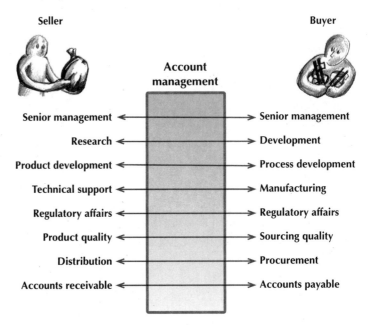

Seller	Account management	Buyer
Senior management	← →	Senior management
Research	← →	Development
Product development	← →	Process development
Technical support	← →	Manufacturing
Regulatory affairs	← →	Regulatory affairs
Product quality	← →	Sourcing quality
Distribution	← →	Procurement
Accounts receivable	← →	Accounts payable

Flexible organizations share information so it can be used wherever necessary

Flexible organizations deal with information differently than more traditional, hierarchical organizations. They realize that information has more value when it's shared. Think of the simple case of customer information in the software business—it can come from technical support, market surveys, letters, meetings at shows, and more. But if that information doesn't get to the right people in the company, it's worthless. And who are the right people? Well, they may be different each day—one day it might be an engineer working on some code, the next day it might be a sales engineer, or the vice-president of marketing. If the information isn't shared, it might as well not exist.

Creating a Framework for Business Value

If you look back at the discussion of the virtual value chain ("Value Chains and the Marketspace" on page 109), you'll find that there are a number of locations in any business process where you can add value. But how you add value affects, and is affected by, your business and how conducive it is to change.

Why is change so important? Because almost anything a business does to benefit from electronic commerce is going to involve some type of alteration (see Figure 12-2). The change might be something as simple as improving a process by doing it electronically instead of manually. But embracing the virtual value chain as a way of doing things, or extracting maximum value from the marketspace, requires more—usually a transformation of your business, or its redefinition.

Incorporating electronic commerce in your business will require some changes

Changing your business for electronic commerce.

Figure 12-2

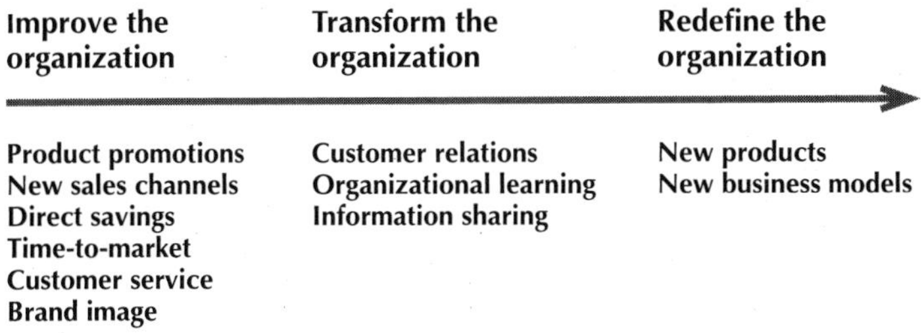

Improve the organization	Transform the organization	Redefine the organization

Product promotions	Customer relations	New products
New sales channels	Organizational learning	New business models
Direct savings	Information sharing	
Time-to-market		
Customer service		
Brand image		

Using Electronic Commerce

You can improve almost any aspect of your business processes to take advantage of electronic commerce. For instance, you can create better product promotions to improve sales by adding multimedia to Internet presentations and offering more detailed product descriptions on your Web site. It's a fundamental precept of marketing to target information based on customers' backgrounds, or some other demographic or psychographic feature. You can also design your Web site and e-mail services to incorporate information from databases to tailor information to individual clients instead of demographic groups. You might even

Improve your processes by adding multimedia, providing more details, and customizing the information presented

establish the Internet as a new sales channel, perhaps by tying sales directly to an online catalog and order form; or use the Internet as a transmission medium to relay purchase orders to your suppliers.

Use the Internet as a communications medium to reduce costs

Using the Internet as a communications medium can reduce your direct costs of doing business—for example, in a business-to-business environment, purchase orders can be relayed in electronic form, eliminating the need for re-keying crucial information. Product delivery via the Internet is also possible, as long as your product is digital; software can be delivered to the customer and registered over the Internet, eliminating the need for printed documentation and packaging. Getting products and product upgrades to the customer electronically, either directly or via a distributor, can cut the time to market for digital products. Putting an electronic catalog on line, instead of printing and mailing it, also reduces the time it takes to get product information to your customers and distributors, as demonstrated by Fruit of the Loom and AMP (see Chapter 8, "Collaborating on a Distribution Chain," page 151, and Chapter 9, "Maximizing the Usefulness of an Online Catalog," page 171, respectively).

Use the Internet to share information, improve customer support, and enhance your corporate image

Obtaining information about customers and their needs has a direct impact on business practices because of the way it positively affects product design and planning, thereby giving you a market advantage (see Figure 12-3). Furthermore, by putting frequently requested information in a FAQ document or searchable database on the Web, you can also use the Internet to simultaneously improve your customer support while reducing its costs. And, of course, don't overlook the value that using the Internet adds to your corporate image—after all, the Internet is considered cutting-edge technology and your business will be considered forward-thinking by offering goods or services over the Internet.

Using customer profiles.

Figure 12-3

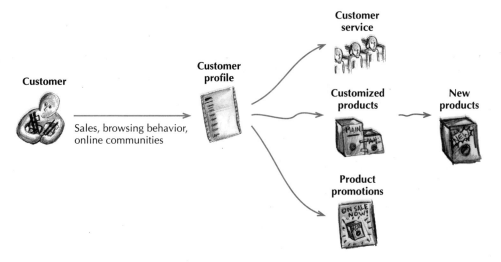

Electronic commerce on the Internet also affords you opportunities to transform your business as you shift from the
value chain to the virtual value chain. For example, customer relations can be changed from one-way asynchronous
communications to two-way interactive communications.
Instead of relying only on telephone conversations restricted
to working hours and subject to telephone tag, you can use
the Web and e-mail to exchange information and opinions
between customers and staff. But remember, this will profit
your operations only if your organization is structured to
exchange information freely, and the members of your
organization actually understand that information is both
freely accepted and given.

Use the Internet for two-way exchanges, free from limitations of time and place

Your business can collect data about customer preferences
and habits by observing what they do at your Web site; you
can then use this information to customize your offerings
and services. To do this, of course, your company has to
have the tools in place both to collect the data in an organized fashion and to analyze it for making decisions. In
Chapters 7 and 9 ("An Electronic Marketplace of Buyers and

Use the Internet to learn about cus-tomer habits and preferences

Sellers," page 133, and "Maximizing the Usefulness of an Online Catalog," page 171) you saw how Industry.net and AMP Connect are collecting data on customer searches and information requests, and using it to refine their offerings and plan new products and services to meet customer needs.

Recall that when it comes to creating values in a virtual value chain, five different activities can be involved—gathering, organizing, selecting, synthesizing, and distributing information. Because you can generate new products or value using each of these activities at any of the points along the value chain, you can, in effect, create a value matrix (see Figure 12-4), where the intersection of each information related activity with each step in the value chain is another opportunity to add value.

Figure 12-4   *A value matrix.*

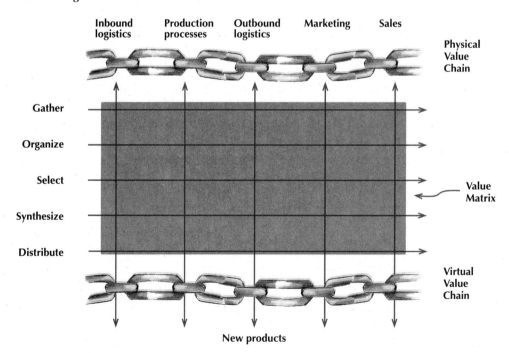

Using the Internet for commerce will also offer opportunities for new products and new business models, often within this framework of the virtual value chain or in dealing with the marketspace. For example, it's entirely possible that Fruit of the Loom could charge another clothier for access to a channel derived from Activewear Online, much in the same way that SABRE became a source of revenue for American Airlines even after it opened up the system to offerings from competing airlines. Or take a look at Federal Express' new BusinessLink service, which ties their shipping and tracking system with electronic processing of orders for participating merchants; they've linked together two important pieces of the sales cycle (ordering and shipping), not by eliminating the middleman, but by using a new (electronic) channel to forge the links between customer, merchant, and shipper.

Use the Internet to tie together different parts of the sales cycle, creating new channels and services

Doing Things Differently in the Marketspace

In the past, many businesses grew by exercising economies of scale. That same principle can also be applied to electronic commerce, but in a more limited sense because other principles can have just as great an impact. If you're planning to offer digital products within the marketspace, there's one fundamental principle that you should be aware of—the Law of Digital Assets. Originally formulated by two professors from the Harvard Business School, the Law of Digital Assets points out that, unlike physical assets, digital assets are used but not consumed. In other words, digital assets can be used over and over again. Thus you can create more value for your business by continually recycling your digital assets through a large, nearly infinite, number of transactions. However, this does not necessarily mean that your digital products will remain useful forever. Common industry practices will continue to dictate your need to revise, enhance, improve, and even repackage your products.

According to the Law of Digital Assets, digital assets are used, but not consumed

As you plan your strategy to incorporate electronic commerce into your business, you should be prepared for a number of issues that will arise. These issues can be organized into four categories, as shown in the table below—organizational, implementation, marketing, and legal.

Some Issues Affecting Business in the Marketspace

Category	Issue
Organizational	Building infrastructures for sharing information Managing knowledge Using intermediaries Maintaining flexibility Flattening the organization
Implementation	Using pilot projects Automating processes Planning for expansion and rapid growth Using data warehouses Setting up workflow applications
Marketing	Promoting two-way interactive communications Profiling customers Segmentation Defining & maintaining communities of interest Push vs. pull information flow
Legal	Taxation Customer and corporate privacy Export controls on cryptographic products

Organizational Issues

Implementation requires infrastructure changes

Implementation of electronic commerce is not simply a technology project. It changes current business processes and practices, and usually requires significant organizational changes. Along with changes in organizational structure come changes in the company's communications and information infrastructures. One of the biggest challenges for companies when implementing electronic commerce is managing these organizational changes.

In many cases, crucial organizational changes revolve around the treatment of information and communications. For instance, a comprehensive communications capability should be a fundamental part of your infrastructure. This could be something as simple as electronic mail, or it might be something more involved, such as a Lotus Notes database or a special client/server application. However it's done, though, this communications infrastructure, and the development and encouragement of a culture that uses it, is fundamental to maintaining a flexible organization that can respond quickly to changes and new opportunities.

A comprehensive communications network makes it possible for a flexible organization to respond

As you plan to open your infrastructure for better information exchange, look for opportunities to replace parallel infrastructures with a common shared infrastructure. For instance, don't maintain two separate systems for customer service, one for inquiries via the phone and a second for Internet-based inquiries. Convert them to a common data platform. Even more important is looking for ways to link different departmental systems together. Customer contact information can be captured from a variety of sources (such as sales, support, and marketing), but it needs to be distributed to *everyone* who might benefit from the information, including product designers and engineers, for example, so sharing of the information should be accomplished as effectively as possible.

Use electronic systems to share data and avoid duplication of efforts

Along with this communications and information infrastructure comes the need for management of the knowledge this information generates. In many ways, this isn't a new idea—corporations try to do it all the time. But the increase in the quantity of information in general, and the sharing of information, makes knowledge management even more important. Without it, companies and their employees will be unable to find and take advantage of numerous opportunities, and they may well collapse under a glut of information with which they're ill-equipped to deal.

Information management is crucial, and may necessitate changes in the information infrastructure

Working with business partners on electronic commerce projects requires matching your own communication capabilities with those of your partners. This is one of the aims of **EDI**, for example—the form of data to be transferred among partners, and the means of transferring the data, are standardized. But partners may still be required to alter their internal processes in order to be able to process the EDI data they receive.

Intermediaries can help resolve incompatibilities, avoiding the need for frequent short-term changes

If you're unwilling, or unable, to match capabilities, one course of action is to employ an intermediary. This may prove especially beneficial if you're taking part in a short-term project. AeroTech's CITIS project, discussed in Chapter 11 ("The Beginnings of a Virtual Factory," page 203), is a good example of this—they can provide connections to important data for short-term suppliers to McDonnell Douglas without requiring an extensive outlay of time and money on the part of the suppliers. Nets Inc. is another good example of an intermediary or facilitator (see Chapter 7, "An Electronic Marketplace of Buyers and Sellers," page 133); they provide a common ground where many manufacturers and suppliers can get together to exchange information and set up working partnerships.

Both AeroTech and Nets Inc. are expanding to offer other services that make it easier for partners to perform more of their business transactions (such as posting requests for quotes, trading purchase orders, and making payments) on line, further tightening the links between the companies who participate. Incorporating translation services (for file formats, for instance) as part of the link also makes it easier for partners to communicate when they have different computing systems or procedures.

AeroTech also solves one of the problems associated with sharing information—that of controlling access. In the most flexible information environments, members of the community can not only view someone else's data, but also change it, if necessary. But many companies balk at permitting outsiders access to their information, and allowing those outsiders to make changes is unthinkable. Setting access rights for the partners, and having an intermediary control and monitor access, as well as maintain the data banks, can be quite appealing to companies who want to share data without having to maintain added security measures for outside users.

Intermediaries can also handle data access control

Revamping business processes to accommodate many of the new opportunities offered by electronic commerce is a continual task. There will always be external pressures exerted by technological changes on the Internet, as well as changes expected by your customers in a continuously evolving marketplace. But this prospect should not freeze you into immobility, nor should it keep you from starting a project just because all the pieces aren't yet in place. As Charles Kirk of Fruit of the Loom has pointed out, the speed of Web-based **front-end processes** may well push forward the re-engineering of a business's **back-end processes**. But it doesn't pay to wait until both are completely updated and in sync before implementing them. Or, as George Brill of AeroTech put it, you have to follow Nike's slogan and "Just do it."

All the pieces will never be *ready* at the same time, so don't wait to begin a project

Implementation Issues

Once you've made your plans, there comes the task of implementing them. Sometimes standard information systems practices are enough to form a framework for the processes you need to implement. Certainly, you shouldn't overlook the value of your information systems department and their experience—but it must be tempered with an experience of the Internet, particularly the issues of its dynamics and open systems approach as outlined in this book. For better or worse, things are often done differently on the Internet.

The Internet brings new considerations for information systems

Pilot projects can help to discover some problems early

The case studies in this book share a common thread in the way the companies have approached their projects—they all involved pilot projects. That's a good practice for any large-scale undertaking, whether or not it involves the Internet or is focused on electronic commerce. For electronic commerce, pilot projects involving some of your clients or business partners can be especially valuable. These early designs also help you discover problems in both procedures and perceptions before the system becomes more widely available, and the problems become harder to fix.

Some problems won't be apparent until full-scale implementation occurs

There are, however, some things that a pilot project may not adequately illustrate, things that only show up as the project is scaled up. For instance, data management was often mentioned by the case study managers as a crucial issue during expansion from the pilot study to full implementation. As an example, hand-coding **HTML** pages works for small Web sites in their initial stages of availability, but as your business on the Web grows, or new processes and features are included, you will need an automated procedure for creating Web pages because hand-coding will no longer be a viable option.

Consider relational databases and object-oriented approaches; prepare for growth

Planning for the expansion of your Web site and associated data, and automating as many of the processes involved in maintaining your Web site, are crucial to the success of your efforts. And it becomes even more crucial as you follow the trend towards more interactivity with your customers or support **transactional commerce** processing over the Internet. That's why many of the companies mentioned here use large relational databases and object-oriented approaches to dynamically generate much of their current Web content (see Figure 12-5). And, as you saw in the case of AMP Connect (Chapter 9, "Maximizing the Usefulness of an Online Catalog," page 171), that same data can be used for other purposes as well, such as specialized print catalogs.

Information stored in a single database can be used for different purposes.

Figure 12-5

Legacy sources　　　　**Virtual data platform**　　　**Multiple distribution capabilities**

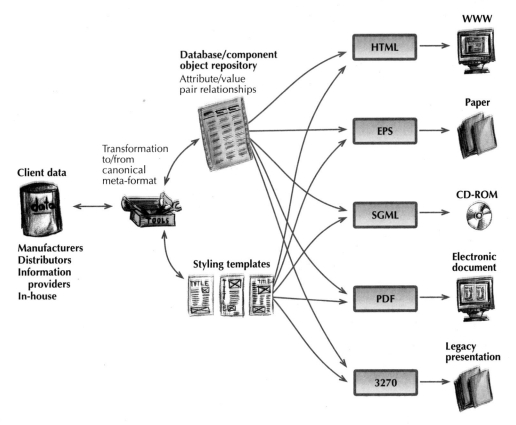

Automating the presentation of Web content also makes it easier to customize the information displayed to your customers. Once you've collected enough data to form a customer's profile, you can use that profile to guide how you present your Web content. It can also be used as a guide for special promotions and product customization.

Expect customer profiling and customized goods and services to become even more sophisticated as electronic

Use profile data to guide your presentation

Use data warehousing and mining techniques to facilitate customization

commerce evolves on the Internet. More sophisticated methods require more data, and you can get much of that data from your electronic dealings with your customers: from their browsing and purchasing habits on a Web site, and their purchase and payment habits from accounts payable, to their requests for assistance from technical or customer support. Because all that data is digital, it can be collected and analyzed—but only if you make the effort to collect and store it. Nets Inc. is an example of a company that is already using data warehousing for their customer data, and is developing data mining techniques to understand their customers' habits and needs. Such approaches make it easier to micro-segment the market, leading to more customization.

Create proprietary solutions when necessary; replace with commercial solutions when available

Much of the technology being developed for electronic commerce is relatively new and immature compared to other electronic technologies. That often means that there's a lot of experimentation going on—not only might your company be experimenting with different electronic commerce projects, but the vendors and developers offering you products are experimenting as well. Don't be surprised if the tools you need to set up an electronic commerce system either aren't readily available or aren't as sophisticated as you've come to expect from other development projects. But there's usually enough to get started with, and things will only improve. Recall how Nets Inc. approached the problem—they developed their own proprietary solutions in house in order to implement features in a timely fashion, but they did not hesitate to replace those proprietary solutions with commercially available products of equal quality when such products became available.

You can spur on refinement of back-end processes by implementing front-ends to support electronic commerce. In other words, you can improve back-end processes to support electronic commerce by automating them as much as possible. A further step would be to use workflow software to move customer orders, making it easier to merge the electronic exchange of orders with both your buyers and your internal processes. Re-keying data often leads to mistakes and time delays; keeping everything digital helps avoid such errors.

Automation of processes and commerce data is essential if you're planning to support microtransactions and micropayments as part of your commerce model. Depending on the types of **microtransactions** you intend to support, you'll have to decide on the smallest amount of information or service that you'll charge for, or how time charges will be broken down. Even if you're planning to implement microtransactions, remember that many users may still prefer subscription accounts because they are easier to control and budget for. Both systems can be offered to your customers, but whichever route you choose, you'll have to see that it's integrated with your existing accounting systems—if that's not possible, you'll have to design new ones that encompass all options. If you look back at Microsoft's new Pay-Per-Incident option for customer support (see Chapter 10, "Electronic Customer Support," page 187), they chose to integrate the charges into the existing system, but redesigned the database and wrote some management software to merge Pay-Per-Incident transactions with the rest of the usual customer support payment options. And in doing so they also provided more flexibility for future types of transactions and customer options.

> Whether you support microtransactions, subscriptions, or both, you'll need to integrate the process with your existing accounting systems

Marketing Issues

Take advantage of the fact that the Internet has evolved into a truly interactive medium; Web sites should include dynamic data and support transactions between buyer and seller. This poses new problems and new opportunities for

> Reach out to small groups and online communities

marketers. As you've read earlier, electronic commerce systems on the Internet can collect information on customer needs and behavioral patterns that will allow for a more personalized relationship between suppliers and their customers. Now marketing departments can reach out to newly created customer groups, such as microsegments (smaller market groups) and online communities.

Effective marketing needs consumer information, but privacy must be considered

Marketers also have to help the company formulate a plan for collecting customer data that takes into account the issue of customer privacy. When it comes to business-to-business commerce, this may be less of a problem, but many consumers on the Internet currently feel that they should be giving away as little information about themselves as possible. It helps to be up-front about what data will be collected from a user's visit to your Web site, and how it's likely to be used.

Customized products are not always cost effective, but electronic commerce makes customized promotions worthwhile

Customization of products and promotions via the Internet doesn't always have to occur on a one-to-one basis, as **microsegmentation** of market niches often proves adequate. But you do have to guard against creating market segments that are too small. The finer the segmentation, the easier it will be to appeal to people's narrow (and probably more passionate) interests. However, make those market segments too small and they may not support the costs of developing specific products, even if the Internet reduces these costs considerably. Customized promotions for digital products are even easier to present on a one-to-one or microsegmented basis, because only the information about the products has to change, not the products themselves.

Create communities of interest to gain insights and build customer loyalty

As a part of your segmentation strategy, you should look for opportunities to create or target *communities of interest.* These communities are excellent forums for providing information about your company and its products, as well as gathering market data. If your business can create communities that satisfy both the communal and transactional needs of your customers or business partners, you should reap the benefits of greater customer loyalty and gain important insights into the nature and needs of your customer base.

Although there's a myriad of ways to combine business information, any assemblage of information must be packaged to meet the needs of the customer. The more relevant the information appears to the customer, the more likely it is to be used, and the more likely it will strengthen a link between you and your customer. The real challenge is to find systems that help you efficiently define and create your information packaging, but still meet the needs of your markets. Recall that the more specialized you make the customer's profiles, the more useful your services and products will be for that customer, and the less likely it will be for that customer to go to a competitor. (Even if the competitor maintains profiles, customers won't want to provide duplicate information at a competitor's Web site.)

Use detailed profiles to make your promotions relevant to your customers

As the Internet has become more of an interactive communications medium, it has focused greater attention on the differences between *push* and *pull* marketing. Marketers that are accustomed to working with the more traditional advertising media such as print and television, have to tread more softly when advertising on the Internet. For instance, e-mail can be a useful vehicle for providing one-to-one notices of products and company information, but many Internet users do not appreciate receiving what they consider to be junk mail. Posting product notices to Usenet news groups is also a good way to reach communities of interest, but be sure that the news groups condone such procedures. Widely broadcasting company or product information on the Internet by bulk e-mail or widespread postings to news groups is usually frowned upon and will most likely lead to a negative corporate image on the Internet. If you're going to use

Advertising through an interactive medium, such as the Internet, requires a different approach from traditional print and broadcast advertising vehicles like e-mail to send information to current or potential customers, get some idea of their receptiveness to such approaches first.

Use checklists to support customer-initiated information pull

As customer profiles get more sophisticated, and Web and e-mail technologies coupled with Web-database links get more capable, it's easier to support customer-initiated *information pull*. As an example, a checklist of product information on a Web form, or in product descriptions in an online catalog, can be used to send the requested information via e-mail or fax, according to the user's profile.

Legal Issues

The issues surrounding electronic commerce that may well have the greatest impact, but still remain to be resolved, are the legal ones. This includes issues surrounding privacy, taxes on electronic commerce, and export controls of products using encryption technologies.

Privacy issues have legal as well as marketing ramifications

The issue of personal privacy is so large that it cannot be adequately covered in this book.[2] It includes concerns about gathering and reusing data on a person's browsing habits at a Web site, tracking information on customer purchases, and the anonymity of **digital cash** (recall the discussion of digital cash in Chapter 3, "Handling Money on the Net," page 35). Broadcasting product information via e-mail or newsgroups is considered by some to be an invasion of their privacy, so you need to be aware of your customers' preferences—these will change from region to region, profession to profession, and country to country.

---

2. Many books are available on this subject, including: *Who Owns Information?*, by Anne Wells Branscomb, Basic Books, 1994; *Who Knows: Safeguarding Your Privacy in a Networked World*, by Don Tapscott, & Ann Cavoukian, Harvard Business School Press, 1996; and *Mind Your Own Business: The Battle for Personal Privacy*, by Gini Graham Scott, Plenum Press, 1995.

Unlike personal privacy, business privacy is fairly well-defined in the legal sense, and businesses have many weapons in their legal war chest to protect the confidentiality of their data. Whenever you're working to establish a business partnership or community of businesses, you need to be able to work out explicitly what data will be shared, and to whom it will be accessible, if you want the project to succeed.

One of the issues surrounding the privacy of individuals and their electronic communications is related to encryption controls. Various branches of the United States government have expressed concern that encrypted, anonymous payment schemes, such as e-cash, would allow easy laundering of money by criminals, as well as tax evasion. These are a few of the reasons why the Executive Branch has been pushing key escrow, sometimes referred to as a third-party key recovery system. (The Clipper chip was one such proposal.) This is a system where in addition to the key pair used in **public key cryptography**, a third encryption key is generated for that session only, and kept by a trusted party for use by government agencies when they see fit. Such circumstances might include tapping encrypted communications between suspect parties. Various organizations committed to preserving an individual's privacy, such as the Electronic Frontier Foundation, have objected to the initial proposals for key escrow and the means by which keys would be made available to government agencies.

Law enforcement and government officials are concerned about the use of encryption and anonymous methods of payment

Under regulations in force in early 1996, software companies in the United States were not allowed to export encryption stronger than 40 bits. Many United States vendors believed this restriction hobbled their ability to offer their products to new markets overseas who were awaiting strong encryption. A new policy came into effect in November 1996, allowing 56-bit encryption technology to be exported,

Encryption export laws exist, and jurisdiction now resides with the Commerce Department but it also required that encryption vendors include techniques for third-party key recovery within the next two years. It was also this new policy that switched jurisdiction over encryption exports from the Justice Department to the Commerce Department.

Encryption can be disabled before shipping and later reactivitated with a token

We're likely to continue to see changes in encryption technologies and export controls for the next few years. For example, as this book went to press, Hewlett Packard had proposed a security system called the International Cryptography Framework (ICF). ICF units are exportable with any type of encryption because the encryption is disabled when shipped, and remains so until activated by a software or hardware token. The purchaser of the product would have to obtain the token from a government-approved server that enforces policies about permissible encryption algorithms and encryption key lengths. So, for example, someone buying an ICF product in Europe would go to a government-approved third party for ICF tokens that enabled 56-bit encryption, while someone in the United States would be able to obtain tokens that enabled 128-bit encryption.

Issues of taxation are complicated by the decentralized nature of the Internet

Issues surrounding sales taxes are particularly problematic, at least for the lawmakers. If a Massachusetts company is using a Web server located in Washington, and an **Internet service provider** (ISP) headquartered in Virginia, which states, if any, are entitled to taxes on the goods or services sold? So far, the issue remains unanswered. States and counties have retreated from attempts to tax the revenues of ISPs and the Treasury Department issued a document in late 1996 recommending that the United States government proceed slowly in taxing Internet-generated revenues and electronic commerce, or risk severely retarding the progress of electronic commerce in its formative stage.

Keeping Pace with the Internet

The Internet is not a static environment. To the contrary, it seems to have introduced an even faster pace of change to the software world than ever before. As more options become available, so too will customer expectations, and the competitive landscape will continue to change. Businesses conducting electronic commerce on the Internet must also be prepared to change as the technologies and markets change, moving from static data publishing, to increased interactivity, to real-time transactions, and finally to a merging of business processes between business partners (see Figure 12-6).

The evolution of business functionality on the Internet.

Figure 12-6

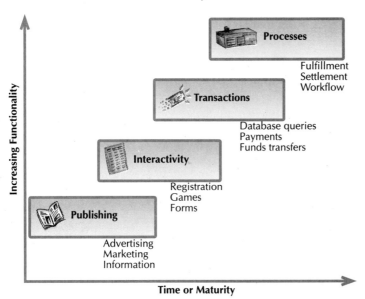

Try to think of the Internet as a new interactive medium of communications when you're planning to incorporate it into your plans for electronic commerce. This means moving beyond the static display of information, which is the way many businesses first used the Web. Static information may

Use the Internet for two-way, interactive communication with customers be of some business value, but the greatest opportunities lie in other, more interactive uses of the Internet.

The increasing ties between multimedia and the Internet are just one example of adding interactivity to Web-based business. In most cases, business sites offering only static published data about products no longer satisfy the needs of their customers. For instance, you've seen how product catalogs can be expanded to include more and more information about products in a greater variety of formats—at AMP Connect and Industry.net, for example, customers can view product specifications and application notes, as well as download wire-frame or rendered **CAD** files for their own designs. With these systems, the data is presented in a dynamic way, customized to the needs or known preferences of the user. The *one size fits all* approach doesn't work on the Internet any more. Interactivity at business sites will continue to increase, tying technologies like Internet telephony and videoconferencing to Web sites, for example.

While interactivity, especially via customer registration and forms-based information transfer, helps the growth of electronic commerce, transactional processing is even more important. Tying information presented on the Web and information exchanged with customers to corporate databases, and moving some of that data to payment systems such as EDI, **ACH**, or **EFT**, all further integrate your processes for efficiency and speed. This can give you a competitive advantage. You'll also find opportunities to link your business processes with your buyer's processes for more efficiency. As partnerships and other business associations expand on the Internet, eventually you'll see the sharing of business processes as well as information. These need not be long-lived associations, as the current business environment seems to be pushing businesses to form short-term associations to get the job done in a dynamic marketplace.

Chapter Thirteen

The Future of Electronic Commerce

Electronic commerce on the Internet is still at an early stage of development. Many of the technologies that form its infrastructures are still experimental or at least not available in the large scale required by the Internet. Also keep in mind that the evolution of electronic commerce will be influenced by all sorts of interested parties (see Figure 13-1). As you'll discover in this chapter, if anything regarding the future of electronic commerce is certain, it's that this situation will soon change for the better.

Figure 13-1

Many different institutions, industries, and other parties with vested interests will affect the progress of electronic commerce.

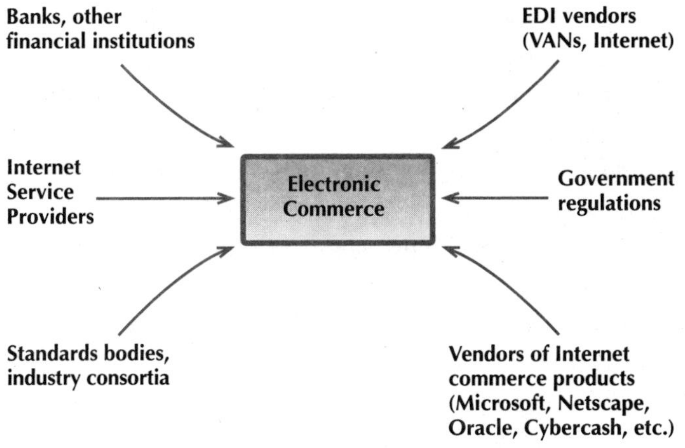

As a close to this book, this last chapter examines some of the developments that will affect electronic commerce in the near term.

Technologies

Because electronic commerce covers so many different aspects of communications and networking, quite a few technologies have an impact on electronic commerce. The following presents pointers on what to look for, and what you will find happening, in the most important of these technologies.

The Internet vs. Private Nets

The stability of the Internet must be considered

So far, the Internet has been able to meet the demands of its users. But 1996 was the first year when some began to question whether the Internet was capable of scaling up further, and whether it could reliably meet the communications demands that will be placed upon it. Highly publicized service outages from respected **Internet service providers**, such as Netcom, AT&T Worldnet, and America Online, have served to raise the possibility of a failure of part of the Internet, bringing into question the robustness of the Internet for business uses.

New protocols are emerging to help reserve bandwidth and prioritize traffic

Protocols are being developed to allow Internet users to reserve bandwidth for applications, and for prioritized traffic. For example, the Resource Reservation Protocol, or RSVP, has been developed to help reserve bandwidth for multimedia transmissions such as streaming audio and video and videoconferencing; this same protocol can be used to reserve bandwidth for other applications as well, such as priority e-mail for **EDI** messages or **FTP** for file transfers. Routers supporting RSVP are only now becoming available; it'll be some time before a great deal of the Internet routinely supports RSVP.

ISPs are also starting to offer their own end-to-end networks that cross the United States independently of the Internet's main backbone, but still link to it as needed. Aimed at businesses, these networks can be used to speed along business traffic with minimal impact from increased consumer Internet traffic. These private commercial networks also make it easier for companies to form **virtual private networks** (VPNs) with added security, replacing private corporate networks that use leased lines. Using these commercial networks can be less costly than leased-line networks, even with the additional rates incurred. Private networks also offer another advantage: they link to the Internet, allowing for communication with other partners and customers without requiring special set ups.

ISPs are building supplementary networks

Because the Internet is an internetwork, or a network of networks, it has both weak and strong links. You should shop around for the best service provider, one that offers service and transmission quality guarantees, good technical support, and is accessible from many locations around the country, or perhaps from around the world. But in the absence of service guarantees from providers, selecting an ISP can be a tough call. As opposed to private networks, traffic can be switched from carrier to carrier as it travels over the Internet, so a single ISP's guarantee of service cannot be expected to encompass the entire Internet. Nevertheless, work is being done to make it easier to choose an ISP. Informal ratings of ISPs coupled with service guarantees from the ISPs are the start.

A good ISP offers quality service, transmission, and technical support

Security

As Chapter 3, "Handling Money on the Net," introduced, there are many options for securing communications on the Internet. A great deal of work is being done with **public key cryptography**, and this will continue to lead in the marketplace. Nevertheless, there is no single dominant solution in a wide field of options and proposals.

The security market
has yet to determine
the most appropriate
level at which
to implement
security options

Part of the problem with the security market is determining at what level of computing and networking to insert security measures (see Figure 13-2). At the moment, solutions are available for use at the application level (such as security protocols for e-mail and the Web), at the session level (**SSL**, for example), and at lower levels in the network (securing IP packet-level transmissions on the Internet, for instance). De facto standards are evolving rapidly; SSL for protecting data transmitted over the Web, and **S/MIME** and **PGP** for protecting e-mail messages.

Figure 13-2   ***Use of security standards in networks.***

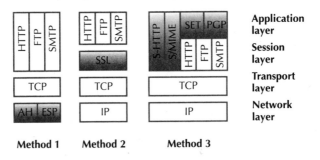

Standards will emerge for sharing encryption algorithms and digital certificates

Many developers of security products have been focusing narrowly on either their individual applications or on a limited range of applications. As we see more applications using cryptography for electronic commerce, we're faced with having to manage multiple **digital certificates** in different formats—at least until some standard is developed. Initiatives like **CryptoAPI** and Intel's **Common Data Security Architecture** (CDSA) are an attempt to provide layered security services that make it easier to share encryption algorithms and digital certificates between applications rather than write the required software from scratch. Initially, CryptoAPI was meant for computers running Microsoft Windows NT or Microsoft Windows 95, while Intel aimed to provide more of a cross-platform solution with CDSA. Eventually, you can expect the two systems to interoperate.

Infrastructures

Although the Internet's infrastructure has evolved over 20 years, it has remained fairly decentralized. Many of the technologies covered in this book have yet to establish the type of robust, secure, easy-to-access, and easy-to-use infrastructure that is required for daily business use. Notable among these components still in an embryonic stage are electronic payment systems, digital certificates, and **public keys**.

For the past few decades, banks and institutions that offer credit cards have created national and global electronic infrastructures for **electronic funds transfers** and credit card authorizations. These infrastructures operate over private networks and, at least for the near term, are unlikely to move to the Internet. But these same institutions are opening **gateways** between their services and the Internet, making it easier for businesses to connect to their systems. These financial infrastructures are reaching out to a larger customer base and offering new services by embracing the Internet as another communications medium, thereby extending their own infrastructures.

Financial institutions are extending their private networks to interface with the Internet

In the meantime, companies like CyberCash, DigiCash, and First Virtual Holdings are trying to create their own Internet-based infrastructures to link buyers and sellers. These infrastructures are also linked to the existing financial systems, either directly through the vendor (CyberCash, for example) or through partnerships with banks. For the moment, these Internet-based systems are independent of each other and lack interoperability, causing buyers and sellers alike to be confused about which systems they should use. Strategic alliances among developers, financial institutions, and other software developers (such as those producing **Web browsers** and **Web servers**) are likely to tip the balance. Initiatives like **JEPI** may help solve this problem, but many commercial developers are going their own individual ways, and may

New commercial endeavors are linking to existing financial systems, but lack of interoperability remains a problem

propose their own solutions before JEPI gets sufficient backing among both developers and users.

Digital cash, in particular, suffers from infrastructure problems because, while it's intended to be the digital equivalent of real cash, each bank issues its own electronic cash **tokens** that are not compatible with systems used by other banks. Worrying about different foreign currencies when you travel from country to county is bad enough, but worrying about exchanging digital cash between banks even within the same country (depending on which bank you use and which merchant you buy goods from) would be intolerable.

This incompatibility of digital cash systems will remain a problem for consumer-to-business commerce for the next few years at least, but it won't necessarily be a problem for business-to-business commerce. EDI is a standardized way of transferring purchasing and financial information, one that is usually negotiated between business partners before any transactions occur. (Of course, the time required to set up EDI has been one of the reasons for its rather limited usage.) This approach of negotiating procedures will extend to other businesses as they use EDI over the Internet, and these businesses are likely to follow similar procedures with payment systems other than EDI. In the absence of suitable infrastructures for these other payment systems, intermediaries such as Nets Inc. will continue to provide standardized methods of handling financial transactions between buyers and sellers.

Digital certificates and **public key** systems have no pre-existing *trust network* comparable to existing financial infrastructures. Everything needed for the distribution and verification of digital certificates is being built from the ground up. Commercial firms like CyberTrust, Nortel, and Verisign are issuing digital certificates to individuals as well as businesses, and they have been ramping up their efforts with electronic commerce on the Internet in mind. However, a fully developed hierarchy of **certificate authorities**, for either the United States or globally, has yet to be established. Furthermore, interoperability between certificate authorities is not guaranteed, as more than one public key algorithm can be, and is, employed.

Other problems arise as public key pairs are issued. The user is the ultimate lynchpin in securing the **private key** of the pair. If the owner of the private key loses the key, or if the key is stolen or compromised in some other way due to the owner's negligence, the key pair must be revocable. The infrastructure required to do this in a routine, fast manner has yet to be fully developed. And there are questions as to whether or not the proposed hierarchy of certificate authorities can be scaled up to handle millions of digital certificates and key pairs as electronic commerce becomes mainstream.

Infrastructures must be built to handle a high volume of digital certificates and key pairs

Online Catalogs
Online catalogs are likely to continue to be an important part of electronic commerce, for both consumer-to-business commerce and business-to-business commerce. Dynamically generated custom catalogs and searches drawing data from corporate databases will be crucial, and will be the standard way of doing things for some time.

Custom catalogs dynamically generated from corporate databases will be the norm

A number of software vendors are offering many different ways of creating and maintaining online catalogs. But very little about the catalogs themselves is standardized. In fact, many may think that catalog standardization is not necessary under the current conditions. After all, customers visit a company's Web site, find out details about the products and services it offers, and decide if their needs will be met. When they visit a different Web site, things might be done a little differently, but the procedures are generally the same.

Some standardiza-
tion in the delivery of
product data is likely

But imagine the benefits if customers could collect data
about related products from a number of different catalogs,
and then compare the products within their own catalog.
That would be possible only if the logic of the catalog and
the form of the product data were standardized in some
way. Intermediaries could also offer the service of creating
custom catalogs (see Figure 13-3) on a scheduled or as-
needed basis. In fact, standardizing this information would
also make it possible for customers to use software agents
that would automatically query different catalogs, collect
product information and present it as a recommendation to
purchase or a comparison of new offerings. Researchers
and developers have started to create and test cataloging
standards so online catalogs will be interoperable. If you're
interested in such a system, check out the Web sites at
CommerceNet and The Fisher Center for Information Technology and Management at the University of California, Berkeley.

Figure 13-3 *A reseller or other cybermediary can compile information from
many manufacturers' catalogs and present them to the buyer.*

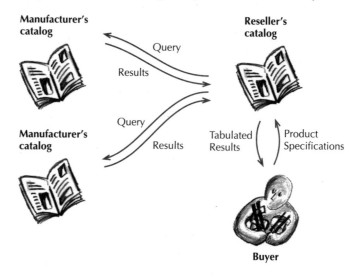

EDI

As discussed in Chapter 3, "Handling Money on the Net," the original electronic commerce applications using networks are commonly referred to as EDI. Many large corporations have implemented EDI, and they are routinely using it with their suppliers to simplify management of their supply chains and the handling of their financial transactions. The Internet offers a low-cost alternative to using a **value added network** (VAN) for transmitting EDI data. By itself, this won't make EDI more appealing to smaller businesses, because they would still need to integrate EDI data with their internal systems, but it will help to further the acceptance of EDI.

Using the Internet for EDI is less expensive than private networks

Three things are happening in the EDI world, partially spurred on by the current popularity of the Internet. First, standards bodies and developers for EDI are extending the standards to simplify negotiations between business partners and to add support for real-time EDI. Second, more vendors are offering products to conduct EDI over the Internet. Finally, VANs themselves are supporting Internet access for conducting EDI.

New EDI products and standards are emerging

Another trend worth following is the move to offer Internet-based electronic commerce and EDI as an integrated package. In some cases, intermediaries such as Nets Inc. are coupling Web browsing of online catalogs with EDI-based **back-end processing**. Other companies, such as Actra and Open-Market, offer Web-based electronic commerce server software that links to EDI systems.

EDI is being integrated with other software

Electronic Mail

Although the World Wide Web has received a lot of focus in this book, other Internet-based services, such as electronic mail, can be equally important to electronic commerce. For example, EDI VANs routinely use e-mail for transferring EDI

New security protocols will make Internet e-mail as secure as EDI e-mail

data between partners. In the past, businesses have been reluctant to use Internet-based e-mail for electronic commerce because it lacks the necessary security, directory services, and other options businesses have come to rely on. But that's changing as newer protocols are being developed by the IETF.

For instance, S/MIME is becoming an ad hoc standard for securing multi-part e-mail, such as EDI documents, on the Internet. This is already being implemented for electronic commerce; Premenos' Templar software and Actra's Business Document Gateway both use S/MIME for transferring EDI data over the Internet.

A protocol for standardized mail receipts is in development

One option that's been missing from Internet e-mail is a standardized way to acknowledge receipt of a message. The protocol for this is still being reviewed by the IETF, but we should see standardized mail receipts for Internet e-mail before long. That, coupled with **digital signatures** and S/MIME, will help make e-mail more robust and suitable for handling non-repudiation and data transfer through the Internet.

Microtransactions

Micropayment pilot studies are in progress

Although **microtransactions** and micropayment schemes have been mentioned a number of times in this book, they are both certainly technologies that are still in their infancy. Limited pilot projects are now underway to test some of the technologies proposed for micropayments. For example, Carnegie Mellon University is now testing in its libraries the NetBill system developed by Professor Marvin Sirbu; and Digital Equipment Corporation's Millicent system was tested in house for most of 1996, with plans for public trials slated for 1997.

CyberCash, with its CyberCoin software, is the first company to offer a commercial system that supports microtrans-actions. Funds for these cash transactions, typically from 25 cents to 10 dollars, are drawn from a consumer's existing bank account. CyberCash has already initiated a number of strategic alliances to support the system—First Union, First USA Paymentech, First Data and its affiliated banks, and Michigan National Bank have already committed to offer or pilot the CyberCoin service in 1996. Headgames (online games) and Quote.Com (real-time stock quotes) are two of the companies planning to use CyberCoin in payment for their services.

Microtransactions using CyberCoin software are also being tested

Expect to see cybermediaries who will handle the process-ing of microtransactions for businesses. ClickShare is an early example of such a cybermediary, accumulating charges on information that's purchased from electronic publishers located at their site. Future cybermediaries will probably not restrict their clients to a single Web site, al-though consolidation at a site can be a good move for marketing and advertising.

Cybermediaries are likely to handle transaction processing

Software Agents

One of the hot, and perhaps over-hyped, technologies advanced over the past few years has been software agents, self-learning programs that users can instruct to perform acts on their behalf. A variety of uses for software agents have been proposed. Two of immediate interest to electronic commerce are retrieving select product information and negotiating the sale of an item.

An Internet software agent developed by Arthur Anderson Inc. has already demonstrated the first task; their software agent accesses data from various Web-based audio CD dealers to find the best price for a particular selection.

Software agents for comparison-shopping already exist

Similar agents could be constructed to visit numerous online catalogs, extract information on selected products, and present that data to the user in a personalized buyer's catalog (see Figure 13-4). Sales negotiations are a more complex process, and agents capable of performing such tasks are still in the research phase. Much of this work is being done at Stanford University and CommerceNet.

Figure 13-4 *A buyer can instruct a software agent to find and compare product information from multiple catalogs.*

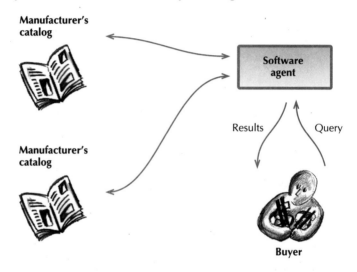

Manufacturer's catalog

Software agent

Results Query

Manufacturer's catalog

Buyer

Smart Cards

Smart cards will evolve to include embedded micro-processors

Although **smart cards** have been around for more than a decade, they have not yet seen widespread use. Pre-paid or stored-value cards are currently in use for public telephones, tollbooths, and mass transit systems in the United States and overseas. But the real impact of electronic commerce, especially tied to the Internet, will come with the development of smart cards that include an embedded microprocessor. These smart cards will not only be used for Internet-based purchases, but will also be able to serve as electronic purses that can be used for everyday purchases at stores.

The technology to support electronic commerce using smart cards is still being developed, and it is being field-tested on a limited basis. Mondex International (in which MasterCard recently bought a majority interest) is conducting one of the largest field trials in England. The Mondex smart cards use the digital cash system developed by David Chaum and DigiCash.

Smart card technology is being tested in England

Another major effort is the CAFE project, involving the European Commission, DigiCash, Siemens, Ingenico, and other European companies. Their goal is to use smart card technology to provide a means for representing the European currency unit (ECU) as a common medium of exchange throughout Europe.

Smart cards have yet to make a significant impact on consumer markets, but the pieces to make that possible are now starting to be put in place. For example, Verifone, one of the leaders in the point-of-sales hardware market for merchants, has developed a low-cost smart card terminal for merchants as well as a smart card reader that attaches to a user's personal computer. The Personal ATM is a countertop device about the size of a human hand, which lets consumers use a phone line to download money into a smart card in their home. Hayes Microcomputer Products, Inc. has also created the SmartCard Modem that allows users to use a phone line to update personal smart cards.

Soon you will be able to download money to your smart card from home

Institutions

Technology alone doesn't provide answers to all of the problems. Whatever develops will have to function within society. Making electronic commerce really work will depend as much on what our governing and financial institutions do, as it will on the technologies that develop.

Centers of Trust

Trust between buyer and seller is an important element in all financial transactions, but it is difficult to establish in electronic commerce. When businesses conduct commerce with one another, reputations can be checked and verified independently of the Internet. Business-to-business deals that are electronic extensions of real-world deals already have an element of trust that's built upon previous negotiations and transactions.

That same trust is more difficult to establish in consumer-to-business commerce on the Internet. You may know the old joke that no one knows you're a dog on the Internet. Now take that a step further for online, commercial transactions—how can one get a sense of a potential business partner from its electronic storefront or from an e-mail exchange? Could that partner be a dog? If all a purchasing manager knows about a supplier comes from what can be seen on that supplier's Web site, he or she has every right to be somewhat suspicious.

On those occasions when the Internet is the sole link between parties, where the transaction is abstract (no signing of a paper check or handing over of a receipt, for instance), more has to be done to establish trust in the relationship. Digital certificates and digital signatures for transactions may well handle some of this. Another possibility is for customers to deal with Internet merchants who are certified by a neutral, trusted party. eTrust is the first such attempt at certifying trusted merchants on the Internet, with a full-scale program planned for 1997. Other organizations will join eTrust before long.

Even with certifications, merchants and other Internet-based sellers will have a difficult time establishing the same level of trust with a buyer as banks enjoy. At least for consumer-based electronic commerce, you may well see banks leveraging the public's trust by offering them more and more commercial services.

Cybermediaries

You can expect to see more cybermediaries, and new types of intermediaries, pursuing electronic commerce on the Internet. Rather than cutting out the middleman, as some gurus have predicted, electronic commerce will require new intermediaries, mainly because the information space is so complicated and unstructured. Consider the Web, for example. Even with search engines like Yahoo, Lycos, Info-Seek, and Alta Vista, finding the needed information can be difficult. And the Web is still growing at an incredible rate, which will only make this glut of information (the infoglut) worse. Time is always at a premium, so if you can get someone to do a task for you, or even part of a task, you'll come out ahead—and that's the function of an intermediary.

Lots of people will save time by using intermediaries to find what they need on line

Cybermediaries will be able to exist even in the presence of software agents. You might think that a software agent capable of constructing a buyer's catalog for an individual would eliminate the need for an intermediary. But the likelihood is that intermediaries, such as Nets Inc., will serve as information sources for the agents. They may also employ agents of their own for special uses. In any case, the two will coexist.

Even software agents will not soon replace intermediaries

Governments

When it comes to money and commerce, governments always have something to say. You've already seen that government agencies are struggling to balance an indi-

The Clipper Chip is not yet dead

vidual's right to privacy with the need to monitor illegal actions, such as money laundering. The United States government's attempt to require the Clipper chip in new communications devices was originally defeated, but it's an ongoing battle with new variations.

Key escrow may eventually garner support

Governmental restrictions on exporting encryption software and hardware have eased slightly, but still keep the global marketplace from being a level playing field. Key escrow, having the government or a trusted third party keep a master encryption key, may be a solution but it has not yet received popular support from developers or other nations.

Final Market Forecast

As a final glance into the future, here's a brief look at markets for electronic commerce.

The consumer market for electronic commerce will explode when a personal computer is no longer required

The consumer-to-business market will continue to grow, driven by purchases of home computers and other Web-enabled devices (such as WebTV), as well as developments in new media for delivering increased bandwidth. For example, work is moving ahead on **cable modems**, Digital Subscriber Lines (DSL), satellite access, and even Asynchronous Transfer Mode (ATM) to the home. Consumer acceptance of electronic commerce will increase when it no longer requires the use of a personal computer; when electronic commerce extends to non-computer devices such as televisions, automatic teller machines, point-of-sale terminals, and other devices linked to smart cards (see Figure 13-5). These efforts will take us into the next decade.

Tomorrow's payment systems will allow the consumer to make purchases in many ways.

Figure 13-5

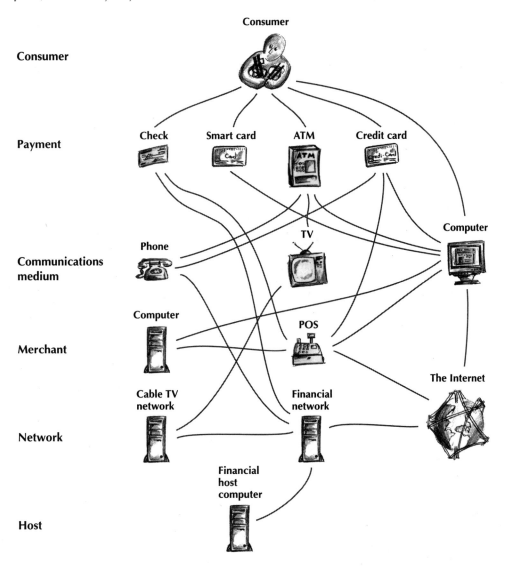

Consumer

Consumer

Payment

Check   Smart card   ATM   Credit card

Computer

Communications medium

Phone

TV

Merchant

Computer

POS

The Internet

Network

Cable TV network

Financial network

Host

Financial host computer

Businesses will
integrate EDI with
the Internet and
adopt new electronic
payment systems

In the business-to-business market, short-term partnering
and more supplier associations will drive the need for faster
ways of conducting supply and financial transactions
(see Figure 13-6). EDI on the Internet will have its place, if
only because of the installed base of EDI and its prior integration with business practices. But other systems will be
equally important, as corporate purchasing cards and other
electronic systems of payment are integrated with business
processes, either directly or through intermediaries.

Figure 13-6   *Transactions will be enhanced by electronic partnering.*

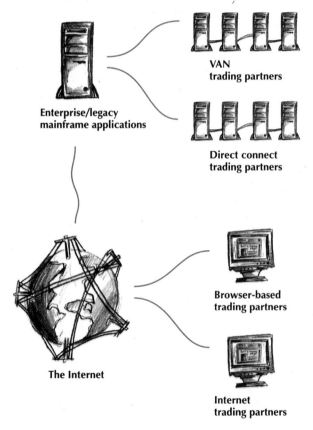

Enterprise/legacy
mainframe applications

VAN
trading partners

Direct connect
trading partners

The Internet

Browser-based
trading partners

Internet
trading partners

Whatever happens, the future of electronic commerce will
be exciting and full of opportunities.

Glossary

ACH *See* **Automated Clearing House**.

ADSL *See* **asymmetrical digital subscriber line**.

ARP The address resolution protocol operates on the network layer and works to help network devices determine an IP address. *See also* **IP address**.

asymmetrical digital subscriber line A protocol for providing high rates of data delivery (6–9 Mbps) over existing copper phone lines.

asymmetric cryptography A cryptographic system where encryption and decryption are performed using different keys. *See also* **public key cryptography**.

Automated Clearing House One of a series of highly reliable nationwide electronic funds transfer systems governed by operating rules which provide for the interbank clearing of electronic payments for participating financial institutions

back-end processes Computing applications running and using data stored on large mainframe computers and other legacy computers or servers.

blind signatures This system, developed by DigiCash, allows a buyer to obtain e-cash from a bank without the bank being able to correlate the buyer's name with the tokens it issues.

cable modem A device that offers data transmission bandwidths of up to 30 Mbps over existing cable TV wiring.

CAD An abbreviation for computer-assisted design.

CAM An abbreviation for computer-assisted manufacturing.

CDSA *See* **Common Data Security Architecture**.

certificate authority A trusted company or organization that will accept your public key, along with some proof of your identity, and serve as a repository of digital certificates. Others can then request verification of your public key from the certificate authority. *See also* **digital certificate**.

certificate revocation list Certificate authorities must maintain a list of digital certificates that are no longer valid (not including those expired). *See also* **certificate authority**.

CGI script Common Gateway Interface is a scripting system designed to work with HTTP Web servers. The scripts, usually written in the Perl coding language, are often used to exchange data between a Web server and databases. *See also* **hypertext transfer protocol**; **Web server**.

cipher A set of rules used to transform original information into its coded form.

cipher text The encoded form of a message.

commoditization The process whereby products begin to look similar, their value decreases, and prices go down. Products valued as commodities do not appear to be anything special, and are often sold in price wars.

Common Data Security Architecture Intel's cross-platform applications programming interface that operates at the system level to provide developers with a means of calling cryptographic functions, such as encryption algorithms, through a standardized interface. Some of the companies implementing CDSA in their products include Netscape, Datakey, VASCO Data Security, and Verisign.

CryptoAPI Microsoft's applications programming interface that operates at the system level to provide Windows developers with a means of calling cryptographic functions, such as encryption algorithms, through a standardized interface. Because it's modular, CryptoAPI allows developers to substitute one cryptographic algorithm for another, according to their needs. CryptoAPI also includes options for processing and managing digital certificates. *See also* **digital certificate**.

cryptographic algorithm A mathematical function that combines plain text or other intelligible information with a string of digits (called a key) to produce unintelligible cipher text. *See also* **cipher text**; **key**.

Data Encryption Standard An algorithm or block cipher that uses a 56-bit key and operates on a block of 64 bits. Created by IBM and endorsed by the United States government in 1977, the data encryption standard is relatively fast and often used to encrypt large amounts of data at one time. *See also* **cipher**; **key**.

DCE *See* **distributed computing environment protocols**.

DES *See* **Data Encryption Standard**.

Diffie-Hellman A system designed to allow two individuals to agree on a shared key, even though they only exchange messages in public. This oldest public-key cryptosystem is still in use, but does not support either encryption or digital signatures.

digital cash An electronic replacement for cash.

digital certificate A electronic document, issued by a certificate authority, used to establish a company's identity by verifying its public key. *See also* **certificate authority**.

digital signature This special signature for signing electronic correspondence is produced by encrypting the message digest with the sender's private key. *See also* **message digest**; **private key**.

Digital Signature Algorithm Developed by NIST, this system is based on the El Gamal algorithm. The signature scheme uses the same sort of keys as Diffie-Hellman and can create signatures faster than RSA. (Also known as DSS, or the Digital Signature Standard.)

Digital Signature Standard *See* **Digital Signature Algorithm**.

distributed computing environment protocols DCE protocols define how software objects or modules are stored and can interact across a network. DCE is often used to provide a common interface to networked applications and to provide authentication for network services.

DNS *See* **domain naming service**.

domain naming service This is the network service responsible for converting numeric IP addresses into text-based names. *See also* **IP address**.

DSA *See* **Digital Signature Algorithm**.

DSS *See* **Digital Signature Algorithm**.

EDI *See* **electronic data interchange**.

EFT *See* **electronic fund transfer**.

electronic data interchange The electronic exchange of business documents (such as purchase orders, quotations, bills of lading, and invoices) between companies' computer applications in a standardized form. EDI systems are primarily used by companies wanting to communicate with their suppliers.

electronic fund transfer A system that optimizes the transfer of electronic payments, including remittance information, over secure private networks between banks. Direct deposit of employee paychecks into their bank accounts is one example of the use of EFT.

extranet Two or more intranets connected using TCP/IP; also called shared nets. *See also* **intranet**.

FDDI *See* **fiber distributed data interface**.

FEDI *See* **financial EDI**.

feedback marketing *See* **relationship marketing**.

fiber distributed data interface A standard for 100-Mbps fiber optic networks.

file transfer protocol The protocol used for file transfers between file servers and client computers on the Internet. Depending on your software, you can select files one by one and upload or download them, or you can create a list of files and transfer them as a batch.

financial EDI This system is typically set up between banks and their corporate customers to allow the banks to receive payment authorizations from payers, and make payment settlements to payees. So far FEDI is used strictly for business-to-business transactions.

firewalls Firewalls implement access controls based on the contents of the packets of data that are transmitted between two parties or devices on the network. By providing a single point of control for security on a network, firewalls can provide protection against attacks on individual protocols or applications, and can be effective in protecting against spoofing. Firewalls cannot provide privacy or authentication, nor can they protect a network against viruses. *See also* **packet**; **spoofing**.

front-end processes Computer applications running on client computers connected to servers or legacy mainframe computers.

FTP *See* **file transfer protocol**.

gateway A software program used to connect two networks using different protocols so that they can transfer data between the two. Before transferring, the program converts the data into a protocol-compatible form.

hard goods Physical products, that is, those you can touch and see.

HTML *See* **HyperText Markup Language**.

HTTP *See* **hypertext transfer protocol**.

HyperText Markup Language A standard set of codes used to define Web documents. The browser on the user's computer looks at the HTML to determine how the text, graphics, and other multimedia elements should be displayed.

hypertext transfer protocol This protocol determines how an HTML file is transferred from server to client on the World Wide Web.

IDEA *See* **International Data Encryption Algorithm**.

IMAP *See* **Internet Mail Access Protocol.**

Integrated Services Digital Network This worldwide, totally digital communications network, evolving from existing telephone services, offers greater bandwidth than normal telephone lines, which are slower and require digital-to-analog conversions.

International Data Encryption Algorithm This encryption algorithm, created in 1991, offers very strong encryption using a 128-bit key.

Internet Mail Access Protocol A newer protocol used to handle the retrieval of messages.

Internet protocol This protocol works on the network layer to provide an address space for internetworks, and to handle the routing of packets across an internetwork. *See also* **ARP**; **packet**.

Internet service providers Companies that provide customers with connections to the Internet.

intranet An internal TCP/IP network used for sharing information within the corporation.

IP *See* **Internet protocol**.

IP address A numeric address that identifies a computer on the network.

ISDN *See* **Integrated Services Digital Network**.

ISPs *See* **Internet service providers**.

Java Electronic Commerce Framework This is a series of Java libraries, from Sun Microsystems, that include wallet and security options to help Java programmers handle electronic payments. *See also* **wallet**.

JECF *See* **Java Electronic Commerce Framework**.

JEPI *See* **Joint Electronic Payments Initiative**.

Joint Electronic Payments Initiative This initiative, led by the World Wide Web Consortium and CommerceNet, is an attempt to standardize payment negotiations. On the buyer's side (the client side), JEPI serves as an interface that enables a Web browser, and wallets, to use a variety of payment protocols. On the merchant's side (the server side), JEPI acts between the network and transport layers to pass off the incoming transactions to the proper transport and payment protocols.

key A string of digits, which when used with a cryptographic algorithm, produces cipher text. *See also* **cipher text**.

marketspace A new term for the market where electronic commerce is conducted. It encompasses the transition from physically defined markets to markets based on, and controlled by, information.

mass customization *See* **relationship marketing**.

MD5 An algorithm used for encryption.

message digest The representation of a body of text as a single string of digits created using a one-way hash function. *See also* **one-way hash function**.

microcash Small denomination digital tokens.

micromerchants Those who offer their wares on the Internet in exchange for e-cash or digital cash.

microsegmentation Using more and more detailed customer preferences to delineate smaller market groups.

microtransactions Low-cost, real-time transactions using microcash.

middleware Transaction processing software that enables a client computer application to access data from multiple databases.

MIME *See* **multimedia Internet mail extensions**.

multimedia Internet mail extensions An e-mail message using the MIME protocol can consist of more than one part; these parts might be graphics, video or sound clips, or other types of multimedia. This e-mail protocol extends the capabilities of earlier e-mail messaging protocols.

NAPs *See* **network access points**.

network access points On-ramps to the high-speed Internet backbone maintained by Sprint, PacBell, MFS, and others.

one-way hash function This is a formula used to convert a message of any length into a string of digits called a message digest. The length of the function determines the length of the digest, and no key is required. *See also* **key**; **message digest**.

OpenEDI A recent series of specifications designed to make EDI transactions simpler to specify and set up, as well as to use over the Internet. These specifications may make it possible for businesses of all sizes to use EDI over the Internet. *See also* **electronic data interchange**.

packet The fundamental grouping of data for transmission on a digital network. A packet consists of a sequence of bits that includes control information for transmitting the data, as well as the data itself.

PDA *See* **personal digital assistant**.

PEM *See* **privacy-enhanced mail**.

personal digital assistant Small portable electronic computing device.

PGP *See* **Pretty Good Privacy.**

points-of-presence Local access points to a national or international communications network. Users dial into their networks by calling local phone numbers, rather than a toll-free number or a long-distance call to a centralized location. Both commercial service providers (such as AOL) and Internet service providers maintain POPs. *See also* **Internet service providers**.

point-to-point protocol This protocol governs TCP/IP transmissions over serial (modem) connections. *See also* **Internet protocol; transmission control protocol**.

POP *See* **post office protocol**.

POPs *See* **points-of-presence**.

post office protocol One of the most essential Internet protocols for e-mail, POP is used to handle the retrieval of messages. *See also* **Internet Mail Access Protocol** and **simple mail transport protocol**.)

PPP *See* **point-to-point protocol**.

Pretty Good Privacy PGP security applications for Internet e-mail use a variety of encryption standards and are freely available for all major operating systems. Messages can be encrypted before using an e-mail program, and some mail programs can use special PGP plug-in modules to handle encrypted mail.

privacy-enhanced mail An Internet standard for securing e-mail using either public keys or symmetric keys. PEM cannot handle the newer multipart e-mail supported by MIME, and it requires a rigid hierarchy of certificate authorities for issuing keys. *See also* **public key; symmetric encryption**.

private key A key used to encrypt a message but kept private to the originator.

protocols The rules that determine everything about the way a network operates. Protocols govern how applications access the network, the way data from an application is divided into packets for transmission through a cable, and which electrical signals represent data on a network cable.

proxy server Proxy servers adopt a store-and-forward approach to protecting crucial data and applications. They terminate the incoming connection from the source and initiate a second connection to the destination, insuring that the incoming user has appropriate access rights to use data requested from the destination before passing that data on to the user.

public key The key used by a message's recipient to decrypt a message; can be divulged to as large an extent as is necessary or convenient.

public key cryptography An encryption method that uses a pair of keys: one public and one private. Messages encoded with either key can be decoded by the other. Public-key cryptography uses asymmetric encryption algorithms. *See also* **asymmetric cryptography**.

RC2 and **RC4** These algorithms, designed by Ron Rivest (the R in RSA Data Security Inc.), use variable key size ciphers for very fast bulk encryption. A little faster than DES, the two algorithms can be made more secure by selecting a longer key size. RC2 is a block cipher and can be used in place of DES. RC4 is a stream cipher and is as much as 10 times faster than DES. *See also* **ciphers**; **Data Encryption Standard**.

relationship marketing Creating custom relationships with each individual customer.

RSA This public-key encryption algorithm (named after its designers, Rivest, Shamir, and Adelman of RSA Data Security Inc.) supports a variable key length as well as variable blocksize of the text to be encrypted. The plain text block must be smaller than the key length. The common key length is 512 bits. *See also* **public key**.

secret-key cryptography *See* **symmetric encryption**.

Secured Electronic Transaction Developed by the MasterCard/VISA consortium, SET is a combination of a protocol designed for use by other applications (such as Web browsers) and a standard (recommended procedures) for handling credit-card transactions over the Internet.

secure hypertext transfer protocol Designed specifically to support the hypertext transfer protocol, S-HTTP provides authentication for servers and browsers, as well as confidentiality and data integrity for communications between a Web server and a browser.

secure multimedia Internet mail extensions This is a newer proposed standard that uses many of the cryptographic algorithms patented and licensed by RSA Data Security Inc. S/MIME depends on digital certificates, and thus also depends on some kind of certificate authority, whether it be corporate or global, to ensure authentication.

secure sockets layer Like S-HTTP, this protocol provides authentication for servers and browsers, as well as confidentiality and data integrity for communications between a Web server and a browser. However, SSL secures the communications channel by operating lower in the network stack—between the application layer and the TCP/IP transport and network layers. SSL can be used for transactions other than those on the Web, but it's not designed to handle security decisions based on authentication at the application or document level.

secure wide-area networks These protocols include methods for authentication and encryption of packets, as well as a method for exchanging and managing the keys required for the authentication and encryption processes. S/WAN protocols also help to insure interoperability between router and firewall vendors.

SET *See* **Secured Electronic Transaction**.

S-HTTP *See* **secure hypertext transfer protocol**.

simple mail transport protocol One of the most essential Internet protocols for transferring e-mail between servers. *See also* **post office protocol**.

simple network management protocol This protocol is used for controlling network devices such as routers, bridges, and switching hubs.

smart cards A credit card-sized plastic card with a special type of integrated circuit embedded in it. The integrated circuit holds information in electronic form and controls who uses this information and how.

S/MIME *See* **secure multimedia Internet mail extensions**.

SMTP *See* **simple mail transport protocol**.

SNMP *See* **simple network management protocol**.

spoofing This is when one party masquerades as someone else on line.

SSL *See* **secure sockets layer**.

S/WAN *See* **secure wide-area networks**.

symmetric encryption Using this method, both the sender and the recipient possess the same key, which means that both parties can encrypt and decrypt data with that key. *See also* **asymmetric cryptography**.

TCP *See* **transmission control protocol**.

TCP/IP Protocols These protocols define how data is subdivided into packets for transmission, and how applications can transfer files and send electronic mail. *See also* **Internet protocols; protocols; transmission control protocol.**

telnet The Internet standard for terminal emulation and remote host access.

tokens Strings of digits representing a certain amount of currency. The issuing bank validates each token with a digital stamp.

TPAs *See* **trading partner agreements**.

trading partner agreements Specifications agreed upon by two or more companies doing business together which define the forms of the data that will be exchanged via EDI.

transactional commerce Customer-specific transactions that integrate real-time interactivity (such as the generation of Web pages on the fly) with information in corporate databases.

transmission control protocol This protocol determines the maximum transmission size (that is, the packet size) and fine tunes transmissions accordingly. It is used when 100 percent reliability of the transmission is required. *See also* **packet; user datagram protocol**.

Triple DES An algorithm based on DES. This method encrypts a block of data three times, with three different keys. *See also* **Data Encryption Standard**.

UDP *See* **user datagram protocol**.

uniform resource locator The means for identifying a resource on the Internet. A URL begins with the name of the protocol needed to get the data from the server, followed by the text name of the resource. For example, a Web page is a resource located on the Internet and it requires the use of the HTTP protocol. So, the URL for Microsoft's technical support home page is http://www.microsoft.com/support/mtshome.htm. A URL can include the IP address of a resource in lieu of the text name, for example: ftp://130.43.6.3 (which is ftp.support.apple.com). *See also* **IP address**; **protocols**.

URL *See* **uniform resource locator**.

user datagram protocol This protocol determines the maximum transmission size (that is, the packet size) and fine tunes transmissions accordingly. It is used when 100 percent reliability of the transmission is not required. *See also* **packet; transmission control protocol**.

value added networks Networks that are maintained privately and dedicated to EDI between business partners.

virtual corporation An entity composed of geographically disperse workers who share their work and communicate only by electronic means, with little, if any, face-to-face contact.

virtual private networks Networks that are essentially private, but use the Internet in lieu of expensive leased phone lines between offices.

VPNs *See* **virtual private networks**.

wallet A helper application for a Web browser used to pass an encrypted credit card number from a buyer, through the sales merchant, and on to the server maintained by the credit company (CyberCash or Verifone, for example) for authentication and approval. *See also* **Web browser**.

Web browser A software program that allows you to connect with network servers in order to access HTML documents and their associated media files (that is, Web pages) and to follow links from document to document, or page to page. The server may be on a private network or the Internet. Helper applications (such as a wallet) can be incorporated with the browser to handle special file types and applications. *See also* **HyperText Markup Language**; **Web server**.

Web server A software program that manages data at the Web site, controls access to that data, and responds to requests from Web browsers. *See also* **Web browsers**.

Index

I

ICF (International Cryptography Framework), 242

IDEA (International Data Encryption Algorithm), 82

identification, 67

IEEE (Institute of Electrical and Electronic Engineers), 221

IETF (Internet Engineering Task Force), 221, 222

IIS (Internet Information Server), 119

IMAP (Internet Mail Access Protocol), 32

implementation issues, 230, 233–37
  CITIS (Contractor Integrated Technical Information Service) system, 206–11
  open standards, 207–8
  providing services, 208–10
  security issues, 210–11

Industrial Locator, 134

Industry Net, 134

Industry.net, 133–49, 244. See also Nets Inc.
  advantages of moving to the Web, 135
  association communities and, 142
  background of, 134
  buying members and selling clients in, 136
  description of Web site, 136–42
  implementation of Web site, 136–39
  levels of Web services on, 138
  listings of engineering specialties, 140–42
  as Web hosting service, 135

Industry.net Report, 146

information
  fulfillment and, 16
  strategies for integrating electronic commerce and, 219–20
  virtual value chains and, 103–6

information pull, customer-initiated, 240

information sharing, 12–14, 113–14

infrastructure, future developments in, 249–51

Institute of Electrical and Electronic Engineers (IEEE), 221

institutions, future of electronic commerce and, 257–60

integrators, 109, 110

integrity, 38

interactive communications, 237, 243–44
  customer relations and, 227
  push vs. pull marketing and, 239

intermediaries (brokers), 14, 19, 109–13, 204. See also cybermediaries
  new types of, 112
  services offered by, 144–45
  sharing information with, 17

International Cryptography Framework (ICF), 242

International Standards Organization (ISO), 28

International Telecommunications Union (ITU), 221

Internet, the. See also electronic commerce; World Wide Web (the Web); and specific topics
  application protocols, 30–32
  business market on, 1, 2–3, 37, 89, 90, 101–2. See also electronic commerce
  future of, 262
  online communities and, 114–16
  communities based in (See online communities)
  consumer market on, 89–101. See also electronic commerce
  acceptance of new technologies in, 97–101
  custom relationships with customers, 92, 96
  demographics and, 93–95
  future of, 260
  growth of, 91
  Internet access methods and, 93
  loyalty of customers and, 95–97
  corporate image and, 226
  evolution of business functionality on, 107–244
  future of (See future of electronic commerce)
  network infrastructure of, 27–32
  network protocols, 28–30
  security systems (See security)
  structure and growth of, 23–27
  tracking innovations related to, 220–24

Internet DMZ, 191

Microsoft Internet Information Server (IIS), 119, 127

Microsoft Merchant Server, 119, 120, 122, 125–28

microtransactions, 54, 237
 future developments in, 254–55

middleware, 62

Millicent system, 254

MIME (Multimedia Internet Mail Extensions), 32

Mondex International, 257

multimedia, 94, 244

N

NAPs (Network Access Points), 23–24

National Automated Clearing House Association, 51

National Institute for Standards and Technology (NIST), 82, 149, 217

NetBill system, 254

Nets Inc., 133, 136, 232, 236. See also Industry.net
 building on an existing client base, 142–43
 catalogs, 136–37, 144
 database approach of, 136–38
 development philosophy of, 147
 future plans of, 147
 long-running transaction and, 145–46
 market models, 144, 145
 as a one-stop shop, 143

Network Access Points (NAPs), 23–24

networks. See also Internet, the
 cable television, 34
 in general, 4–5
 infrastructure of, 27–32
 other than the Internet, 32–34
 private, 246–47
 telecommunications, 34

newsgroups, 12

non-repudiation, 67, 70

O

OneServer Web server software, 158

one-way hash functions, 73–74

online catalogs (See catalogs, online)

online communities, 109, 112–16, 133
 buying members and selling clients in, 136
 of interest, 238–39

OnNET, 85

OpenEDI, 57

open market model, 144, 145

open standards, 220
 CITIS implementation and, 207–8

open systems, 28

Oracle Corporation, 107

ordering systems, 14
 Broder Bros., 154
 Fruit of the Loom, 160–62
 Gateway, 117–30
 just-in-time (JIT), 167

order tracking, 120

O'Reilly's WebBoard, 155

O'Reilly's WebSite server program, 155

organizational issues, 230–33

OSI Reference Model, 28

P

packets, 28

payment systems, 14–16, 26–27, 35
 Nets Inc.'s, 147–49
 requirements of, 38–41
 tools for implementation of, 60–62
 types of, 41–59
  credit cards, 42–48
  digital cash, 51–55
  EDI (electronic data interchange), 56–59
  electronic checks, 49–51

Pay-Per-Incident (PPI) system, Microsoft, 188–91, 193, 194, 198–200

PDA (personal digital assistant), 41

peer-to-peer communications, 28

PEM (Privacy- Enhanced Mail), 85

Personal ATM, 257

PGP (Pretty Good Privacy), 80–81, 85

PNC Bank Corp., 147, 148
POP (Post Office Protocol), 32
POPs (Points-of-Presence), 134
PPP (Point-to-Point Protocol), 30
privacy, 39, 40, 66, 67
  business, 241
  digital cash and, 51
  personal, legal issues, 240, 241
private networks, the Internet vs., 246–47
product data sheets, 15
protocols
  application, 30–32
  network, 28
    TCP/IP, 24, 29, 30, 32, 208
  security-related, 45, 47
public-key cryptography, 70–74, 251
  certificate authorities and, 76
  distribution of public key, 74–76
purchase order, 7
push vs. pull marketing, 239

R

RC2, 82
RC4, 82
registration, online, eliciting customer
    profiles by using, 178
Rivest, Ron, 82
RSA, 82
RSVP (Resource Reservation Protocol), 246

S

sales cycle, electronic commerce vs.
    traditional, 3–4, 9
sales taxes, 242
Sanmar, 169
Schneier, Bruce, 79
searching the AMP Connect Web site, 178–
    81
secret-key encryption (symmetric encryp-
    tion), 69–70
Secure HTTP (S-HTTP), 83, 84
Secure MIME (S/MIME), 83–85, 254
Secure Sockets Layer (SSL), 83, 84

Secure Wide Area Networks (S/WAN), 83, 87
security, 65–88, 232–33. See also encryption
    (cryptography)
  CITIS system and, 210–11
  digital cash and, 55
  digital certificates, 74–77
  future developments in, 247–48
  Internet security systems, 81–87
    common key algorithms, 82
    e-mail protocols, 84–85
    firewalls, 85–87
    Web application protocols, 84
  Internet standards, 83
  Microsoft customer support system and,
    190–95, 199
  threats and solutions, 65, 66
security-related protocols, 45, 47
segmentation of market niches, 238
service and support (See customer service
    and support)
SET (Secured Electronic Transaction)
    protocol, 27, 47, 63, 83
shippers, 16
shipping order, 7, 8
shopping cart metaphor, 126–27
S-HTTP (Secure HTTP), 84
signatures
  blind, 52
  digital, 39, 73
Sirbu, Marvin, 254
SmartCard Modem, 257
smart cards, 41, 256–57
S/MIME (Secure MIME), 83–85, 254
SMTP (Simple Mail Transport Protocol), 32
Snickelways Interactive, 152, 154, 155, 157,
    160, 169
SNMP (Simple Network Management
    Protocol), 31
software agents, 255–56, 259
software.net, 5
spoofing, 86
Spot Shop, The (Gateway), 120, 123, 125–26
SSL (Secure Sockets Layer) protocol, 45, 83,
    84, 211
standards
  Internet, 220–23
  open, 220

CITIS implementation and, 207–8
surveys, customer, 14
S/WAN (Secure Wide Area Networks), 83, 87
symmetric encryption, 69–70

T

TCP (Transmission Control Protocol), 30
TCP/IP protocols, 24, 29, 30, 208
  for intranets and extranets, 32
technical support (See customer support)
technologies, future, 246–57
Technology Adoption Life Cycle, 97–98
telecommunications networks, 34
tokens, digital cash and, 52, 54
TPAs (Trading Partner Agreements), 56
traditional commerce, 3–4
transactional commerce, 108
transactional processing, 234, 244
Transaction Manager software, 193
transaction processing software, 62
transactions, 36–38. See also payment
    systems
  traditional vs. electronic business, 4, 7–10
Triple DES, 82
trust
  future of electronic commerce and, 258–
  59
  online communities and, 113, 250
trust network, 250

U

UCAR Composites, 212–13
UDP (User Datagram Protocol), 30
unexpected buying, 143

V

value chains, 102–6
  virtual, 103–6, 219, 224–25, 227, 228
value matrix, 228
VANs (Value Added Networks), 33, 38, 56
  future developments in, 253

Vendor Management Inventory (VMI) system,
  Fruit of the Loom, 152, 167
Verifone, 45, 46, 257
virtual corporation, 203
virtual factory, 203–4
VirtualPIN, 45
Virtual Private Networks (VPNs), 34, 87, 247
virtual value chains, 103–6, 219, 224–25,
  227, 228
Visa, 27, 47
VMARK's HyperSTAR middleware, 155
VMI (Vendor Management Inventory), 152,
  167
VPNs (Virtual Private Networks), 34, 87, 247

W

wallet (helper application), 44, 45
Web applications, security protocols for, 84
WebBoard, 155
Web browsers, 36
  defined, 13n
Web hosting services, 61, 135
web of trust, concept of a, 85
Web Response System, 188–91, 193–200
Web servers, defined, 13n
Web sites
  AeroTech Service Group, 211–15
  AMP Connect, 178–81
  Fruit of the Loom, 160–63
    full-scale development of Web site,
    157– 60
    pilot Web project, 152–56
  Gateway 2000, 120–21, 123–26
  Industry.net
    description of Web site, 136–42
    implementation, 136–39
  Microsoft customer support system, 195–
    98
WebSite server program, 155
World Wide Web (the Web), 12

X

X Windows, 209

Dave Kosiur

rejoined the world of writing about technology full time in 1996. In earlier lives, his work spanned the widest range of timescales possible. When studying oceanic and geochemical reactions, his time frames spanned thousands of years, but when working as a marketing analyst for Internet software, he responded to the constant changes so common to the Internet. Somewhere along the way, he's managed to combine the long-term views of geology with the fast-paced business developments of PC and Internet software. Dave got his start writing about technology while working for Chevron Corporation before moving on to produce *Connections*, a technical newsletter on Macintosh networking, for five years. After writing *the* award-winning reference on Mac networking, *The Macworld Networking Bible* (IDG Books, 1992; 2nd edition, 1995) and selling his newsletter, Dave turned his full-time attention to the Internet in 1992. Dave's articles regularly appear in *PC Week*, *Sunworld Online*, and *ZD Internet Magazine*. In addition to electronic commerce, he's been focusing on electronic mail, ATM & IP networks, cryptography, component software, networked objects, and electronic software distribution. Dave holds a B.S. in Physics and a M.S. in Natural Sciences from the State University of New York at Buffalo, and a Ph.D. in geochemistry from UCLA. He can be contacted at drkosiur@ix.netcom.com.

The manuscript for this book was prepared and submitted to Microsoft Press in electronic form. Text files were prepared using Microsoft Word for Windows 95. Pages were composed by The Water Mill Group using Adobe Page-Maker 6.5 for Windows, with text in Optima and display type in Optima Bold. Composed pages were delivered to the printer as electronic prepress files.

Cover Graphic Designer
Becker Design

Interior Graphic Designer
Kim Eggleston

Interior Graphic Artist
Travis Beaven

Principal Compositor
Steve Sagman

Principal Proofreader/Copy Editor
Devra Hall

Proofreader
James West

Indexer
Maro Riofrancos

Printed on recycled paper stock.

A *business technology* so important,

it deserves a *nontechnical* explanation.

In today's enterprise, the way work gets done has changed. People collaborate via groupware, the Internet, and intranets. It's a crucial development that nontechnical professionals must understand—and with this book, you can. Here, you'll learn how networking environments are put together, you'll explore the importance of different approaches, and you'll see how collaborative computing can—and can't—advance the goals of your organization. So get an explanation that makes this crucial subject as clear as it ought to be. Get UNDERSTANDING GROUPWARE IN THE ENTERPRISE.

The *Strategic Technology* series is for executives, business planners, software designers, and technical managers who need a quick, comprehensive introduction to important technologies and their implications for business.

Microsoft®*Press*

You work with Microsoft® **Office.**
Now you want to build a great **intranet.**
Congratulations, you're **nearly done.**

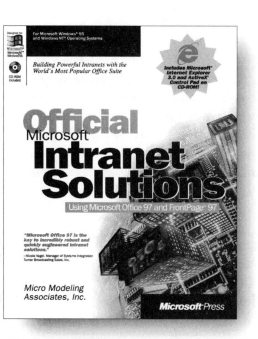

For Microsoft Windows® 95 and Windows NT® Operating Systems

Building Powerful Intranets with the World's Most Popular Office Suite

Includes Microsoft® Internet Explorer 3.0 and ActiveX™ Control Pad on CD-ROM!

Official
Microsoft® **Intranet Solutions**
Using Microsoft Office 97 and FrontPage™ 97

"Microsoft Office 97 is the key to incredibly robust and quickly engineered intranet solutions."
—Nicole Vogel, Manager of Systems Integration Turner Broadcasting Sales, Inc.

Micro Modeling Associates, Inc.

Microsoft Press

You don't need to start from scratch. In fact, once you upgrade to Microsoft Office 97, all you add is Microsoft FrontPage™ 97, Microsoft Internet Explorer, and this book. Here technical managers and developers can discover how to use these popular programs to quickly create awesome, full-featured intranets that are easy for everyone to use—administrators and users alike. So build on the foundation you've already put in place. To find out how, get OFFICIAL MICROSOFT INTRANET SOLUTIONS.

U.S.A.	**$39.99**
U.K.	£52.99 [V.A.T. included]
Canada	$54.99
ISBN	1-57231-509-1

Microsoft Press

To understand the future of information flow, you have to understand the pipeline.

U.S.A. **$19.99**
U.K.   £18.49
Canada $26.99
ISBN 1-57231-513-X

If you work with and plan for the Internet, video conferencing, or business communications, you need UNDERSTANDING BANDWIDTH. Here you'll find clear, comprehensive explanations from well-known technology observer and analyst Cary Lu. And in short order, you'll understand the issues and technologies surrounding bandwidth, as well as their strategic importance. Get UNDERSTANDING BANDWIDTH, and open up your company's information pipeline.

The *Strategic Technology* series is for executives, business planners, software designers, and technical managers who need a quick, comprehensive introduction to important technologies and their implications for business.

***Microsoft*®Press**

Register Today!

Return this
Understanding
Electronic Commerce
registration card for
a Microsoft Press® catalog

U.S. and Canada addresses only. Fill in information below and mail postage-free.
Please mail only the bottom half of this page.

1-57231-560-1A   ***UNDERSTANDING***   *Owner Registration Card*
                        ELECTRONIC COMMERCE

_____

NAME

_____

INSTITUTION OR COMPANY NAME

_____

ADDRESS

_____

CITY   STATE   ZIP

Microsoft®*Press*
Quality Computer Books

For a free catalog of
Microsoft Press® products, call
1-800-MSPRESS